Without Decay

Scripture Reveals Its Own Preservation

James Ridley

Ridley House Books

WITHOUT DECAY

Volume One, 1st Edition, 2023

Doctrinal Review by Pastor Marshall Stevens, Pastor Jim Bailey, and Pastor Jerry Scheidbach.

Editing by Lynn Squire.

Proofreading by Pastor Neil Warthan, Lora Justice, David Squire, Jessica Craighead, Anne Grant, Tommy Craighead, Mike Farrell.

Cover art by Tonya Ridley.

Publisher: Ridley House Books, LLC, California, USA.

All Scripture quotations are from the precious King James Bible. Rights in the Authorized (King James) Version in the United Kingdom are vested in the Crown. Reproduced by permission of the Crown's patentee, Cambridge University Press.

ePUB Edition ISBN 979-8-9885774-0-9; Softcover Print Edition ISBN 979-8-9885774-1-6; Hardcover Print Edition ISBN 979-8-9885774-2-3.

Ridley House Books supports the human right to individual free expression, and the value of *copyright*. As such, this material is Copyright © 2023 by James Ridley and Ridley House Books, LLC, which reserves all rights. No part of this publication may be reproduced, stored in a system, or transmitted in any form or by any means — electronic, mechanical, photocopy, recording, or any other method — save for brief quotations in book reviews, Sunday school teaching, or pulpit preaching, without the prior permission from the author or publisher. Diligent effort has been made to ensure this material does not infringe on the rights of others. This publication is designed to provide accurate and authoritative information in regard to the subject matter covered. While the publisher and author have used their best efforts in preparing this book, they make no representations or warranties with respect to the accuracy or completeness of the contents of this book and specifically disclaim any implied warranties of merchantability or fitness for a particular purpose.

FOR RIGHTS AND PERMISSIONS, CONTACT RIDLEY HOUSE BOOKS, LLC

BY ELECTRONIC MAIL AT AUTHOR@RIDLEYHOUSEBOOKS.COM.

CONTENTS

Dedication	IV
Foreword	V
Preface	VII
Introduction	1
1. How It All Started	3
2. Accuracy and Precision	9
3. Safe from Injury	19
4. Substantial Evidence	33
5. Necessary and Sufficient	49
6. Lively Oracles	65
7. Purposely Stitched	83
8. Systematics	99
9. Now and Later	117
10. By God's Finger	135
11. Surviving Originals	153
12. Enduring Originals	167
13. Conveyance	179
Afterword	191
About the Author	195
A Note from the Author	197
Reference Index	199

This volume prayerfully dedicated

To my closest friend and wonderful wife, Tonya Faye.

For my sisters: Georgia, Jude, Jane, and Jen.

In acknowledgement of the debt I owe to my boyhood friend, Bryan A. Austring, for introducing me to the Author and Finisher of all faith.

Foreword

Ask any born-again child of God what their most important possession is, and the answer is salvation. To know we are forgiven of our sins; that our home is secure in heaven; that we are passed from death unto life, is an eternal possession which surpasses anything this world could offer.

We know our Lord Jesus Christ, at a great price, purchased salvation for us. Without Him, we cannot afford such grace. We also know the gospel is our means of salvation. Jesus Christ died for our sins according to the Scriptures. He was buried, and He rose again the third day, according to the Scriptures. These facts are indisputable.

Yet, without the Scriptures, we cannot know the gospel, and we do not know what we need to know — to have faith. The Bible tells us "Faith cometh by hearing, and hearing by the word of God" (Romans 10:17). Take the word of God out of this verse and you have nothing specific to hear which produces saving faith. "For by grace are ye saved through faith" (Ephesians 2:8).

Yes, salvation is our most important possession. But the word of God is equally important, for without it, we cannot know the truth. Jesus said the word of God is truth in John 17:17. Without the truth, we do not know what to believe; we might easily believe in something less than the truth. The new birth — salvation — comes by the incorruptible seed of the word of God (1 Peter 1:23). Listen to what David said to God in worship about the importance of God's word: "I will worship toward thy holy temple, and praise thy name for thy lovingkindness and for thy truth: for thou hast magnified thy word above all thy name" (Psalm 138:2).

As God exalts His word above His name, I am also thankful for this truth: "Jesus Christ the same yesterday, and to day, and for ever" (Hebrews 13:8) and "For I am the LORD, I change not" (Malachi 3:6). He changes not. So isn't it important we understand His word never changes?

What if the critics are right? What if through the need to copy and copy and copy, and to translate from language to language, the word of God decays? And what if the words we have today are not as pure as those originally given?

Where would we be if the Bible has missing words, or some added words, or some words mistranslated? We totally depend on the words to give us faith — for salvation.

We must realize if the words of God decay, we do not have His word today. Our faith would rest on some expert — not the word of God. Alas, we know our great God promised to preserve His words. He told us, "Heaven and earth shall pass away, but my words shall not pass away" (Matthew 24:35).

I have known author James Ridley for well over 30 years. His vast array of experiences in many areas of life gives him great perspective. He is a man faithful to our LORD and I depend on him for so much in my ministry. Centering his studies on the word of God, he wrote this book to help us realize it is very reasonable to believe and understand God has kept His words, all of them, for us — *Without Decay*.

This book will help you see Scripture's preservation in a manner you had not considered. Its purpose is to help you completely trust in the Bible as the perfect, preserved words of God.

— Pastor Marshall P. Stevens, American Canyon, CA

Preface

Once I placed the twelve-foot, three-legged wood ladder next to the majestic apple tree, I donned over my shoulders a fruit harvesting bag. My grandmother told me the torn-and-oft-repaired heavy canvas bag dated from the 1930s (which I believed, given its tattered condition). Atop the ladder, having blazed a trail through the branches, I filled the bag with ready-to-pick, but not-quite-ripe Gravenstein apples.

The apples weren't huge, and not sweet to eat, but these hardy apples were perfect for canning applesauce, baking apple pies, making apple jams and jellies, and other confectionery wonders. We spent several days picking and boxing the apples. We gave away many to friends in the Dry Creek Valley outside Healdsburg, California. And we set aside plenty for the making of delightful foods.

We had special machines for peeling and coring each apple. Oh, what a sight to see a dozen relatives filling the entire kitchen at the ranch house, stepping over one another, staying focused on the all-important canning task. People processing the apples occupied every available space, charging through many hours, preparing and cooking and canning these stalwart fruits.

Outside my grandmother's recollection, we find no recipe. Every batch of applesauce became a masterpiece of artful canning perfection, with a taste never matched! My sisters, mom, aunts, and grandma had a genuine talent for cutting the apple pieces to the right bite size. The applesauce in stores and restaurants is a lesser puree — but this — is a magical delight of spectacular taste.

After boiling the Mason jars, lids, and rings in super-heated water, the applesauce found its way into the hot jars, avoiding cracking. After synching the lid and boiling for a time, someone gracefully placed the jar on a metal rack over a double layer of bath towels on the kitchen table. Soon the table overflowed with many dozens of sumptuous vases of tart and sweet goodness. Because of the heat, each jar sat untouchable for over two hours. Soon, we heard the most magnificent "pop" as jars cooled enough to draw the lid to a final vacuum. Sealed.

Months later we could remove the ring, hear the "swoosh" of unsealing the lid, and open a can of apple preserves to encounter the sweet smell, splendid taste, and marvelous texture just the same as the day when this delicious dessert found its way into the Mason jars. The previous year's worth of growing, picking, preparing, and canning had achieved the purpose.

I am grateful I get to look back at my childhood and remember this simple, but powerful tale. While writing this volume, this story frequently surfaced in my mind and in conversations with others. As a child, I never appreciated the value of preserving food for later use. I get it now. It's amazing to me we could open the jar, and enjoy the protected apples, so many months later.

So much more than those wonderful apple preserves, the words of God are kept in splendid condition throughout time by the LORD's magnificent methods. Today, we get to hold those words in our hands; to read them; to hear them, because He eternally preserves those words — they are *Without Decay*.

Like life, with its many turns and circumstances, the Bible pages contain wonderful stories about many people and about Jesus Christ. As I weave my way through the Bible, I see so much more than just a storyline with interesting facts. God's word is so much more than history, with unique characters and fantastic scripts. More and more, I adore the various writing styles, narratives, and prophecies. As we travel along the Bible journey, we see songs, letters, and limitless sterling details. Painting these pictures in my mind captivates my imagination. One verse adds to the next, multiplying each thread of the story as it comes alive and stitches into my thinking. It's almost like my thoughts are the threads of a loom progressing back and forth, to and fro, as the weaver spins a beautiful tapestry woven from the words.

Unfortunately, there is today a melancholy spirit in societies around the world, brought on by a decades-long abandonment of God's words. For many around us, the Bible anchor is dragging and they are drifting. With all my might, I have tried to make the essence of this book help my fellow citizens, Christian or not, return to a love for the Holy Bible. To navigate the obstacles of life, we must return to the trustworthy pages of Scripture, giving them first place as we approach each day.

Psalm 18:28 is our guide point: "For thou wilt light my candle: the LORD my God will enlighten my darkness."

My foremost intent in this book is to stir your curiosity in the words of the Bible. The language itself is marvelous, but the **impact** of the language is eternal!

Join me on this journey, as I show you some beautiful details about the Wonderful Words of Life.

—Author

Introduction

The loom is a strange machine with many moving parts. We don't give it much thought, but we all enjoy what it does. Weaving on a loom creates cloth, fabrics, or tapestries. There are many types of looms, but the basic operating principle is to hold some threads steady while other threads run back and forth between them. This crisscrossing effect gives the fabric strength, beauty, and durability.

As each weft thread (the loose ones) travels back and forth on a shuttle, the warp threads (the tight ones) move up and down on harnesses and heddles, remaining taut on the front and back beams of the loom. The weaver crafts his tapestry following a prescribed pattern. With dexterous movements, the artist lifts and lowers the warp threads, allowing the weft threads to be woven in and out. Thread after thread, with great precision and accuracy, the weaver artistically fashions a durable cloth, intended to last a very long time.

I compare God's works of inspiration and preservation to these intersecting warp and weft threads. As the inspired words launch from the Bible page, the safe-guarding blanket of preservation keeps them safe from all decay. Let's not take this for granted, but "stop and smell the roses." The supernatural Scriptures teach us much about their own safe keeping. Their time-tested durability did not happen by accident.

On one hand, many books report about inspiration. On the other hand, few books comment on the Scripture's intrinsic perspective about its maintenance. Throughout the Bible is a gentle, hushed mystery that the preservation of the words is so tightly interwoven with the inspiration of the words — they are inseparable and unalienable.

In this book, you shall discover some of the many methods and movements by which the LORD wove His complete and perfect fabric of words. Like the warp threads, He fastens the inspiration of those words. Like the weft threads, He provides resilience to their safekeeping.

In the first several chapters, I will outline some core principles about the Bible's reliability. As we spring forward, I will reveal some of the complimentary fibers showing the Bible's perspectives on its own preservation. In Volume Two, having already built a foundation and begun the core subject, I will dive into several additional areas where the Bible reveals its own safekeeping.

Important notes:

1. The Bible teaches us the words of Scripture are lively. They are vigorous, vital, and they manifest life; they continue. Lively, and similar words, describe the quick and powerful nature of God's words. No book is alive in the same way as the Bible.

2. To be respectful, I capitalize the word LORD (and He, His, and Him when referring to the LORD), unless a Scripture quote reads otherwise. Also, out of reverence to the beauty of the English language, and in keeping with seven being the number of perfection, I keep the letter "u" in Saviour.

3. The phrase *without decay* means the Scriptures are beyond the impact of decay; they are impervious to any force of man. The Scriptures are in a sound state and do not gradually pass to a less perfect state.

4. I use the phrase *word of God* or *God's word* or similar statements in the traditional sense. The words from God are collectively the word of God.

5. I use the word *prime* as an adjective, meaning first in importance or rank; first in order, time, or sequence; first in excellence, quality, or value.

In the recipe of daily life, there is no ingredient more important than the *words* of God. I hope after reading this book, you will consider the Scriptures as simple, established truth, easy to understand. For those who have not gained salvation, I hope this book will convince you of a new faith in Jesus Christ.

— James Ridley, American Canyon, California

Chapter One

How It All Started

Beginning marches toward its dawn. Before human existence, God is. From nothing, He established what we call the universe and Planet Earth with its history. None were there, but God. At His choosing, out of His everlastingness, His essence, thoughts, and utterances graced from His lofty throne into words. God spoke — and His words punctually arrived at their duty station to begin the creation. The LORD transmitted His Heavenly presence into earthly genesis.

God is our beginning. "For in six days the LORD made heaven and earth, the sea, and all that in them is, and rested the seventh day: wherefore the LORD blessed the sabbath day, and hallowed it" (Exodus 20:11). The Word of God launched all substances. "In the beginning was the Word, and the Word was with God, and the Word was God. The same was in the beginning with God. All things were made by him; and without him was not any thing made that was made" (John 1:1–3).

God spoke. By His words, He set into constructive motion the vastness of all creation, earth, and all its constituents. By His words, He fashioned the beauty of the firmament; He formed the lands; He gave life to plants and animals; and He breathed life into the man-of-clay, forged in His image.

God spoke. By majestic words, He stretched the heavens like a curtain. With His words, He laid Earth's durable foundations. It is His thunderous voice which assembled and calmed the waters which covered the mountains! He sent the springs among the hills, growing both grass and herb; the first food broke through the ground. He planted the trees and made them full of sap; He built houses for nesting birds.

God spoke. By His words, He gave the sun for the day and appointed the moon for the night. When God takes away the breath of man, beast, bug, or plant, they return to dust. By His Spirit all life and things are created; He renews the face of the earth. The glory of the LORD shall endure for ever: the LORD shall rejoice in his works (Psalm 104).

God holds it all together. "For by him were all things created, that are in heaven, and that are in earth, visible and invisible, whether they be thrones, or dominions, or principalities, or powers: all things were created by him, and for him: and he is before all things, and by him all things consist" (Colossians 1:16–17). Psalm 33 declares all the work the LORD did in creation and teaches "the word of the LORD is right; and all his works are done in truth" (Psalm 33:4).

Fresh and First

Very few things in life are as exhilarating as a breath of fresh air. Ladies love to receive fresh flowers. How exciting to hold a freshly minted $100 note! The smell of fresh-baked cookies soothes the savage beast! We enjoy driving on a freshly paved street. Every time we meet with something fresh or first, it stirs our emotions and imaginations!

So much more, the Bible is all about crisp *firsts*. Page after page, there are many, many firsts. So marvelous are some of these fresh starts, we can hardly describe them! Just the name Genesis says it all — it was the first, the beginning, the initiation of all things! The Bible is the holy, primary fruit of Heavenly words loaned to us for our journey on Planet Earth. Jesus even says to the Heavenly Father, "Sanctify them through thy truth: thy word is truth" (John 17:17).

Oh, may we approach the words of God with a fresh attitude and at first light every day! Scripture is the most eminent, exalted, and highest of all literature in the world.

Drink up the words of God as they *refresh* your palate and spark your thoughts of the Saviour, putting Him *first*!

> For an angel went down at a certain season into the pool, and troubled the water: whosoever then first after the troubling of the water stepped in was made whole of whatsoever disease he had. (John 5:4)

Over and over with fresh words, the Holy Ghost descended upon Ezekiel multiple times — on the **first day** of the month (Ezekiel 26:1, 29:17, 31:1, and 32:1).

The LORD Jesus miraculously conquered the grave, and the disciples found it empty on the **first day of the week**: "And very early in the morning the first day of the week, they came unto the sepulchre at the rising of the sun. And entering into the sepulchre, they saw a young man sitting on the right side, clothed in a long white garment; and they were affrighted. And he saith unto them, Be not affrighted: Ye seek Jesus of Nazareth, which was crucified: he is risen; he is not here: behold the place where they laid him. Now when Jesus was risen early the first day of the week, he appeared first to Mary Magdalene, out of whom he had cast seven devils" (Mark 16:2, 5–6, and 9). "That Christ should suffer, and that he should be the first that should rise from the dead, and should shew light unto the people, and to the Gentiles" (Acts 26:23).

> For I delivered unto you first of all that which I also received, how that Christ died for our sins according to the scriptures; and that he was buried, and that he rose again the third day according to the scriptures. (1 Corinthians 15:3–4)

> I exhort therefore, that, first of all, supplications, prayers, intercessions, and giving of thanks, be made for all men. (1 Timothy 2:1)

> How shall we escape, if we neglect so great salvation; which at the first began to be spoken by the Lord, and was confirmed unto us by them that heard him. (Hebrews 2:3)

New

A new house, a new car, new shoes, even a new pen, can bring joy. The new smartphone consumes us. It thrills girls and boys to get new birthday or Christmas gifts — toys, trikes, and yes, sometimes even new t-shirts. We get excited about new things.

The Holy Bible is the lively words of God and they renew our spirit every time we read them! Watch as the words of Scripture reveal wonderful new things!

Coming soon, the Christian's NEW home: "For, behold, I create new heavens and a new earth: and the former shall not be remembered, nor come into mind" (Isaiah 65:17). "For as the new heavens and the new earth, which I will make, shall remain before me, saith the LORD, so shall your seed and your name remain" (Isaiah 66:22). "And I saw a new heaven and a new earth: for the first heaven and the first earth were passed away; and there was no more sea" (Revelation 21:1).

Christ makes each person new: "Therefore if any man be in Christ, he is a new creature: old things are passed away; behold, all things are become new" (2 Corinthians 5:17).

God gives a new song: "O sing unto the LORD a new song: sing unto the LORD, all the earth" (Psalm 96:1).

For the broken, desperate, and confused, the LORD gives: "A new heart also will I give you, and a new spirit will I put within you: and I will take away the stony heart out of your flesh, and I will give you an heart of flesh. And I will put my spirit within you, and cause you to walk in my statutes, and ye shall keep my judgments, and do them" (Ezekiel 36:26–27).

Beginning

The runners take their stance on the line, poised to spring. Anticipation is palpable as the official moves to the designated spot near the starting line. Bang! The pistol cracks and racers launch with lightning fast strides and the crowd goes wild as the frontrunner sprints ahead!

Like the racers, as the sun breaches the horizon into day and brings new light, we should run to the Bible. Like God's mercies, fresh every morning, His words bring new beginnings to last through the day. Our delight must be in the Bible, where we meditate every day and night (Psalm 1:2–3). Breakfast is not enough, for we must eat the bread of life (John 6:35, and 48). Rest, assurance, and comfort begin with the Bible.

Have you ever tried to imagine anything before your birth? It's not possible to know something you have not experienced, read, or been told. Thankfully, God's reliable and faithful word "is true from the beginning" and every one of His righteous judgments endure forever (Psalm 119:160). You can know God by knowing His word. Your spirit refreshes by reading His word.

Jesus Christ is the chief beginner of all our beginnings: "And he is the head of the body, the church: who is the beginning, the firstborn from the dead; that in all things he might have the preeminence" (Colossians 1:18). "That which was from the beginning, which we have heard, which we have seen with our eyes, which we have looked upon, and our hands have handled, of the Word of life" (1 John 1:1).

In Jesus Christ is life: "I am Alpha and Omega, the beginning and the end. I will give unto him that is athirst of the fountain of the water of life freely" (Revelation 21:6). "I am Alpha and Omega, the beginning and the end, the first and the last" (Revelation 22:13).

God's words are like oil, which makes the face shine and "bread which strengtheneth man's heart" (Psalm 104:15).

No Space Between Them

As we explore the inseparable relationship between God's eternalness and His words, the focus is on the Scriptures telling us of their safekeeping. Compared to eternity, man's collective understanding spans only a few millennia we call natural time (or known time). God's term is *preserve*: keeping His words free from decay. Sometimes in the Bible, preservation refers to people, places, or things. Many times, preservation is about words.

In this life, God's nature often seems mysterious. By the words of Scripture, we learn about His eternal nature. All around us, we can see things that God created. His eternalness paints across the blue sky, and the tiniest of creatures magnify its immeasurable depth. If we stop to ponder the majesty and beauty of God, taking a moment to read His words, the mystery fades away.

Many centuries after the creation of Earth, the LORD Jesus Christ stepped from eternity into the flesh, leaving off sin. Just as the prophets spoke, He came to "seek and to save that which was lost" (Luke 19:10). When He dwelled among us, He lifted the shroud of mystery about salvation, eternity — and His nature. Regardless of one's belief, Jesus walked on Planet Earth. As the Word, He became human. He is also the Living Word, and Scripture is the Word in written form. Jesus Christ served perfectly the will of the Heavenly Father. As the Son of God, He kept all the laws. As the Last Adam, He is the great high priest who willingly sacrificed His life to become sin for each person. According to Matthew 3:15, the LORD Jesus fulfilled all righteousness, but never divested His exquisite nature and eternal existence.

The authenticity of God's words is not a superficial veil. The truth of Scripture runs through all the words. They are not merely coated with the appearance of truth. The Bible is not a packaged marketing course. Its words so much more keep their inherent Heavenly authority throughout, and at every depth. The Apostle Paul's letter to the Christian church in Rome eloquently expresses the reliability of the words of Scripture toward salvation and every aspect of life.

> But what saith it? The word is nigh thee, even in thy mouth, and in thy heart: that is, the word of faith, which we preach. (Romans 10:8)

> So then faith cometh by hearing, and hearing by the word of God. But I say, Have they not heard? Yes verily, their sound went into all the earth, and their words unto the ends of the world. (Romans 10:17–18)

For us, we only understand the start of something. With God, He exists. Before the beginning — is the Word. At the beginning — is the Word. Since the beginning — is the Word. At the end of Planet Earth, the Word continues. **God spoke.** It all started with words.

The Bible must be considered as the great source of all the truth by which men are to be guided in government as well as in all social transactions. — Noah Webster

CHAPTER TWO

ACCURACY AND PRECISION

ACCURACY IS HOW MUCH a thing avoids mistakes, and how close the thing conforms to truth. Accuracy is about exactness. According to Noah Webster, "The accuracy of ideas or opinions is conformity to truth. The value of testimony depends on its *accuracy*; copies of legal instruments should be taken with *accuracy*." For example, the speedometer in a car is required to measure the actual ground speed. Satellite orbits must adhere to strict accuracy, or the orbit decays, killing the mission. The checkout machines at the grocery store must read the bar code accurately to register the correct price. *Accuracy*: free from mistakes.

Precision is the ability of accurate measurements to repeat many times. "Precision in the use of words is a prime excellence in discourse; it is indispensable in controversy, in legal instruments, and in mathematical calculations. Neither perspicuity nor precision should be sacrificed to ornament." This is the definition of precision given by Noah Webster in his 1828 *American Dictionary of the English Language*. A centimeter on tape is the precision quantity for the construction of furniture and buildings. A Troy ounce is for the truthful weighing of precious metals. A second of time is both simultaneously tiny and very great. The second is vital to every aspect of our lives, including traffic lights, commerce, and air travel. *Precision*: repeatedly consistent.

Some Bible examples of precision combined with accuracy include the buoyancy of the ark resulting from the accurate measurements given by God and the precision construction by Noah and his family. Another is the LORD creating the universe in six 24-hour days. Jesus Christ stated accurately He will rise again the third day. As promised, He resurrected precisely three days later.

In Judges, we read of men possessing precise skills with accurate targeting.

> Among all this people there were seven hundred chosen men lefthanded; every one could sling stones at an hair breadth, and not miss. (Judges 20:16)

As a young man, David ended the giant by precisely launching a stone which accurately punctured Goliath's skull.

> And David put his hand in his bag, and took thence a stone, and slang it, and smote the Philistine in his forehead, that the stone sunk into his forehead; and he fell upon his face to the earth. (1 Samuel 17:49)

The LORD provides precise care of His creatures and brings accuracy in all of life's conduct.

> And hath made of one blood all nations of men for to dwell on all the face of the earth, and hath determined the times before appointed, and the bounds of their habitation; that they should seek the LORD, if haply they might feel after him, and find him, though he be not far from every one of us: for in him we live, and move, and have our being; as certain also of your own poets have said, For we are also his offspring. (Acts 17:26–28)

Accurate. Precise.

Math Is the Creative Language

Mathematics is the fundamental language of creation. The entire field of mathematics was established by God to give structure and unity to His creation. To this description also can be added the terms symmetry, beauty, and elegance. Mathematics extends from real numbers to the complex, and perhaps to realms yet unexplored.[1]

Mathematics is the verifiable instruction set used for the construction of any invention, without regard to complexity or simplicity. Mathematics is the language of accurate measurement and precise accounting.

> Mathematics is the language in which God has written the universe — Galileo Galilei.

Over time, and with much study and application, scientists and engineers achieve greater precision in their craft as they exercise mathematical skills. Nurses and doctors rely on math many times a day when caring for patients. As accuracy increases, so does our capacity for creative works and helpful actions.

Consider the space program: this amazing effort required the most advanced mathematics known to man. The precision and accuracy demanded for launching and recovering spaceships required new mathematical formulas and methods, yet to be discovered. In contrast, the LORD's brilliance to preserve His words far exceeds the acumen of the talented space program scientists and mathematicians. Our LORD maintained the inspiration of His words through effective retention, and He did so by the agents of *accuracy* and *precision*, conducting every step of the plan with purpose.

Just by observing the infinite paradigms of nature and the beauty of the countless celestial bodies, we understand the boundless intelligent design of God. The language of mathematics, well beyond our ability to understand, started and completed every marvelous creation. When Jehovah saw all which He made (i.e., created, constructed), He labeled it as beyond comparison! God spoke and all of Creation came into existence (Genesis 1).

Jesus Christ is eternal, existing before and after the earthly creation. It is His will which keeps all time, space, and matter in a delightful concert and uninterruptible cohesion. Apostle Paul instructed the Colossian church that LORD Jesus had made all creation.

---

1. Excerpted from Mathematics: The Language of Creation, by Don B. DeYoung and Glen W. Wolfrom, Creation Research Society Books, 2017

> For by him were all things created, that are in heaven, and that are in earth, visible and invisible, whether they be thrones, or dominions, or principalities, or powers: all things were created by him, and for him: and he is before all things, and by him all things consist. And he is the head of the body, the church: who is the beginning, the firstborn from the dead; that in all things he might have the preeminence. (Colossians 1:16–18)

As a discipline, mathematics plays an interpretive role in explaining and revealing the hidden beauty of numbers and their patterns, which are inherent in nature.[2]

What Is the Order of Creation?

When considering the magnitude of God's creation, it's often easy to dismiss the grandness of scale and attention to detail the LORD carefully crafted into every aspect. We recognize only the LORD could achieve the vastness of the assemblies named Planet Earth and the Universe. When God creates, He does so with unmatched accuracy and precision — from the tiniest of elements, such as the neutron, to the largest of complex galactic systems, unimaginably distant from our station. Throughout Scripture we see the LORD organizing the order of things.

In the tabernacle, order prevails.

> And thou shalt bring in the table, and set in order the things that are to be set in order upon it; and thou shalt bring in the candlestick, and light the lamps thereof. (Exodus 40:4)

In King David's largest psalm, we find order.

> Order my steps in thy word: and let not any iniquity have dominion over me. (Psalm 119:133)

---

2. Talwanga Matiki, Mediterranean Journal of Social Sciences, Vol 5, No 23, November 2014

When Apostle Peter declared the Gospel unto the Gentiles, he did so with an orderly rehearsal.

> But Peter rehearsed the matter from the beginning, and expounded it by order unto them. (Acts 11:4)

Consider the events of John 19, leading up to the crucifixion of the LORD. Step by step, watch as the LORD headed for His cross to lay down His life, and finally the soldiers giving Him vinegar. With His mission of redemption finished, He gave up the ghost.

The order of creation is time, then space, and last, matter (or mass).[3] We may name this order the *time-space-matter* continuum. God creates time first, so there is something to record; He then creates space so there is a place to put something, and He then creates matter so there is something to put into space for a fixed amount of time. With purpose and intent, He compounded all things, placing the earth at the center of His focus, where He breathed life into the first Adam and all his progeny. As the day yields to its opposite night, His handiwork keeps its glorious state. His lastingness expresses from the first day into the next day and the next, and so forth.

With each rising of the sun across the horizon, the day is afresh with His mercy. As the sun sets for the evening, He continues the promised protections. He brings strength to each day. As promised, all creation yields to His command. Preservation is natural for the LORD (Psalm 19). This is preservation on the planetary scale!

By Jesus Christ, all things consist. Apostle John wrote, "And this is the record, that God hath given to us eternal life, and this life is in his Son" (1 John 5:11). God is life. In the inspired text of Scripture, this life reveals itself for all to read. Thankfully, the LORD Jesus fittingly preserved all His words throughout mankind's brief span of time on earth, and from everlasting to everlasting. Were it not for God's words, your person and mine cease to exist. When "God said" and furnished His creation, He spoke the worlds, the heavens, and all creatures into existence. Jesus Christ, the Living Word, brings life.

---

3. Dr. Jason Lisle, Spacetime: Virtual Particles, Time, ... and the Trinity, December 7, 2007, from https://answersingenesis.org/physics/spacetime/

> That which was from the beginning, which we have heard, which we have seen with our eyes, which we have looked upon, and our hands have handled, of the Word of life. (1 John 1:1)

With intent comes order. It's impossible to suppose upon Jehovah God a notion of dis-orderliness or entropy. Should any created thing decay or change, it does so because of man's sin, an aberration to God's perfect design.

We must not think of God as disarrayed or occasionally unkempt. With the Father, order and regularity are paramount in the whole creation. Scripture provides a solution to every situation in life and does so with a planned arrangement. There is harmony in the building blocks of grace. As Peter assembles those blocks, he starts with a foundation.

> Grace and peace be multiplied unto you through the knowledge of God, and of Jesus our Lord, according as his divine power hath given unto us all things that pertain unto life and godliness, through the knowledge of him that hath called us to glory and virtue. (2 Peter 1:2–3)

Consider the local church. It's made of members whose core purpose is unity. There is one body, one Spirit, and one hope; one LORD, one faith, one baptism; and one God and Father. In His churches, He gave apostles, prophets, evangelists, pastors, teachers; bishops, and deacons (Ephesians 4 and Philippians 1).

As the LORD Jesus founded the first church (Matthew 10), He set an order and standards within the called-out assembly. Each member is accountable to the Head of the church (1 Timothy 3:15). In Apostle Paul's instruction to the confused church at Corinth, he closes a multitude of behavioral instructions with this simple statement: "Let all things be done decently and in order" (1 Corinthians 14:40). To leaders and members in the church, you must keep your life decorous and your mind disciplined and your appearance well-groomed. Keep order in day-to-day activities. Accountability and unity are the marks of order in the church.

Also, by a simple illustration, the LORD Jesus describes the precision and accuracy stemming from the Father's management of every human.

> Are not two sparrows sold for a farthing? and one of them shall not fall on the ground without your Father. But the very hairs

of your head are all numbered. Fear ye not therefore, ye are of more value than many sparrows. (Matthew 10:29–31)

From the Word of Life come the accurate words of grace and truth, precisely granting the greatest gift by the Gospel of salvation (John 1 and Ephesians 1). In God, there is no arbitrary thing.

> Every good gift and every perfect gift is from above, and cometh down from the Father of lights, with whom is no variableness, neither shadow of turning. (James 1:17)

Order.

PRESERVE

> To save or keep from injury or destruction; defend from evil; uphold; sustain; *save from decay*; keep in a sound state; to keep or defend against corruption.[4]

Preserving a substance halts or retards decay. The substance remains sound and prosperous, rather than declining to a state of destruction or impairment.

Meats cured with salts or caramel pecan ice cream frozen with refrigeration are fine examples of prolonged protection. Other foods are vacuum-packed, removing most or all air before sealing. In each case, the goal is longer shelf life. In a similar fashion, but with so much more grandeur and everlasting liveliness, the words spoken and written by the Father, the Word, and the Spirit remain without decay. The Great Protector divinely wraps and eternally shields His words, and does not permit them to degrade, cloud, or lose strength.

Establishing and maintaining this universal conservation effort is done with resolve, not recklessness. For sure, earthly examples can help us understand

---

4. From the American Dictionary of the English Language, Noah Webster, 1828, from https://webstersdictionary1828.com/Dictionary/preserve

the methods and mechanics of preservation. However, Bible custodianship is a Heavenly act; a Holy Spirit working, not subject to human boundaries.

Wonderfully, the Protector moves upon the spirit of man toward the goal of preservation, which is the entire essence of Psalm 121. The psalmist describes the direct action of God, including "made heaven and earth", "not moved", "shall preserve", and "even for evermore."

As Inspiration Is to Cause, Preservation Is to Effect

For brevity's sake, I will examine the province of inspiration, where it directly relates to a particular Scripture or as it helps to illustrate preservation, but I am not dismissive of the inextricable link between both. Inspiration (like the warp thread) and preservation (like the weft thread) warrant equal amounts of faith and comprehension.

Grasping the doctrine of preservation will infuse your mind with a clear discernment regarding the matter of inspiration. Those safely-kept-inspired words of the Lord, detailed in Hebrews 4:12, divide the body and soul of a person and can penetrate the innermost thoughts and intentions of the heart. The liveliness of the words persists in each sentence, paragraph, section, and book. The perfect word blossoms as He weaves inspiration with preservation. If you do not have faith, reading this material will prove interesting but frustrating, detailed, but dull.

One thread seen in the final chapter of the canon well illustrates this matter of cause and effect. The Apostle John signifies (proves, shows) by an angel as to The Revelation of Jesus Christ given to Him by the Father. John writes about carrying the record of the words of God, of the testimony of Jesus Christ, and of the things he saw. Surely, with the commandments came also the tools to achieve the directive. With a quill in hand, John writes. He lays into plain view for all to see, "Blessed is he that readeth, and they that hear the words of this prophecy, and keep those things which are written therein: for the time is at hand" (Revelation 1:3).

Notice the clarity on cause and effect: the preaching is about the written word of God being read and followed (cause), and with the *cause* comes blessing (effect). As a vessel, John is uniquely qualified to record The Revelation of Jesus Christ, as the LORD chose him to write such a large volume of the New Testament. As John obeys the commandment to write to the seven churches, it's critical to note the trumpeting Voice, which commands John to write in a book. The Voice tells John to send the book to the seven churches in Asia. Each letter, to each church, contains the judgments against the named church and the way of their escape.

In striking action, the LORD Jesus upbraids each church, because they have **caused** their own sorrow. Because He is a merciful Saviour, this is not the end. John bears the record also of the **effect** of their obedience to the Saviour. The result of overcoming their impending perdition is to eat the tree of life; be relieved of the second death; eat of the hidden manna; receive a new name; have power over nations; retain his name in the book of life; be clothed in white raiment; be made a pillar in the temple of God; and finally, to sit near the throne of the LORD Jesus (Revelation 2–3).

John wrote. Sometime later, he dispatches the book to each of the seven churches. How did each church receive its copy of the letter?

It's plausible John dissected the sheets of the scroll into sections and sent each section to the respective church. This I doubt, as I do not see John tampering with the rolls. It is also possible John kept the entire book as a single volume and forwarded it to each church, likely by a ready custodian, and each church subsequently read all sections, passing it on to the next church in the order. This option, while possible, is also implausible. Another option is other believers quietly withdrew each letter from Patmos, compiled, copied, and duplicated each one, and sent them to all the churches. Each church then receives a copy of all seven letters sent to all seven churches.

The historical record is unclear. Scripture does not reveal how the letters arrived at the churches. Someday, when we enter Heavenly Jerusalem, we shall learn the answers. The most likely scenario is this: after John survived his time on Patmos and later returned to Ephesus, he carried the book with him and oversaw its copying and distribution to at least the seven named churches.

Regardless of how the letters reached the churches, they surely did. This certainty is enough evidence to establish the veracity of the Scripture account. For all hearers and readers, the Holy Ghost preserved these letters in the canon of Scripture. The Revelation is the final summary and culmination of all the previous sixty-five books of Scripture. Imagine an unfinished Bible without The Revelation of Jesus Christ. It's like a cake with no frosting; a car with no steering wheel; or a book with the last chapter ripped out.

We rightly say the words in the Holy Bible are God-breathed (i.e., words inspired through chosen men). Mankind receives its breath from the Creator, established by the records found in the Pentateuch (Genesis 3), and near the end of the Gospel according to the Apostle John (chapter 21), and from Elihu, who stated there is a spirit in man and the inspiration of the Almighty grants understanding (Job 32:8). Preservation is the act of the Lofty Preserver shielding His inspired words (which existed before time), recording them on Earth for a limited period, ensuring they endure in perpetuity. Scriptural preservation primarily benefits the reader and hearer. We have today the reliable Bible which teaches each person many principles, but especially how to be restored by salvation in Jesus Christ. Galileo Galilei said, "All truths are easy to understand once they are discovered; the point is to discover them."

"Concerning thy testimonies, I have known of old that thou hast founded them for ever" (Psalm 119:152).

Chapter Three

Safe from Injury

With distress at every turn, King David exclaims, "Help, LORD."

In peerless majesty, King David records the twelfth Psalm. He boldly proclaims midway through the prose, "The words of the LORD are pure words: as silver tried in a furnace of earth, purified seven times. Thou shalt keep them, O LORD, thou shalt preserve them from this generation for ever" (Psalm 12:6–7). This is the platinum Bible passage about preservation. The LORD is keeping the *words* safe. David already knows God's words are inherently and reliably pure; he knows the purity extends to the written text. This is not the pure like pure chocolate or pure water, but a pure which is so uncorrupted, mere human analogy cannot compare. Amidst severe troubles and enemies all around, King David clings tightly to the singular thing he can rely upon without exception — the *words* of the LORD.

What Are the Boundaries of Infinity?

Space — the final frontier. The mission is to go boldly where no man has gone before. The iconic television show *Star Trek* escorted the viewer into imaginary escapades to worlds in the great beyond. Writers wrote each script intending to spur the beholder into discoverable, albeit fictional, space expeditions. The fantastical series remains a mainstay of television entertainment.

The abundant marketing and sales of the series, the full-length movies, the recordings, and so many promotional products are all but immeasurable. The *Star Trek* franchise has impacted everything from costumes to makeup; lunch boxes to nightlights to shoes; conference themes to soda pop bottles to automobiles; from the youngest child to the senior citizens. Even some of the early cellular telephones emulated Captain Kirk's "communicator." We simply cannot dismiss the influence of the voyages of Starship Enterprise.

Even this long-running and gripping series is limited by the perspective of the talented scriptwriters. Indeed, even at warp speed, the properties of time, space, and machine restrict the ability of the USS ENTERPRISE to travel through vast horizons. How many times did Scotty inform Captain Kirk, "She hasn't got the power!" Despite all the capabilities of this fabulous starship, even the crew of NCC-1701 could not strike into eternity, being limited by physical elements.

When one ponders the principles and certainties of everlastingness, the mind delves into so much more than what meets the eye or present thought. The concept of eternity — ***infinity*** — is altogether inconceivable in the mind of man while in this transient lifetime. I am mortal. You are mortal. Our own humanness hems us in. Thankfully, someday, this mortality shall be preserved in immortality. Even the greatest minds of all societies of all ages struggle to comprehend the concept of eternity as humans buckle involuntarily to the consequences of sin.

The LORD Jesus often taught in parable statements. We too can learn from various earthly examples about Scripture's story of its own preservation. Let's look at a few illustrations to stitch together masterful preservation crisscrossing the tapestry of Scripture, as it bulwarks the inspiration of God's words.

Deep Space Voyagers

The Voyager 2 and Voyager 1 spacecraft actually fulfilled portions of the fantastical voyages of the Starship Enterprise and have rigorously trekked where no man (or any earthly object) has gone before. The design, construction, and operation of these superb spacecraft certainly qualifies as the pinnacle of scientific success. Both vessels launched only weeks apart in the summer of 1977, under very difficult circumstances. Both crafts achieved every aspect of their missions, and so much more.

Here is just a glimpse of the communication abilities of the Voyagers.

> The command computer subsystem (CCS) provides sequencing and control functions. The CCS contains fixed routines such as command decoding and fault detection and corrective routines, antenna pointing information, and spacecraft sequencing information. The Attitude and Articulation Control Subsystem (AACS) controls spacecraft orientation, maintains the pointing of the high gain antenna toward Earth, controls attitude ma-

neuvers, and positions the scan platform. Uplink communications is via S-band (16-bits/sec command rate) while an X-band transmitter provides downlink telemetry at 160 bits/sec normally and 1.4 kbps for playback of high-rate plasma wave data. All data are transmitted from and received at the spacecraft via the 3.7 meter high-gain antenna (HGA). Electrical power is supplied by three Radioisotope Thermoelectric Generators (RTGs). The current power levels are about 249 watts for each spacecraft. As the electrical power decreases, power loads on the spacecraft must be turned off in order to avoid having demand exceed supply. As loads are turned off, some spacecraft capabilities are eliminated.[1]

Traveling through space at fabulous speeds, with unparalleled navigational accuracy, these vessels inspected the major planets of our solar system, collecting and later transmitting fascinating data back to the home base on Earth. The scientists programmed these fine craft with a language all their own. It strikes awe in our minds: these machines communicate with the words **loaned to them by their creators**. Arriving on-station, on time, as close as is safely possible to their intended marks, the Voyager vehicles conducted themselves according to precise configurations and in unmatched operation, with pre-programmed direction from their masters.

After some years, with their planet-visiting missions completed, each vehicle began its long journey into the farther reaches of space beyond our solar system. In basic terms, these vessels have now crossed the theoretical boundary where the solar winds from our sun cease and the strength of those winds diminishes and can no longer push back the stellar winds of the surrounding stars. This sector is called the heliopause — the zone where the interstellar medium and solar wind pressures balance.

Approaching five decades of space travel, these crafts now speed through interstellar space into imperceivable endlessness. And yet, considering the unimaginable vastness of the expanding universe, Voyager 2 and Voyager 1 have only just begun. Using the word achievement falls far short in describing the handiwork of JPL and NASA, the many ingenious corporations, the myriad of scientists and engineers, and countless vendors and support staff. The vast number of scientific and artful inventions of the space program are much more impactful today than the Voyager missions.

---

1. Jet Propulsion Lab, The Voyager Spacecraft, from https://voyager.jpl.nasa.gov/mission/spacecraft

One of several influential ways these marvelous chariots of inquiry show conservation is in the power plant providing the direct current energy for all the onboard systems:

> Electrical power is supplied by three MHW-RTG radioisotope thermoelectric generators (RTGs). They are powered by plutonium-238 and provided approximately 470 W at 30 volts DC when the spacecraft was launched. (Early) in 2011, 34 years after launch, such an RTG would inherently produce 359 watts or about 76% of its initial power. By October 2011 the power generated by Voyager 2 and Voyager 1 had dropped to about 57% of the power at launch.[2]

The teams who built the Voyager 2 and Voyager 1 discovery platforms intended to engage the data collection mission of both craft for as long as possible. Striving against the limits of budgeteers, the pioneers discreetly committed the Voyager missions to visit the four outer planets, not just the two planets in the budget. Their invention required great technical skill and far-reaching resourcefulness to mitigate the many risks of such an endeavor. Keeping each vehicle energized for the journey required resolute study well beyond typical scientific careers.

Preserving electric capacity became the prime directive, granting each of the Voyagers the long-term energy to collect information and send words back to the terrestrial base. In 2023, we are told, these paragons of space excursion continue to transmit the tiniest of radio data back to Earth. They continue to use their words.

While these vehicles are at the summit of brilliant engineering, there is a component of both craft having little to do with the mission of collecting data from the solar system and everything to do with the preservation and communicating of a message:

> Both Voyager space-crafts carry a greeting to any form of life, should that be encountered. The message is carried by a phonograph record — a 12-inch gold-plated copper disc containing sounds and images selected to portray the diversity of life and

---

2. Jet Propulsion Lab, The Voyager Spacecraft, from https://voyager.jpl.nasa.gov/mission/spacecraft

culture on Earth. The contents of the record were selected for NASA by a committee chaired by Carl Sagan of Cornell University. Dr. Sagan and his associates assembled 115 images and a variety of natural sounds. To this, they added musical selections from different cultures and eras, and spoken greetings from Earth-people in fifty-five languages.[3]

While the plutonium and other elements of the RTG reactors decay over time, the scientists expected the golden record to last well beyond the reactors.

The record is a time capsule and an interstellar message to any civilization, alien or far-future human, who may recover either of the Voyagers. The golden records also included ideographic instructions on one side, intending to communicate to the recipient how to playback the digital and analog content. Affixed to each craft is a stylus, but not a record player.

Why record such information into gilded albums? With tremendous forethought, the Voyager artists intentionally built into each spacecraft a most impressive method to transmit messages to other beings the crafts may encounter along their journeys. They relied on language — **words** — to attempt communication with those creatures. With all seriousness and urgency, Dr. Sagan and his fellows dedicated their efforts to a project never attempted before.

Rising to the challenge of their commission, they knew these one-of-a-kind recordings must be embedded into the finest of materials, to achieve the required durability. The simple prime directive: defend the recorded discs so the message survives. Hence, they built the gold discs to endure the known harshness and the unknown brutalities of space. The undertaking to manufacture these shiny albums contracts one enterprise — the feat of preservation.

The creators of each Voyager's gilded message went to extensive efforts to ensure the survival of their Earth message to future recipients. With every decision, they carefully ensured the longevity of every component. This was no happy accident — it had purpose and careful planning. The fabrication standards were the highest, avoiding "second-best" for all the materials and methods chosen. Dr. Sagan and his team, through the gold records, were the stewards, watching over the *words* to others, whether alien or earthly.

---

3. Wikipedia, The Voyager Program, from https://en.wikipedia.org/wiki/Voyager_program

The essence of preservation is to make sure the preserved thing lasts for its intended use. As such, the vessels of the Voyager program illustrate the means of the Scriptural journals by transporting the **words** (the messages on the golden disc recordings) of an intelligent designer (the human engineers) to any potential recipients (other species or future humans). Forever, not just five decades — the LORD's enduring words are much more worthy of safety.

Juxtapose all the marvel and creativity in the Voyager Program with the immense scale of transmission and preservation of God's eternal words during the brief life of Planet Earth — and you get a sense of the Bible's journey through the centuries.

ETERNAL — existing at all times without change.

FOREVER — for a limitless time.

INFINITE — without limits; boundless.

Ponder for a moment all the effort put into selecting the contents, determining the exact dimensions, metering the weight and composition of the records, carefully recording the music and messages and images into the medium, manufacturing the discs to exquisite precision, and ultimately covering the discs with lacquer. Indeed, they intended for the plutonium power cells and the resplendent discs to last for a very long time. While quite extraordinary in every comprehensible way, these golden records pale compared to the inspiration of God's words recorded in the sixty-six-book library we call the Holy Bible.

Even these long-lasting machines, and the irreplaceable gold journals they host, do not hold a candle to God's retention policy of His RECORDS! With God's words, there is only one time period — *infinity*. Heaven and earth will pass away, but not the *words* of God. The most direct Scriptures describing the infinite retention period (a certainly human oxymoron) of God's expressed words are of course Psalm 12 and Psalm 105, which declares, "He hath remembered his covenant for ever, the word which he commanded to a thousand generations" (Psalm 105:8); and Psalm 147:5, which heralds, "Great is our LORD, and of great power: his understanding is infinite."

Owing to the notion that the warp thread of inspiration interlaces with the weft thread of preservation in the whole of Scripture, consider:

> Jude, the servant of Jesus Christ, and brother of James, to them that are sanctified by God the Father, and preserved in Jesus Christ, and called. (Jude v. 1)

Psalm 121 focuses on the act of God upon the spirit of man, bringing him help, preserving his soul, and keeping him safe from evil.

> The LORD shall preserve thee from all evil: he shall preserve thy soul. The LORD shall preserve thy going out and thy coming in from this time forth, and even for evermore. (Psalm 121:7–8)

The princely prophet Isaiah, obedient to the Holy Ghost of God, records the indictment from Jehovah, saying,

> Now go, write it before them in a table, and note it in a book, that it may be for the time to come for ever and ever. (Isaiah 30:8)

While the 20th-century Voyager spacecraft are fine examples of endurance in this twenty-first century, their lifespan of some decades is a smidgen in Earth-time. Contrariwise, God's words proceed from eternity. Those words initiated creation-time ("in the beginning"), they persist during Earth-time ("from this generation"), and they prevail beyond man-time ("for ever").

While the gold-plated copper discs of the Voyager business are substantially impervious from physical decay for a significant period, these also have an imminent end, as things made by man degrade with time. As a side note, it is an act of faith to think the golden discs exist today. In 2023, the small amount of data transmitted by the space couriers is not enough to convince any earth person. While the vehicles and payloads likely continue, it is impossible to physically verify this. We believe it by *trusting the instruments and data* at the Jet Propulsion Lab. Why is it so difficult to trust the Holy Bible (the instrument) and the words (the data) it transmits?

Conversely, the Scriptures — *words* marshaled from the timeless stations of Heaven and penned by God's earthly agents, are immune from decline — because the Author is also the shielder of those words. In Psalm 12, King David emphatically stated it is Jehovah who upholds and sustains the pure words forever. And let us be clear — King David is not instructing the LORD or giving Him direction, but is acknowledging the sovereignty of Jehovah in the matter of preserving the words. King David knew the place to go for God's help. In the golden Voyager discs we see fabulous design and beautiful manufacturing methods. When the LORD uses methods and forms, His Scriptures are sheltered from the spoiling storm of decay. God energetically defends His words from the mal-handling of polluted men.

Numbers

Mathematics is indispensable in the fabrication of any invention or the effort in any craft. From the simplest device to the most complicated system, someone forms or finishes each with mathematics. Consider, if you will, the number 2 wooden pencil and the Golden Gate Bridge, both of which are marvelous devices. The first is quite simple, and the last is utterly complex, the one and the other employ mathematics in construction and operation. Indeed, the pencil and the giant bridge stand firm on the act of intelligent design — because the exercise of numeric calculation requires brilliance and capability in the language of creation.

You need only read Genesis 1 to understand the creation. God existed at our beginning and He started creation — using His *words*. How spectacular of God to breathe into the clay-man the breath of life, turning him into a living soul! The works of the LORD are manifold, and in wisdom, He made everything.

The Scriptures are clear — God supernaturally created all existence. He made us so we can know Him, praise Him, and worship Him! With this axiom in mind, take just a few moments to examine three basic constructs of arithmetic — circle, Pi, and line. These epitomize the properties of creative language.

Circle

One of the simplest shapes in all of creation is the circle. Hundreds of times each day, we encounter circular objects. There are contact lenses, silos, lampshades, coins, buttons, coffee cups, and the steering wheel. We find the notion of the circle repeated in Scripture:

Prophet Isaiah recorded:

> It is he that sitteth upon the circle of the earth, and the inhabitants thereof are as grasshoppers; that stretcheth out the heavens as a curtain, and spreadeth them out as a tent to dwell in. (Isaiah 40:22)

A song of degrees revealed:

> As the mountains are round about Jerusalem, so the LORD is round about his people from henceforth even for ever." (Psalm 125:2)

Joshua defeated Jericho:

> And it came to pass on the seventh day, that they rose early about the dawning of the day, and compassed the city after the same manner seven times: only on that day they compassed the city seven times. (Joshua 6:15)

King Solomon recorded the emplacement of Wisdom:

> When he prepared the heavens, I was there: when he set a compass upon the face of the depth. (Proverbs 8:27)

Pi

We express the remarkable number named Pi as 3.14159... and an endless progression of decimals with no perceivable nor calculated repeating pattern. We write Pi, a *mathematical constant*, as the ratio of the circumference of a circle divided by the length of its diameter. Pi is unparalleled. The pre-eminence of Pi implies it is impossible to solve the ancient challenge of squaring the circle with a compass and straightedge.

The Bible often describes Pi by words. "And he made a molten sea, ten cubits from the one brim to the other: it was round all about, and his height was five cubits: and a line of thirty cubits did compass it round about" (1 Kings 7:23). Notice the **diameter** from one brim to the other. Then notice the **circumference** as a compass of thirty cubits. To date, the fraction explaining Pi remains unsolved. Twenty-two divided by seven is close but left wanting. The statistician likely labels this divide and carry effort as absurd (or irrational).

But the Creator has answered the conundrum, as we find in Apostle Paul's first letter to the church at Corinth.

> Because the foolishness of God is wiser than men; and the weakness of God is stronger than men. For ye see your calling, brethren, how that not many wise men after the flesh, not many mighty, not many noble, are called: but God hath chosen the foolish things of the world to confound the wise; and God hath chosen the weak things of the world to confound the things which are mighty. (1 Corinthians 1:25–27)

Thankfully, even the simplest things of God are superior to the most complex things of man.

Line

The shortest distance between two points is a line. A line has one dimension — length. It extends in two directions for infinity (∞) and without perceivable boundaries.

Because of the limitations of men, our minds cannot comprehend the dimensions of a construct with no limits. This concept befuddles even our greatest minds in the arts and sciences when musing on the line. Scripture uses terms such as eternal, infinite, change not (unbending), everlasting, continuing (straight), and "for ever."

Our best efforts and deepest thoughts betray us as we attempt to fathom the many dimensions of the Creator. We commonly refer to three or four dimensions (including time) and some physicists estimate ten dimensions of space (and possibly more). These extremely complex mathematical paradigms are imperceivable to most humans.

Thankfully, the LORD has granted brilliant talent to mathematicians and physicists. Delightfully, the Scriptures are reliable, regardless of the number of dimensions in which He abides. He remains in like fashion as Pi — constant, and as the line, unbounded. Consider: "Jesus Christ the same yesterday, and to day, and for ever" (Hebrews 13:8). Won't it be wonderful when we slip the surly bonds of Earth and enter His eternal presence?

The Scripture is plentiful with examples of the boundless existence of the Creator.

> I am Alpha and Omega, the beginning and the ending, saith the LORD, which is, and which was, and which is to come, the Almighty. (Revelation 1:8)

> And the four beasts had each of them six wings about him; and they were full of eyes within: and they rest not day and night, saying, Holy, holy, holy, LORD God Almighty, which was, and is, and is to come. And when those beasts give glory and honour and thanks to him that sat on the throne, who liveth for ever and ever, the four and twenty elders fall down before him that sat on the throne, and worship him that liveth for ever and ever, and cast their crowns before the throne, saying, Thou art worthy, O LORD, to receive glory and honour and power: for thou hast created all things, and for thy pleasure they are and were created. (Revelation 4:8–11)

> The counsel of the LORD standeth for ever, the thoughts of his heart to all generations. (Psalm 33:11)

Speech, language, and voice — words from Heaven — are the unending string which binds the earth.

> Their line is gone out through all the earth, and their words to the end of the world. (Psalm 19:4)

The longevity of mercy and truth is like the unending structure of the line.

> For the LORD is good; his mercy is everlasting; and his truth endureth to all generations. (Psalm 100:5)

Isaiah shows the LORD's salvation is infinite.

> Lift up your eyes to the heavens, and look upon the earth beneath: for the heavens shall vanish away like smoke, and the earth shall wax old like a garment, and they that dwell therein shall die in like manner: but my salvation shall be for ever, and my righteousness shall not be abolished. (Isaiah 51:6)

Mercifully, the LORD Jehovah has, for an immeasurable linear distance, through the saving work of Jesus Christ, forgiven our sins and healed our iniquities. "As far as the east is from the west, so far hath he removed our transgressions from us" (Psalm 103:12).

The principle stands true. The LORD Jehovah states He will not remember (recall to His memory nor our account) any of our sins or iniquities forgiven through Jesus Christ. "And their sins and iniquities will I remember no more" (Hebrews 10:17).

Hallelujah! Oh, how marvelous and Oh how wonderful! The counsel of our Creator is available today by reading His Bible!

Perpetuity

Describing something as perpetual means it continues uninterrupted; it has no end.

The circle has no end.

The line has no end.

Just imagine — two totally different concepts with equal outcomes. Understanding the notion of perpetuity is vital to gaining a deep sense of the transmission of Bible texts through the ages. Scripture expresses perpetuity in many references, such as perpetual generations, perpetual statutes, perpetual offerings; perpetual property rights, reproaches, pain, backslidings, desolations, or perpetual sleep.

Drink in the beauty expressed in the Scriptures: "Now unto the King eternal, immortal, invisible, the only wise God, be honour and glory for ever and ever. Amen" (1 Timothy 1:17).

Worship

A most wonderful historical account of God's interactive accord with man hails from Solomon's reign over the unified Hebrew people. Upon completing the most magnificent temple, now it was time to dedicate and present the resplendent temple to the Temple Owner. Consider this: the LORD Jehovah met in person with Solomon. The building of this temple was Solomon's greatest achievement as a man of faith. They hosted a multi-day feast, discharged thousands of bloody animal sacrifices, and made prayers of dedication. The Hebrew people united toward this worshipful engagement.

The recorded journals validate the fire from Heaven which consumed the offerings. And then came a rest, and peace! The splendor of this temple and the marvelous fire of God awed everyone, including the enemies. And those former invaders were terrified at the greatness and power of the Temple Owner. Precious is the glory of the LORD, arriving in such volume, and so filling the new temple, the priests could not remain for the smoke of God. Jehovah listens! The High and Lofty One adored this worship. All of this building and grandeur and exaltation results in a splendid reply from Jehovah God:

> For now have I chosen and sanctified this house, that my name may be there for ever: and mine eyes and mine heart shall be there perpetually. (2 Chronicles 7:16)

> And the LORD said unto him, I have heard thy prayer and thy supplication, that thou hast made before me: I have hallowed this house, which thou hast built, to put my name there for ever; and mine eyes and mine heart shall be there perpetually. (1 Kings 9:3)

Hallelujah! The Master of the temple heard Solomon's prayer, just as He promised. He was pleased. The LORD Jehovah fastened His eyes and assigned the strings of His heart to this temple made with hands. Thereupon the Great Protector scribed His name! The human heart may cycle for thousands of millions of beats in a lifetime, but the heart of God has no end of days nor declining compassion.

This earthly temple was a savory sampling of the Temple which is in Heaven. Perpetual! Jehovah adores the earthly building which emulated the eternal temple per His instructions. Imagine how much more He cherishes the Eternal Temple not made with hands!

With marvelous attention to detail, the Apostle John tells of the Heavenly temple in Revelation 11:19: "And the temple of God was opened in heaven, and there was seen in his temple the ark of his testament: and there were lightnings, and voices, and thunderings, and an earthquake, and great hail." In Revelation 15:5 he writes, "And after that I looked, and, behold, the temple of the tabernacle of the testimony in heaven was opened." And in Revelation 15:8 he writes, "And the temple was filled with smoke from the glory of God, and from his power."

John 21:25 says an Earth-sized library of books barely contains all the works of the LORD Jesus Christ. With a lifetime of study, the Bible student merely "scratches the surface" to comprehend the LORD's capacity to uphold and safeguard His ceaseless word. But the endeavor to learn the words of God is worth all the effort!

"Thy word have I hid in mine heart, that I might not sin against thee" (Psalm 119:11).

Chapter Four

Substantial Evidence

No amount of work without faith pleases the Heavenly Father. The highest quality work falls short. When we consider the crisscrossing threads of language and protection in the loom of Scripture, it is by *faith* we trust God has kept His words *without decay*.

> But without faith, it is impossible to please him: for he that cometh to God must believe that he is, and that he is a rewarder of them that diligently seek him. (Hebrews 11:6)

While the physical properties of *preservation* are necessary, it is the **spiritual aspects** of safekeeping which set it apart from all others.

On December 14, 1856, Dr. Charles Haddon Spurgeon preached a now-famous sermon about faith.

In his preaching, he used the word faith more than one hundred times. It is not a long sermon but is poignant. Laying the arguments before the listener, he states,

> The first thing in faith is knowledge. A man cannot believe what he does not know. That is **a clear, self-evident axiom**. If I have never heard of a thing in all my life, and do not know it, I cannot believe it (emphasis added).[1]

---

1. Dr. Charles Haddon Spurgeon, Faith, a sermon, from https://www.spurgeon.org/resource-library/sermons/faith

He adds further:

> But a man may know a thing, and yet not have faith. I may know a thing, and yet not believe it. Therefore assent must go with faith: that is to say, what we know we must also agree unto, as being most certainly the verity of God. Now, in order to faith, it is necessary that I should not only read the Scriptures and understand them, but that I should receive them in my soul as being the very truth of the living God, and I should devoutly with my whole heart receive the whole of the Scripture as being inspired of the Most High, and the whole of the doctrine which he requires me to believe to my salvation, after which he makes clear that a person must agree with the acquired knowledge.[2]

And finally, Dr. Spurgeon admonishes: faith requires leaning (resting, reclining) on the truth now received when he preached,

> But a man may have all this, and yet not possess true faith; for the chief part of faith lies in the last head, namely, in an affiance to the truth; not the believing it merely"; and "Recumbency on the truth was the word which the old preachers used."; and "Now, true faith, in its very essence rests in this — a leaning upon Christ. It will not save me to know that Christ is a Saviour: but it will save me to trust him to be my Saviour. I shall not be delivered from the wrath to come by believing that his atonement is sufficient, but I shall be saved by making that atonement my trust, my refuge, and my all.[3]

From his preaching, Dr. Spurgeon affirms: trusting in the *inspiration* of the Scriptures brings trust in the *preservation* of the Scriptures. The English Scriptures he preached were from multi-generational copies, which hailed from multi-generational copies of the older-language first writings. It seems

---

2. Dr. Charles Haddon Spurgeon, Faith, a sermon, from https://www.spurgeon.org/resource-library/sermons/faith

3. Dr. Charles Haddon Spurgeon, Faith, a sermon, from https://www.spurgeon.org/resource-library/sermons/faith

clear he concluded by faith those Scriptures are reliable for reproof and instruction in righteousness.

Huge Investment to Preserve Mankind

Deep inside a mountain on a remote island in the Svalbard archipelago, halfway between mainland Norway and the North Pole, lies the Global Seed Vault. It is a long-term seed storage facility, built to stand the test of time — and the challenge of natural calamities or man-made disasters. The Seed Vault represents the world's largest collection of crop diversity.

Identifying the vulnerability of the world's gene banks sparked the idea of establishing a global seed vault to serve as a backup storage facility. The Vault's location is ideal for long-term seed storage, for several reasons: a) Svalbard offers a remote location which is difficult to reach; b) while the entrance may be visible, the Vault itself is over 100 meters into the mountain; c) the area is geologically stable, and the humidity is low; d) the Vault is well above sea level, protected from ocean flooding; and, e) the permafrost and thick rock provide a cost-effective and fail-safe method to conserve seeds, even without external power sources.

The Vault is the ultimate insurance policy for the world's food supply, by securing, for many decades, millions of seeds representing every important crop variety available in the world today. It is the final backup.

The Faith Framework

How marvelous! Scientists and farmers from all societies are taking great care to ensure the crops they oversee survive future catastrophes. In a proper way, these pioneers of food safety are working to ward off decay and conserve the seeds in a fixed physical condition for the posterity and prosperity of the human species. Their tireless effort is to preserve seeds of necessary plant foods should natural disasters occur, or should a pestilence deplete a particular crop, or should a discrete genetic strain become otherwise corrupted throughout the planet.

Without expert preservation scientists, the seed collections could not last long. Despite the extensive effort, intricate care, and immense expense to keep the seed strains protected from spoil and decomposition, these specimens are corruptible because of their earthy nature.

The Prophet Isaiah recorded: "The voice said, Cry. And he said, What shall I cry? All flesh is grass, and all the goodliness thereof is as the flower of the field: the grass withereth, the flower fadeth: because the spirit of the LORD bloweth upon it: surely the people is grass. The grass withereth, the flower fadeth: but the word of our God shall stand for ever" (Isaiah 40:6–8). No matter the effort and science put into preserving the genetic seed stock in one of the coldest places on planet Earth, it will never be fool-proof and will eventually succumb to the Earth's imminent destruction. But the indefectible seed of the word of God endures well beyond the lifetime of the Global Seed Vault.

Halting or interrupting the putrefaction process ensures the seed gems stay safe, not declining into uselessness. To most of us, the safekeeping of seeds for this purpose involves methods beyond the imagination. We understand, however, the motive for employing such extraordinary measures — continuation. The vault is in fact a high-tech, self-contained root cellar.

Only a small population of humans will ever be privileged to visit the seed vault — to see it for themselves, which sounds like a grand adventure! A greater swath of the human population will in life perhaps read about or hear stories of the Global Seed Vault. It is a marvel of human achievement, and its story is worth telling. An even smaller populace will actually contribute to the contents and upkeep of the genetic ark, while never setting foot inside the frigid fortress walls.

Perhaps scientists may work in their laboratory with materials returned from the underground chamber. It may be the farmer who carefully plants the progeny of the seed stock formerly housed at the fortress island. And elementary students and curious folk may see photographs of the cavernous refrigerator; hear recordings of sounds from the catacomb, or perhaps hear the stories from those who visit the secure room where kernels are safe and isolated from the ravaging forces of nature and man.

But for all those things, the greatest majority of souls on Planet Earth must rely upon the authenticity of the accounts about the seed vault. To consider the story truthful, a person must consider the qualities of the information about the Global Seed Vault, and evaluate the facts before them. They must judge the accuracy of the message (the record or journal) and they must evaluate the integrity of the messenger — approving or rejecting the messenger's mastery of the subject. Then and only then shall the receiver of the message conclude whether the information is true or false.

In consideration of the Scripture, the reader must read the text, account for its message, rely upon the Holy Ghost as messenger, and conclude whether the Scripture before them is genuine or counterfeit. An honest examination of the Bible can only arrive at one conclusion — they are the Wonderful Words of Life!

Perhaps you encountered a living document which changes from time to time, being republished as the author deems appropriate. By definition, such a document is not absolute. Its information is changing (or subject to amendment), and the reader must check whether the message is still reliable. Sometimes documents we use require updating. This is neither the state nor nature of Scripture (thankfully).

The Scriptures are the only document equipped with an eternal faculty for self-interpretation and are, by nature, static, but lively in both application and effect. The Bible student will say they learn sundry things from the same passage, having read it multiple times. Faith drives the communion between the readers' spirit and the Holy Spirit, as he eats up those lively words!

The framework of faith is this: trust (confidence, assurance, and virtue), and expectation.

Consider Again the Seed

A seed is the principal material from which anything springs forth. The Gospel of Jesus Christ is the seed discerned by the mind of man, beginning with the text of Scripture. "The word is nigh thee, even in thy mouth, and in thy heart: that is, the word of faith, which we preach; that if thou shalt confess with thy mouth the LORD Jesus, and shalt believe in thine heart that God hath raised him from the dead, thou shalt be saved" (Romans 10:8–9).

Apostle Peter wrote:

> Seeing ye have purified your souls in obeying the truth through the Spirit unto unfeigned love of the brethren, see that ye love one another with a pure heart fervently: being born again, not of corruptible seed, but of incorruptible, by the word of God, which liveth and abideth for ever. For all flesh is as grass, and all the glory of man as the flower of grass. The grass withereth, and the flower thereof falleth away: but the word of the Lord endureth for ever. And this is the word which by the gospel is preached unto you. (1 Peter 1:22–25)

When a person is fully persuaded in his mind, and correctly acts on those good seeds (words) in their heart, they have taken the first step, or principal action, of faith. By repenting of sin and calling upon the name of the LORD Jesus Christ, the child, woman, or man allows God to transform them spiritually into a new creature — a person of, by, and for faith. This entire transition from stale unbelief to actioned faith is possible by the agency of the *words* of God, transmitted through Scripture, and carefully shepherded by the Holy Ghost into the heart and mind of each person.

Faith comes by hearing the *words* of God. The Apostle Peter contrasts the immense difference between the two types of seeds. In one seed, there is only withering and decay, but in the other, there is endurance. The former seed produces death. The latter seed brings eternal life.

Substance

What is a substance? We commonly say a substance is an actual material which is *seen* or *touched*. A substance is not imaginary nor void, but is measurable. Further, both matter and spirit are substances, and are so much more than just those things meeting the eye. A substance is the essential part of something. A substance may be the subject of a text, speech, or work of art; wealth or possessions; the main points of litigation or contract; strength or integrity of character; something significant or a noteworthy thing; or a chemical formulation. A substance is verifiable by our senses.

Also, when we say something has *substance*, we are saying it has *quality* or is *genuine*; it is *desirable* or *valuable*. Substances include the clock on the wall, the water we drink, the air we breathe, the boards we build with, and the food we eat. Driven nails and medicines for health are substances. The wealth we gain, the wealth we distribute to missionaries, the books we read, or the words we hear are substances.

A substance may be material alive from God's creation, whether small or great, such as described in Genesis, "For yet seven days, and I will cause it to rain upon the earth forty days and forty nights; and every living substance that I have made will I destroy from off the face of the earth" (Genesis 7:4), or substance may be the whole essence of man, as found recorded by King David in Psalm 139:15–16: "My substance was not hid from thee, when I was made in secret, and curiously wrought in the lowest parts of the earth. Thine eyes did see my substance, yet being unperfect; and in thy book all my members were written, which in continuance were fashioned, when as yet there was none of them." In Scripture, the word substance often refers to stuff or possessions, such as we read in Genesis when Abram (Abraham) departs Haran and takes his *substance* with him (Genesis 12:5).

The Hebrews' letter matures our objective thinking by precisely describing faith as the **tangible and measurable** characteristic of our **expectation** of good things found in the **Heavenly realm.** A Christian expects he will depart this earth and join the body of saints in the Heavenly City. The *substance* of the Christian faith is the combination of belief and trust for which the Saviour will provision the promises. To know God, we yield to His Spirit and read His words. We expect He will perfectly and completely supply all we could ask or think. "Now faith is the substance of things hoped for, the evidence of things not seen" (Hebrews 11:1).

The Christian's hope stands firm upon the work of Jesus Christ and His loving redemption of eternal life for every soul. A person knows of the Saviour's work by reading the Scriptures. A person may also trust those Scriptures as tangible and essential truth — *substance*.

Evidence

What is evidence? You probably answer that evidence is the physical material, written details, or verbal testimony given under oath which certifies a violation of some criminal or civil code. Evidence may be eyewitness testimony, video footage of a crime scene, liquid or solid chemical compounds, paper documents, or even other people. While your response is correct, the word *evidence* brings a more piercing declaration: evidence **enables the mind to see the truth.**

Evidence: proof arising from our own perceptions by the senses, from the testimony of others, or from deductions of reason. Our senses furnish *evidence* of the existence of microscopic matter, color, heat or cold, mountain-top excursions, deep-sea creatures, and so forth. The statements and actions of a witness are *evidence* to a court and jury. By use of reasoning skills, the listener establishes truth or falsity about those statements. By deduction in our thoughts, we reason the facts or arguments presented.

Evidence may also be an instrument of writing which contains exhibits or attestations. Evidence makes a concept understandable. Justification of the human spirit is a matter of evidence: "But that no man is justified by the law in the sight of God, it is evident: for, The just shall live by faith" (Galatians 3:11).

In legal terms, evidence pertains to the burden of proof, admissibility, relevance, weight, and sufficiency of what should be admitted into the record of a legal proceeding. Evidence — crucial in both civil and criminal proceedings — may include many different materials or words. Both criminal and civil courts at all levels have rules governing the admissibility of evidence into trials. If evidence is obtained illegally, such as during an unlawful police search, then the evidence (and any other evidence it leads to) may not be used at trial. Evidence which is considered irrelevant or prejudicial to a case also may be deemed inadmissible. Additionally, evidence may be thrown out if the integrity of its handling (chain of custody) is in doubt. There are four general types of evidence: a) **Real** (tangible things, such as audio recordings or weapons); b) **Demonstrative** (a model or story of what likely happened at a given time and place); c) **Documentary** (a letter or other written facts); or, d) **Testimonial** (witness testimony). The basic prerequisites of admissibility are relevance, materiality, and competence. In general, if the evidence is shown to be relevant, material, and competent, and is not barred by an exclusionary rule, it is admissible. Evidence is *relevant* when it has a reasonable tendency to make the fact that it is offered to prove or disprove, either more or less probable. Evidence is *material* if it is offered to prove a fact that is at issue in the case. Evidence is *competent* if the proof being offered meets certain traditional requirements of reliability.[4]

We should consider Scripture as *evidence*. Scripture's literary and historical pedigree suffices to prove the quality and effectiveness of the words on the page. But with Scripture, it goes much farther. What document could be more relevant to the condition of man, or his destiny, than the Bible? What other document could better show man's sin against his creator? Is there another document which more readily shows humanity's need for rescue? What other literary evidence has proven through the ages its competency to convince people of the death, burial, and resurrection of Jesus Christ?

---

4. Adapted from What are the Rules of Evidence?, https://www.findlaw.com/hirealawyer/choosing-the-right-lawyer/evidence-law.html and a Summary of the Rules of Evidence, https://corporate.findlaw.com/litigation-disputes/summary-of-the-rules-of-evidence.html

In view of the rules of evidence, the words of the Bible are **real** because they exist and apply to every aspect of human life and eternal destiny. The words are **demonstrative** because they illustrate the testimony of many factual witnesses. They are **documentary**, being written. The words are **testimonial** because they tell us what God said directly or through His chosen penmen (the proficient witnesses).

Everything and all properties we read in Scripture — the names, dates, and places — the people and interactions; the decisions and assemblies, and so forth, is *evidence* proving God's words did travel by His will from their eternal station to dwell upon earth, and God's Word dwells among us today, in written form (John 1)!

Remarkably, Jeremiah 32 contains the English word "evidence" several times. The chapter shows the prophet is imprisoned in the king's house court after the besieging of Jerusalem. (Notably, King Zedekiah detested Jeremiah's rigorous preaching.) The shuttered prophet received a simple message from Jehovah to buy his cousin Hanameel's field in Anathoth. His cousin then visited Jeremiah to complete the transaction and the wise prophet showed his obedience to the LORD, buying the field.

There are several noteworthy (albeit inconspicuous) sweet tidbits found in this adventurous chronology. First, Jeremiah reserved the rights of redemption and inheritance of the field. Also, even though Jeremiah remained in jail, he gained or possessed silver, which he used to make the purchase. As well, the soon-to-be-traveling prophet could receive visitors and conduct business, even under house arrest. It seems even his captors respected him.

The facts of the story start with the Prophet Jeremiah consenting to the purchase agreement of the field in Anathoth, and finish with Baruch storing two copies of the signed documents in earthen vessels. They sealed one jar and kept one jar open, intending to preserve the documents for a long time. Modern societies have the same function, vested in the County Recorder's office, where official records stay safe (preserved). Jeremiah signed with his own hand and bound himself as the new owner of the real property. By doing so, he promised to redeem (pay in full) the asking price.

From this story we fully understand that these contracts — these credentialed instruments (or deeds of trust) — are genuine and tangible proof of the prophet's financial transaction and ownership of the field. These documents, necessary for the exchange of real property, enable our minds to see the truth-proof (evidence). Baruch assembled evidentiary materials and established a chain of custody to keep the deeds stored for a lengthy time. Marvelously, not only did Jeremiah affix his signature to the purchase agreements, but the nearby witnesses of the covenant also placed their signatures in the recorder's journal. This method is like our modern notary process.

Reconsidering the Framework of Faith

Following the lead of Noah Webster in his 1828 *American Dictionary of the English Language*, I offer this statement about faith:

> Faith is the substantial act of fixing one's entire dependence upon the Saviour in every area of life. Whether historical, speculative, evangelical, emotional, or otherwise — faith substantially abhors fault-searching and evidently adores your affections upon the Holy Spirit; faith demands the assent of your mind to the declared truth of Scripture; faith dispenses with reason and fulfills the evidentiary requirement for the unseen (and very real) Heavenly confidence; energizing faith builds on the historical and grabs hold of the evangelical; active faith excels toward the approval of the Holy Ghost; faith can be practiced and experienced and cultivated, but is never measured by practical applications, successes, or increments (i.e., pragmatism, synthesis or reductionism); faith opposes doubt and rejects fear; faith propels the believer to a fixity upon the reliability and authority of the Scriptures; faith is a firm, cordial belief in the veracity of God and His words; faith is full and affectionate confidence in the certainty of those things which the Certain One has declared!

Through faith, the unknown becomes known, and through faith, the unseen becomes seen (2 Corinthians 4:18). By faith, we receive warnings of things not seen, just like Admiral Noah, highlighted in Hebrews 11:7. While on Planet Earth, we can only see eternal things with a partial view. In Heaven, we shall see those things in full — face to face. For now, we struggle to see clearly because of the opacity of sin. But later, in the Heavenly station, our view will be crisp and transparent.

The natural man, before being born again, cannot fully comprehend the messages from the Creator. He does not value fully that some principles require no reason, no observation, and neither do those precepts warrant appraisal. Trusting the evidence of Scripture is the prerequisite in all matters. As if hearing the gentle breath of God rippling through a grassy meadow, the words of the Holy Bible compel quiet trust by the believer. For the mind to be transformed and renewed, one acknowledges that some things just require faith (Hebrews 11).

Extending Through the Ages

Mankind has desired truth throughout the ages. Since Cain and Abel brought their gifts to the LORD, faith has been the chief component of the relationship between humans and their Creator. Cain rejected faith, relying only on the physical and practical, having his mind clogged with pride and willfulness. Abel's active faith brought "a more excellent sacrifice than Cain, by which he obtained witness that he was righteous" (Hebrews 11:4).

Abel's excellent sacrifice earned him a place in Scripture as a righteous man. Abel clung to the truth of the Creator while Cain chose his own truth. And his so-named truth is unreliable, with its roots anchored in the awfulness of humanity. Because of the offense of the first Adam, judgment came upon all other people, and we are by default condemned. Conversely, by the righteousness of the LORD Jesus Christ, the gift of salvation is available to every person, and with it the spiritual justification of eternal life. Where sin abounds — grace abounds and overflows and reaches far deeper than sin!

> Wherefore, as by one man sin entered into the world, and death by sin; and so death passed upon all men, for that all have sinned. (Romans 5:12)

> But not as the offence, so also is the free gift. For if through the offence of one many be dead, much more the grace of God, and the gift by grace, which is by one man, Jesus Christ, hath abounded unto many. (Romans 5:15)

> Therefore as by the offence of one judgment came upon all men to condemnation; even so by the righteousness of one the free gift came upon all men unto justification of life. For as by one man's disobedience many were made sinners, so by the obedience of one shall many be made righteous. (Romans 5:18–19)

> Moreover the law entered, that the offence might abound. But where sin abounded, grace did much more abound: that as sin hath reigned unto death, even so might grace reign through righteousness unto eternal life by Jesus Christ our Lord. (Romans 5:20–21)

In each case, we learn of our condition and its consequences — and the way of escape — by **reading the words**.

Demonstration

Historical and material evidence shows the warp thread of inspiration and the weft thread of preservation, but only to a limited extent. History can teach us about the prophets and many events. We can catalog evidence of preservation in the many archaeological findings and the study of material preservation. And yet, the LORD exponentially accounts for the priceless utility of His words — in life situations; in salvation; in practice; and in every imaginable thing on Planet Earth.

After all — His words frame the ground you stand upon (Hebrews 11:3). Those *words* reach interminably beyond the limits of history and archaeology, and even beyond the existence of Earth itself. If there is no word from God, then no earth, no seas, no creatures, no humans — nothing! It pleases the Heavenly Father when we anchor our confidence in the Scriptures. With faith in the everlasting words, we know the Creator, and we see His marvelous works.

Earlier, I described a seed as the principal material from which anything springs forth. Let us briefly look at the concourse between faith and the word of God. In Luke 8, after the LORD Jesus finished defining the parable of the sower, the disciples asked Him, "What might this parable be?" As He expounds further, He states his disciples shall hear directly the mysteries of the kingdom of God, but others shall learn from the parables (earthly examples of Heavenly truths).

The LORD had given them the parable itself and now He defines it for them: "The seed is the word of God." People on the sidelines will hear the word of God and not believe because of the devil. Those staying on the hard, rocky ground will hear and believe, but never plant a root, and will eventually fall away to temptation. Those persons whose station is among the thorns will hear, possibly believe, but choke because of the cares and pleasures of the world.

And thankfully, the seed nurtured by those on the good ground, which have an honest and good heart — having heard the word, will keep it and patiently bring forth fruit in due time. Various people groups treat God's words with variableness, but Scripture has no such entropy. As God does not change, neither do His words. When the good heart receives and nurtures the word seed, then faith becomes more tangible (substantive) and his expectation of good things (hope) bolsters his affection for things above.

The Fruit of Faith

Throughout the ministry of the LORD Jesus, He went into many towns and villages healing people suffering from long-term illnesses, and many diseases and maladies. Scripture says He made the sightless to see, the crippled to walk, the deaf to hear, and the unspeaking to rejoice aloud.

We need only see a few examples from the Bible to establish this simple evidence: the results of faith are *effective* and *permanent*.

> And Jesus arose, and followed him, and so did his disciples. And, behold, a woman, which was diseased with an issue of blood twelve years, came behind him, and touched the hem of his garment: for she said within herself, If I may but touch his garment, I shall be whole. But Jesus turned him about, and when he saw her, he said, Daughter, be of good comfort; thy faith hath made thee whole. And the woman was made whole from that hour. (Matthew 9:19–22)

> And Jesus stood, and commanded him to be brought unto him: and when he was come near, he asked him, saying, What wilt thou that I shall do unto thee? And he said, Lord, that I may receive my sight. And Jesus said unto him, Receive thy sight: thy faith hath saved thee. And immediately he received his sight, and followed him, glorifying God: and all the people, when they saw it, gave praise unto God. (Luke 18:40–43)

> But I know, that even now, whatsoever thou wilt ask of God, God will give it thee. Jesus saith unto her, Thy brother shall rise again. Martha saith unto him, I know that he shall rise again in the resurrection at the last day. Jesus said unto her, I am the resurrection, and the life: he that believeth in me, though he were dead, yet shall he live: and whosoever liveth and believeth in me shall never die. Believest thou this? She saith unto him, Yea, Lord: I believe that thou art the Christ, the Son of God, which should come into the world. (John 11:22–27)

In each of these examples, the recipient of Jesus' healing has both **knowledge** and **trust**. Their awareness is *substantial*. The testimonial *evidence* in each of these passages is the power-filled words which Jesus spoke, and the recipients heard and bound upon their hearts. Faith erased the issue from the woman's blood. The blind man, by faith, gained sight. Faith sealed the Saviour's sovereignty into Martha's heart. Faith did indeed change them by hearing the words directly from the Voice of God Himself.

Faith: substantial expectation and evidentiary revelation.

The Delivery Model

The Christian is fond of paraphrasing or quoting one of Apostle Paul's most famous statements: faith comes by hearing the word of God (Romans 10:17). This verse is beautiful and powerful. But if we ponder it for a moment, we realize confidence in the LORD both begins and ends with the Scriptures. The word of God (the Holy Bible) is the vehicle by which believing faith flows into the heart and mind of man. Further, Jesus stated, "If any man thirst, let him come unto me, and drink. He that believeth on me, as the scripture hath said, out of his belly shall flow rivers of living water" (John 7:37–38).

Let us briefly examine the delivery model: **Scripture — Hearing — Faith**.

In Acts 13, we read a spectacular set of stories which magnificently illustrate this model. The scene opens with the college of prophets at Antioch, consumed with the Scriptures and ministry. The Holy Ghost was there. These prophets are so filled with the Holy Ghost there is no spare space for any unwanted thing — no room left for any other spirit! With every part of their beings, they submitted all their attendance to Him.

As they provide sacred service to the beautiful Holy Ghost — **HE SPOKE**!

STOP!

Muse there for just a moment. The Holy Ghost did not suddenly arrive. He made company with these faithful servants. These men of God ministered primarily to Him, being so filled with His presence, they were sensitive to His reciprocated ministry. He made Himself at home! Just like all the times before, He spoke!

After being commissioned, Barnabas and Saul headed out on a missionary trip at the behest of the Holy Ghost. Notice Sergius Paulus, who desired to hear the word of God, who believed, being astonished at the doctrine of the LORD. Watch as the local despisers rejected faith. Observe the listening Gentiles as they pressed the preachers to bring again the Scripture message to the temple the following sabbath. Behold the large colony of the Hebrews as they followed Barnabas and Saul, being persuaded to continue in grace. And finally, marvel at the many more Gentiles believing on the word of God, as they launched into the faith of the LORD Jesus.

If you step back from the details just for a moment, you will see the entire series of events start with the Holy Ghost speaking *words*, and with every turn, the focal point is the *words* of God. Just imagine being a spectator, observing the lives of people eternally changed by the Lively Word!

As we near the end of Acts 13, the situation is becoming heated. There are some angry Hebrews, for certain. Apostle Paul rhetorically states an obvious point, which is so *evident* it is often overlooked.

Boldly he says,

> It was necessary that the word of God should first have been spoken to you: but seeing ye put it from you, and judge yourselves unworthy of everlasting life, lo, we turn to the Gentiles. For so hath the Lord commanded us, saying, I have set thee to be a light of the Gentiles, that thou shouldest be for salvation unto the ends of the earth. And when the Gentiles heard this, they were glad, and glorified the word of the Lord: and as many as were ordained to eternal life believed. And the word of the Lord was published throughout all the region. (Acts 13:46–49)

As Dr. Spurgeon showed us earlier — belief begins with knowledge. If one is to call upon the LORD Jesus, he must first know of the LORD Jesus (and His grace and works, and so forth). But to gain this knowledge, one must first hear of the Saviour and His works. To hear of the Holy One of salvation, a person must have heard at the mouth of the preacher.

After commissioning, the College of Prophets sent the preachers out with the Gospel message, which Paul later recites by letter to the Christians in Rome:

> How then shall they call on him in whom they have not believed? and how shall they believe in him of whom they have not heard? and how shall they hear without a preacher? And how shall they preach, except they be sent? as it is written, How beautiful are the feet of them that preach the gospel of peace, and bring glad tidings of good things! (Romans 10:14–15)

The preacher may be a person, the preacher may be an electronic book, or the preacher may be the pages of paper in a Bible.

This is the delivery model: **Scripture — Hearing — Faith**. It's all about the words.

The sum total of our knowledge is based on faith in our senses. I can never have any knowledge of fire, except I burn myself, nor of getting wet, save through contact with water; and if it is not in reality true that fire burns and water wets, all our knowing and thinking is at an end — Rev. Frederic Bettex

Chapter Five

Necessary and Sufficient

Everyday you encounter things as either *necessary* and/or *sufficient*, often without realizing it.

When a thing is *sufficient*, it means it is enough to make something happen. Similarly, when a thing is *necessary*, it means something will not happen unless the condition of the thing also happens. When two conditions are both necessary and sufficient to meet the result, they must both be true. True and true always arrive at true. In logic and otherwise, the smallest amount of falsehood results in the whole thing being discarded as false. Notably, the Apostle Paul twice tells us of leaven, which requires only a small amount to permeate the whole loaf. For example, a slight hint of rottenness in milk means I throw out the whole jug. Also, the smallest miscalculation causes a satellite's orbit to falter, destroying the mission.

When we think of something which is *necessary* (a thing of necessity), we recognize it to be unavoidable; an absolute requisite; indispensable to the condition, and therefore — **necessary**. When we think of something which is *sufficient*, we rightly describe the thing as adequate for the proposed end; qualified to the task; competent in performance; accomplished, and therefore — **sufficient**.

The cause (start) must be necessary and sufficient to the effect (end) in order to cause the effect, or else the effect does not finish. For example, water provides necessary buoyancy to a ship and must be sufficient for its flotation and voyage. A handyman with the *necessary* plumbing skills is *sufficient* for fixing a leaky pipe. Breathing is *necessary* to sustain life and must be of *sufficient* quantity to meet the demands of the body.

Consider the coin: two sides, an obverse and a reverse. Each side of the coin is both *necessary* and *sufficient* for the other.

Scripture is necessary to understand God's character and nature. The Scriptures are necessary to see our great need, like a mirror reflecting our current condition. To estimate and admit our failings and shortcomings, Scripture is the necessary judge. To receive salvation and partake in redemption, Scripture is necessary. For conduct and polity in the local church, the Scriptures are necessary. Beyond the world around us, the Scriptures are necessary, as they reveal to us the wonders and works of Christ. The Scriptures reveal to the reader the sovereignty and power of God in all His marvelous creations. Healing the wounds caused by sin requires the effect of Scripture. To see the goodness and grace of God; to perceive the love and light of God; appreciate the holiness and justice of God, and to be the object of the mercy and compassion of God — the Scriptures are necessary.

By substantial evidence, Scripture is true — always true:

> For this cause also thank we God without ceasing, because, when ye received the word of God which ye heard of us, ye received it not as the word of men, but as it is in truth, the word of God, which effectually worketh also in you that believe. (1 Thessalonians 2:13)

The doctrines of inspiration and preservation are *necessary* to one another and *sufficient* for each other. Like the ebb and flow of tidal waters or the rise and fall of a piston in a car engine — inspiration always transmits with preservation, and preservation always conducts with inspiration. They are like the conjoined sides of the same coin, each with a distinct purpose, but working hand-in-hand on the same mission.

In the study of the Scriptures, *sufficiency* is the pillar where the student of the Bible anchors his faith and understanding. Like a fresh drink of cool water is to the palate, every situation or impact in life is answerable with the Bible. In splendid harmony with this principle, is the *necessity* of Scripture — that God has given to humankind all things necessary to understand Him and His timeless message. By ushering His eternal breath through the chosen writers, the LORD launched the first publishing company. His method is not, as some claim, eccentric theater.

Psalm 19 is a marquee example about the sufficiency of Scripture. I encourage you to study it deeply. From day to day and night to night, the Heavens declare the mighty handiwork of God. Man cannot hide anything from God. There is no language or speech, from one end of the earth to the other, where God's words are second best. From the highest of heights, to the lowest of depths, His words are perfect, sure, and simple; right, pure, and clean; and they are true and righteous, sweeter than honey, and more desirable than gold. The properties of God's words labeled in Psalm 19 paint the complete picture of Scripture's sufficiency.

The Bible is *sufficient* because it is adequate; because it is more than qualified for the task; because its Author is supernaturally competent in His performance. And in describing the Biblical books and records as *sufficient*, I am compelled to unfold how *necessary* are those Scriptures. Keep thinking.

If and Then

As we examine the Bible prototypes which meet with being both *necessary* and *sufficient*, let us consider the test method of the truth conditional: **if — then**. If a condition is true, then the action carries out. If a condition is false, then the action will not continue.

Amid Apostle Paul's second letter to the Christian church at Corinth, we discern:

1. *If* our earthly house of this tabernacle dissolves — *then* we have a building of God, a house not made with hands, eternal in the heavens.

2. *If* we are at home in the body — *then* we are absent from the LORD.

3. *If* one died for all — *then* are all dead.

4. *If* any man is in Christ — *then* he is a new creature.

5. *If* old things pass away — *then* all things become new.

6. *If* He who knew no sin, absorbed sin for us — *then* we become righteous before God because of Him — despite our sin.

These truth-tested conditionals are all successfully fulfilled by the work of the Holy Ghost (2 Corinthians 5).

Consider: **if** Goliath — **then** David. Jehovah has never once dismissed His protection over His people, even when they were under judgment and chastisement. This future king of the Hebrews, bold and undeterred, pronounced to the dreadful Philistine, before God and man: "Thou comest to me with a sword, and with a spear, and with a shield: but I come to thee in the name of the LORD of hosts, the God of the armies of Israel, whom thou hast defied" (1 Samuel 17:45). If you, Mr. Philistine, come at me with physical weapons, then I will strike back offensively in the LORD's name, and with Holy weapons which you have never experienced! As the cause of defeating the Philistine man-giant was *necessary*, one stone from the spiritual-giant David's rucksack was *sufficient* to destroy this haughty defier of the LORD.

Consider: **if** my people, which are called by my name, shall humble themselves, and pray, and seek my face, and turn from their wicked ways — **then** will I hear from heaven, and will forgive their sin, and will heal their land (2 Chronicles 7:14).

Consider: **if** all humans are sinners — **then** death came by the deeds of one man (the first Adam). As the Gospel is necessary to the salvation of any human, the death, burial, and resurrection of Jesus Christ (the Last Adam) heals the enormous wound of sin.

By reading the Bible, we comprehend these truth-tested conditionals (Romans 5).

As the Apostle Paul wrote his epistle to the Christian church at Rome, he certified the method for communicating the Gospel (Romans 10:13–15). Paul uncloaks the mystery of salvation through one's actionable faith upon the word of God. The preacher's necessary message of the good news is sufficient to their hearing. It is necessary for the sinner-believer to hear the good news of the Gospel and it is necessary for the sinner to call upon the LORD Jesus Christ. Believing (actionable faith) and calling upon His name suffices to rescue the perishing soul from damnation! The words are clear: if a person calls upon the name of the LORD — He will save them.

In his first letter to Pastor Timothy, the Apostle Paul writes a synopsis of the Gospel of Jesus Christ: "And without controversy great is the mystery of godliness: God was manifest in the flesh, justified in the Spirit, seen of angels, preached unto the Gentiles, believed on in the world, received up into glory" (1 Timothy 3:16).

The concept that God's godliness is profoundly mysterious frustrates the faithless. And yet, the Heavenly Father's credentials are concurrently true and perplexing to our hearts — and they should excite wonder and awe in our thoughts! Like little clues, each checkpoint of the mystery of godliness is *necessary* and *sufficient* to uncloak the mystery — all accomplished by faith, so a person can believe upon the LORD Jesus Christ for eternal restoration.

The Christian must not presume his opinion superior to God Himself, for this is certain foolishness. It is the spirit of anti-Christ which insists we must view the Bible with a doubting spirit and critical eye; or from only a historic or speculative viewpoint. Neither the whole nor part of the Scriptures is reducible to simple phenomena with only visible attributes (e.g., reductionism). Indeed, the Scriptures are replete with wise statements, but those ideologies are not the limit. If one letter, word, or sentence is true, then all passages are true, because they hail from the Author of all truth. Approaching the Scriptures for any reason must focus on their supernatural, Holy Spirit-engaging qualities.

Other books on Planet Earth, regardless of their impact on society, remain void of the liveliness shepherded upon Scripture by the Holy Ghost. None is supernatural, save the Holy Scriptures. Webster's Dictionary, Pilgrim's Progress, and the works of various Christian writers may be wonderful books, with deep and lasting effects on many generations — but they are neither inspired nor protected from decay.

When the human mind relies wholly on "reason" for its conclusions, it rejects faith as the superior solution. The false prophet, polluted politician, or prevaricating scientist apply methods of synthesis to the acts of God, inserting his own agenda. Man's vain methods are limited by time and space and matter (and by extension, limited by sin). There is no amnesty for pragmatism, Gnosticism, skepticism, or psychologism in the reading, study, or application of God's indestructible words. The trappings of the few dimensions of man's intellect do not restrain the Creator. He is without beginning and without end, condescending from His lofty emplacement, and He is not to be compared to the finest of earthly elements. "Forasmuch then as we are the offspring of God, we ought not to think the Godhead is like unto gold, or silver, or stone, graven by art and man's device" (Acts 17:29).

Preservation by Pressure

Wood will degrade easily if not properly treated, especially when exposed to weather. The prime reason to treat wood in one fashion or another is to ward off an attack by external forces. Pressure treatment is a process which forces wood preservatives or fire retardants into the wood. Many consider these processes the best and most effective methods to extend and preserve timber life. Preservatives protect the wood from attack by wood-ingesting insects like termites, and wood rot caused by fungal decay. Fire-retardant treatments help the wood char when exposed to flame, reducing smoke and flame.

Uses for treated wood include interior framing, exposed exterior wood, fresh-water and salt-water exposures, and fire retardants for wall, roof, and floor assemblies. The pressure treatment process is used to protect utility poles, railroad ties, structural framing, fence pickets, and deck boards.

Pressure processes are the most permanent method around today for preserving timber. Special closed cylinders are used to apply pressure or vacuum to the wood. These processes have several advantages over the non-pressure methods, and in most cases, produce a deeper penetration and more uniform absorption of the preservatives, because operators can control the various conditions. After the last treatment, a vacuum is frequently used to extract excess preservatives. Repeated cycles cause more penetration of the treatment agent, producing more endurance. Because of controlled pressure and methods, the wood is kept safe from decay for as long as possible.

Principal Principles

In life, there are many fixed principles we accept as true. We say these things are axiomatic: those principles whose truth is so clear at first sight or hearing that no process of reasoning or mechanical demonstration can make it plainer. Those arguments are self-evident, certain, and obvious. Principal truths are invincible from a dispute — else they are uncertain (not principal).

Consider: the sun rises from the east; the hot stove will cause pain and injury when touched; objects which rise must fall submissive to gravity; the human heart has four chambers; and Earth turns on its axis one entire revolution per day. These are principal truths.

All sixty-six books of the Bible are the paramount principal truth. Scripture (the written whole) comprises parts, each inheriting (and never abandoning) the properties of truth cascading from the Heavenly Source. Each and all sections in the written prose of Scripture are standalone truthful. These specimens are simultaneously *necessary* and *sufficient* for the whole. As you consider further the warp thread of inspiration and the weft thread of preservation interwoven on the language loom, examine the following axioms.

Axiom: Scripture is Inspired

Inspiration is the primary act of God upon men to transmit His eternal words to His creation and creatures. Scripture is God-breathed. It emanates from God's triune Godhead. Psalm 119:89 shows us that God's word is stationary, established, and standing firm in Heaven. God anchors His words in eternity. By inspiration, the LORD Jehovah moves upon a holy man, causing his spiritual lungs to be filled with the sweet, eternal breath of the Holy Ghost, as the

Creator conveys His words through the human agent. When God breathes and speaks through the primary scribe — it is an act of inspiration.

God performs inspiration without admixture or amendment by man, as His Word transits the human vessel. Pastor Timothy received distinct instruction about the inspiration of all Scripture:

> But continue thou in the things which thou hast learned and hast been assured of, knowing of whom thou hast learned them; and that from a child thou hast known the holy scriptures, which are able to make thee wise unto salvation through faith which is in Christ Jesus. All scripture is given by inspiration of God, and is profitable for doctrine, for reproof, for correction, for instruction in righteousness: that the man of God may be perfect, throughly furnished unto all good works. (2 Timothy 3:14–17)

Can the Creator, who uses His words to conduct creation, keep those words undefiled by fetid human behavior? Yes!

He spoke the universe into existence. By His breath, a heap of dusty nothingness became the quickened first Adam. By the dynamic stirring of the Holy Ghost in the spirit of man, speech transmits the word from Jehovah through holy men in their tongue and by operation of the hand to write. When the first man lived alone on young Planet Earth, God's interminable Word innately possessed such qualities as eternal, infallible, sharp, adequate, inerrant, active, powerful, profitable, immutable, quick, healthy, furnished, effective, lovely, and plenary. These qualities do not cease or vacillate.

Take a moment to read Psalm 138. Now consider the God of Creation, yielding from His vitalness, who lent to you and me the one entity magnified above His name — **His words**!

In Second Samuel, the noble and sweet (but unworthy) King David magnificently captures the reader's attention to the notion of inspiration.

> Now these be the last words of David. David the son of Jesse said, and the man who was raised up on high, the anointed of the God of Jacob, and the sweet psalmist of Israel, said, The Spirit of the LORD spake by me, and his word was in my tongue. The God of Israel said, the Rock of Israel spake to me, He that ruleth over men must be just, ruling in the fear of God. And he shall be as

the light of the morning, when the sun riseth, even a morning without clouds; as the tender grass springing out of the earth by clear shining after rain. (2 Samuel 23:1–4)

This flawed, but mighty, warrior-king David has matured into a humbled deputy of the Holy Ghost. He journeyed from tending sheep to appointment by God as the King of Israel. Now at the end of his life, the Spirit of Jehovah once again captured his tongue, delivering a mandate to men which rule over others. Fashioned as rushing waters which carve through rock, David is ready to host God's words, as the Rock of Israel melted him and excited his spirit. King David experienced inspiration before. In a genuine moment of time, the Father breathed His sacred utterances from eternity into the human vessel. This is a pristine example of inspiration, just as with any other prophet.

Scripture is chock full of wonderful exhibits when the LORD speaks through His preachers. The Hebrews' letter begins with dovetailing traditional teaching with contemporary known facts about the LORD Jesus Christ. The correspondence connects the diverse manners of the past fathers and prophets with the most recent events of the day, speaking to the Hebrew leaders by His Son, the appointed heir of all things (Hebrews 1:1–2). As well, the essence of 1 Corinthians 2:13 reveals how plainly the LORD speaks to man through His Spirit, but not in the words which man's wisdom teaches.

Throughout history, the Holy Ghost has moved upon the sundry prophets. Luke 1:70, Acts 3:21, and 2 Peter 3:2 are candid constituents of interwoven inspiration and preservation, revealing the survivability of Scripture. As noted previously, the Holy Ghost makes clear in Hebrews 1:1–2, that the LORD, in the past, spoke through His prophets and spoke in the last days of a time extending through the apostles and direct disciples. Back then, He gave some apostles and prophets, and today He continues the same leadership model in the churches through evangelists, pastors, and teachers — for the perfecting of the saints, for the work of the ministry, and for the edifying of the body of Christ (Ephesians 4:11–12).

Scripture is inspired.

Axiom: Scripture is Resilient

Near the end of 2 Chronicles, we read of King Hezekiah taking counsel with his princes and priests and subsequently issuing a commandment to be posted in all the cities of the Hebrew people. The simple directive? Reinstate the true worship of Jehovah.

Describing the Bible as resilient is to say the words of the part or the whole of Scripture are more than able to withstand trouble and difficulty. Certainly, some hearers did not welcome King Hezekiah's decree, and likely others worked to undermine it. Regardless, King Hezekiah relied upon the copies of the centuries-old written Scripture at his disposal when making the decree. For a great length of time, those copies and the preceding copies had survived many ordeals when published from generation to generation.

The king's summons required all the people to assemble for worship, "for they had not done it of a long time in such sort as it was written." All of this included the promise that God's wrath is preventable: "serve the LORD your God, that the fierceness of his wrath may turn away from you." Further, the families and descendants are supposed to receive compassion from those who took Israel captive to Babylon. Hezekiah's promise on behalf of God could not be more clear: "For if ye turn again unto the LORD, your brethren and your children shall find compassion before them that lead them captive, so that they shall come again into this land: for the LORD your God is gracious and merciful, and will not turn away his face from you, if ye return unto him." (2 Chronicles 30:5–9).

Fast forward to the New Testament. It is not presumptuous to state that Jesus Christ and His apostles spoke words other than those recorded, such as the conversation they had while transiting the cornfield on the sabbath day, or while preparing the ship to set sail on the Sea of Galilee.

Consider the time when, as a child, the LORD Jesus exchanged dialogue with the lawyers and teachers in the temple (seemingly for some number of hours). We do not know all the verbal communion, just the expressed sample. What about the words Jesus wrote on the ground? Reading the narrative, it starts with discussion, and then the Saviour writes. Those are good words, and perhaps useful or encouraging. However, at the Author's choosing, He did not include those words in the canon of Scripture.

Additional words are not germane to our understanding of the Gospel nor the working out of our faith. But still and all, the LORD satisfies all our needs in the everlasting journal, in which there are no over-abundances, and certainly nothing missing. Scripture does not deserve nor demand amendment from man's vocabulary, regardless of eloquence, degree, or letters.

Sundry sections of the Scriptures admonish us to not tamper with the words.

> Ye shall not add unto the word which I command you, neither shall ye diminish ought from it, that ye may keep the command-

ments of the LORD your God which I command you. (Deuteronomy 4:2)

Know therefore this day, and consider it in thine heart, that the LORD he is God in heaven above, and upon the earth beneath: there is none else. Thou shalt keep therefore his statutes, and his commandments, which I command thee this day, that it may go well with thee, and with thy children after thee, and that thou mayest prolong thy days upon the earth, which the LORD thy God giveth thee, for ever. (Deuteronomy 4:39–40)

For I testify unto every man that heareth the words of the prophecy of this book, If any man shall add unto these things, God shall add unto him the plagues that are written in this book: and if any man shall take away from the words of the book of this prophecy, God shall take away his part out of the book of life, and out of the holy city, and from the things which are written in this book. (Revelation 22:18–19)

Scripture is resilient.

Axiom: Scripture is the Royal Commentary

What is a commentary? Basically, it is writing which focuses on, and possibly magnifies, the prime subject which it comments on. A commentary explains or illustrates the obscure, making it clear. As a book, it holds comments or promotes annotations and can be a historical narrative. A commentary does not displace but formally shapes itself to bolster the integrity of the subject. Commentary runs in parallel with the primary subject.

Much fine academic work has achieved detailed lexicons of cross-references in the Scriptures, often compiling more than one-half-million entries. But not even half of the story has been told. The preeminent commentary on Scripture is Scripture itself. This highest and noblest position of the Bible as its own expositor issues from God's authority as the sacred bookwright. The LORD Jehovah does everything far greater than first class. Given the limitless magnitude of the Scriptures and the many writing styles, we need little effort to realize the Bible is the fountain which endlessly flows Living Water in the hearts of children, women, and men. Come unto me, the LORD Jesus says, and receive the water! Drink His water and you will never thirst!

It is possible to reveal so much more about Scripture. Let us glean from several exhibits of the Bible commenting upon itself:

Amid Christ's ministry, right after upbraiding the Pharisees, we find a group of Sadducees attempting to trap Him again into a difficult situation from which there is no escape. The question before the Saviour regarded which of the brothers shall remain married to the woman in the resurrection after she buried seven husbands. How ironic — this is the group of sad fellows who claim expertise in the law and prophets; who say there is *no resurrection*. Imagine attempting to trap the Creator into an inescapable conundrum!

The Apostle Matthew journals the LORD Jesus directly:

> Jesus answered and said unto them, Ye do err, not knowing the scriptures, nor the power of God. For in the resurrection they neither marry, nor are given in marriage, but are as the angels of God in heaven. But as touching the resurrection of the dead, have ye not read that which was spoken unto you by God, saying, I am the God of Abraham, and the God of Isaac, and the God of Jacob? God is not the God of the dead, but of the living. (Matthew 22:29–32)

It's quite marvelous when the LORD Jesus quotes Scripture text, He is teaching the historical record of what God said to them in the far past, and what He says to them in the present day! With a small amount of *commentary*, you will see this passage as a skillful example of Scriptural *self-commentary*. Most likely, the LORD Jesus quoted Exodus 3, which is found in the religious primer for any Saducee student. Just imagine the power of God, shown by the burning of a bush which flames cannot consume. Only the Master of the flame can control fire and accomplish such a wonder! The Sadducees, as spiritual pygmies, did not understand the Scriptures they were so familiar with. Neither did they understand the tenacious power of the Word upon the hearts of men.

Jesus Christ repudiated their wicked, hypocritical hearts with Scripture itself. You can almost see the steam erupting from their ears! Standing right before them was the Author of the Exodus journal, and yet, they rejected Him and His words. Three times in the Exodus passage, the LORD Jehovah described His position and stated His name as the God of Abraham, Isaac, and Jacob.

Emphatically, He constrained Moses to tell the Hebrew people He is **"I AM THAT I AM."** Hallelujah!

Then observe the LORD Jesus as He carefully interrogated these sad fellows with eternal truth asking them, "Have you not read the Scriptures that were spoken unto you by God?" Take notice of the agency of the Godhead who does the speaking — in the past, in their current conversation with Christ, and in our hearts and minds today, all these centuries later. These Pharisees knew something very important: the phrases "Scripture says" and "Scripture reads" are equivalent to "God says."

How could those words spoken by God many centuries prior be now read by these morose Sadducees as they studied the Pentateuch? The answer: the Publisher prevents decay of the Scriptures throughout all centuries. The question is rhetorical, because they are required to know and study the Exodus record (as with the rest of the Pentateuch), and likely they had most or all of it memorized. They knew the truth and refused the Great Commentator! They had elitist head knowledge, but dismissed heart knowledge. These fellows, ironically, claim eminence over the Scriptures, but cannot "see the forest for the trees."

Another example of this royal commentary is near the end of Apostle Paul's letter to the Christian saints in Rome. He reminds them to be unselfish and proactively care for one another; he implores them to be like-minded toward one another and to be in unity of mind and mouth, as they glorify God, following the example of Christ Jesus. The thread running core in Romans 15 is the blessing upon the Gentiles because of the spiritual moves of the saints in Jerusalem.

Apostle Peter also wrote, "Knowing this first, that no prophecy of the scripture is of any private interpretation" (2 Peter 1:20). Scripture did not start from any human. No single person or institution of religion holds all the keys to interpreting the Scriptures. Who are we to "own" God's intentions, thoughts, or words? Interpreting the Scriptures yields to the agency of the Holy Ghost working through the Christian's spirit, to provide understanding to the best of their ability.

And further, after the Thessalonican brethren rescued Paul and Silas and sent them to Berea, we find the Berean brethren are nobler than others because they "received the word with all readiness of mind, and searched the scriptures daily, whether those things were so" (Acts 17:11). With the dawning of each day, the Bereans learned new doctrines and watched the works of God play out before their eyes! These wondrous things needed verification — accomplished by inquiring at the oracles of Scripture.

Scripture is the noblest of commentaries.

Axiom: Jehovah is not Flawed

This crystal-clear statement is unfortunately clouded to some, requiring re-statement. The Heavenly Father Jehovah, the Holy Ghost, and the Son Jesus Christ are without flaw. Marvel at this sweet declaration:

> Happy is he that hath the God of Jacob for his help, whose hope is in the LORD his God: which made heaven, and earth, the sea, and all that therein is: which keepeth truth for ever: which executeth judgment for the oppressed: which giveth food to the hungry. The LORD looseth the prisoners: the LORD openeth the eyes of the blind: the LORD raiseth them that are bowed down: the LORD loveth the righteous: the LORD preserveth the strangers; he relieveth the fatherless and widow: but the way of the wicked he turneth upside down. The LORD shall reign for ever, even thy God, O Zion, unto all generations. Praise ye the LORD. (Psalm 146:5–10)

King David also declared,

> As for God, his way is perfect: the word of the LORD is tried: he is a buckler to all those that trust in him. (Psalm 18:30)

And finally, King David aptly stated the perfectness of the law of God: "The law of the LORD is perfect, converting the soul: the testimony of the LORD is sure, making wise the simple" (Psalm 19:7). God the Father is free of all blemishes and stains. The Holy Ghost of God contracts no defect. In the Son of God — in the person of Jesus Christ — is no fault or blemish, nor spot or wrinkle.

In Matthew 5:48, the LORD Jesus Christ stated the Heavenly Father is perfect. The Father, the Son, and the Holy Ghost are not flawed.

Axiom: Humans are Flawed

There is scarcely any person on Planet Earth who can honorably claim to consider themselves impeccably splendid (although many try). Most reasonable people, regardless of their religion or station in life, understand this natural, universal law: people make mistakes — even the most humble and capable among us.

Surely, no honest person can claim eminence above King David, who, in the aftermath of his great immoral offense against the Heavenly Throne, repented, recognizing the evil he had committed, and confessed to his Creator.

> For I acknowledge my transgressions: and my sin is ever before me. Against thee, thee only, have I sinned, and done this evil in thy sight: that thou mightest be justified when thou speakest, and be clear when thou judgest. Behold, I was shapen in iniquity; and in sin did my mother conceive me. (Psalm 51:3–5)

King David also exclaimed,

> The fool hath said in his heart, There is no God. They are corrupt, they have done abominable works, there is none that doeth good. (Psalm 14:1)

Notice King David's commentary in the next verses, expanding the truth of verse one:

> The LORD looked down from heaven upon the children of men, to see if there were any that did understand, and seek God. They are all gone aside, they are all together become filthy: there is none that doeth good, no, not one. (Psalm 14:2–3)

The once great King Solomon penned in the preacher's book,

> For there is not a just man upon earth, that doeth good, and sinneth not. (Ecclesiastes 7:20)

The princely prophet Isaiah so pronounced indictment upon the condition of all men when he wrote,

> But we are all as an unclean thing, and all our righteousnesses are as filthy rags; and we all do fade as a leaf; and our iniquities, like the wind, have taken us away. (Isaiah 64:6)

The LORD Jesus Christ unreservedly stated it is the heart of man which produces the defiling evil.

> And he said, That which cometh out of the man, that defileth the man. For from within, out of the heart of men, proceed evil thoughts, adulteries, fornications, murders, thefts, covetousness, wickedness, deceit, lasciviousness, an evil eye, blasphemy, pride, foolishness: all these evil things come from within, and defile the man. (Mark 7:20–23)

Man, in his natural and darkened state, is faulty in spirit and soul, requiring rebirth, repair, and sealing. Many among us are like the Apostle Peter, a man who is rash and impulsive (John 18:10). Some of us are like Moses, strong and skillful enough to kill an Egyptian (Exodus 2:11–15). None are good, as says Paul in his letter to the Christian church at Rome (Romans 3:12). Men fail. The most cautious men fail. Women are faulty. Children are defective. None among us has mastered the moral excellencies of this life.

The first man, Adam, all his descendants, (including you and I), are flawed — but by Scripture's promises, **not without hope for restoration and repair**.

> For I will take you from among the heathen, and gather you out of all countries, and will bring you into your own land. Then will I sprinkle clean water upon you, and ye shall be clean: from all your filthiness, and from all your idols, will I cleanse you. A new heart also will I give you, and a new spirit will I put within you: and I will take away the stony heart out of your flesh, and I will give you an heart of flesh. And I will put my spirit within you, and cause you to walk in my statutes, and ye shall keep my judgments, and do them. (Ezekiel 36:24–27)

Scripture. Necessary. Sufficient.

"Neither have I gone back from the commandment of his lips; I have esteemed the words of his mouth more than my necessary food" (Job 23:12).

Chapter Six

Lively Oracles

The fans at a baseball game grow *lively* when their team hits a home run. Children swinging at the park or running through the sprinkler are *lively*. A dog fetching a bouncing ball is *lively*. Bears fishing salmon from the river are *lively*. A Redwood tree swaying in the wind and a wildflower launching forth in the spring are *lively*. Lively congregations sing hymns and *lively* pastors preach. King David's enemies were around him *lively* (Psalm 38:19).

Being lively is to be full of energy, spirit, and movement. **Lively is vigorous and vital.** Liveliness is a manner which denotes life; to exist and continue.

There is, however, a caveat to our understanding of alive. As humans, we are **alive**, but always have our luggage with us — eventual termination. The properties of *static* and *alive* in our limited human paradigm are contradictory because we change and will someday cease. For example, the use of cryopreservation methods to halt the effects of death is futile. When the human body ceases at death (no longer lively), the person passes into eternity.

In contrast, Scripture, which has no end and does not diminish with time, inherits from God the properties of *static* (consistent and reliable) and *living* (energetic and eternal). With God, we always know what to expect. He says what He means, and He means what He says. With God, there is no variableness — not even a hinting shadow of changing course.

> For I am the LORD, I change not. (Malachi 3:6)

> Of old hast thou laid the foundation of the earth: and the heavens are the work of thy hands. They shall perish, but thou shalt endure: yea, all of them shall wax old like a garment; as a vesture

shalt thou change them, and they shall be changed: but thou art the same, and thy years shall have no end. (Psalm 102:25–27)

Then Simon Peter answered him, Lord, to whom shall we go? thou hast the words of eternal life. And we believe and are sure that thou art that Christ, the Son of the living God. (John 6:68–69)

And being made perfect, he became the author of eternal salvation unto all them that obey him. Jesus Christ the same yesterday, and to day, and for ever. (Hebrews 5:9; 13:8)

Hast thou not known? hast thou not heard, that the everlasting God, the LORD, the Creator of the ends of the earth, fainteth not, neither is weary? (Isaiah 40:28)

Oracle

The word *oracle* is primarily a noun. In Latin, *oraculum*, is from the word *oro*, meaning *to utter*. In the Holy Canon, the **oracle** is the place where the Eternal Orator delivers His message, typically in answer to human inquiry.

Oracle: A Person

A person reputed as uncommonly wise, whose determinations are without dispute, or whose opinions are of eminent authority, is called an oracle. Among pagans, the oracle is the answer of a deity to an inquiry of an important matter, usually respecting the success of a battle. Among Hebrews and Christians, oracles are the communications, revelations, or messages delivered by God through prophets and apostles.

In space exploration, we consider Neil Armstrong the oracle of moon landings. In physics, Albert Einstein is an oracle. Linus Torvalds, developer of the Linux kernel, is an oracle in computer science. In 1954, practitioners injected nearly one million of the "polio pioneers" with the inactive Salk vaccine for polio and Dr. Jonas Salk became an oracle in virology.

Moses sought and received God's wisdom on the mountain. He first received the lively commandments from God and delivered them to the Hebrew people, and Moses is the man through whom the words of God flowed. In this context, God employed Moses as the oracle to deliver His message. The prophets Isaiah, Elijah, Ezekiel, Jeremiah, Ezra, and Habakkuk — all oracles of their day. In Samuel's day, many sought him for uncommon wisdom and close posture with God. In King David's day, they described Ahithophel, "as if a man had inquired at the oracle of God" (2 Samuel 16:23).

Without a doubt, Isaiah's career-long vision designates him as an oracle — a vessel where God stores His words for later publishing among His people. The Scripture record from the Prophet Isaiah is central to the story of the life of Jesus Christ. So much of the Isaiah text illustrates beautifully that we must seek the oracle of God.

Isaiah's inspirational delivery of the messages show him as an oracle:

> Come ye, and let us go up to the mountain of the LORD, to the house of the God of Jacob; and he will teach us of his ways, and we will walk in his paths: for out of Zion shall go forth the law, and the word of the LORD from Jerusalem. (Isaiah 2:3)

> For thus saith the LORD that created the heavens; God himself that formed the earth and made it; he hath established it, he created it not in vain, he formed it to be inhabited: I am the LORD; and there is none else. I have not spoken in secret, in a dark place of the earth: I said not unto the seed of Jacob, Seek ye me in vain: I the LORD speak righteousness, I declare things that are right. (Isaiah 45:18–19)

> And it shall come to pass, that from one new moon to another, and from one sabbath to another, shall all flesh come to worship before me, saith the LORD. (Isaiah 66:23)

Oracle: A Place

Often we see the oracle is a building, sometimes a field, or sometimes a brook. Regardless of the station, an oracle is recognizable by attributes — things which set it apart. Preeminently, the oracle is the eye-catching place where God's message dwells, where God gives the answers, where communion commences between Jehovah and His people. The oracle — peculiar among all other venues on Earth.

To commemorate leaving Egypt, God commanded the children of Israel to sacrifice the Passover at the special place where He put His name (Deuteronomy 16). At this place, God received their offering; at this place, the people of God worshiped their Creator. The words of God made this rest stop into the oracle place, and the Hebrew journey continued toward the Promised Land.

Encountering the LORD again at Mount Sinai, Moses completed the LORD's song. He was a clean vessel through whom the Lively Voice spoke. Moses met with God at the fiery mountain-top oracle. Where the word of God is, there is the oracle. The heavens and the earth, which declare His handiwork, are the noble host for the words of the Eternal Creator.

> Give ear, O ye heavens, and I will speak; and hear, O earth, the words of my mouth. My doctrine shall drop as the rain, my speech shall distil as the dew, as the small rain upon the tender herb, and as the showers upon the grass: because I will publish the name of the LORD: ascribe ye greatness unto our God. (Deuteronomy 32:1–3)

After four decades of danger and distress, their destination came into clear view. Just over the Jordan River, the entrance into the land of milk and honey was within reach. As Joshua led the Hebrews across on dry land, they rested at Shechem. Sloping from either side of the valley floor were Mount Ebal and Mount Gerizim. These gentle giants formed a long, narrow valley, almost like a natural amphitheater. It was here they prepared to worship as Joshua commanded construction of a special altar, just as Moses instructed in Deuteronomy 27.

Great stones — massive in dimension and weight — formed the altar. These great stones were like those which covered Jacob's well (Genesis 29:2); those great stones which Solomon rested his grand house upon (1 Kings 7:10); or the great stone which Joseph of Arimathea rolled upon the tomb of Jesus Christ (Matthew 27:59–60). In reverence for God, no iron tool touched the altar stones, and none was artificially squared.

Six tribes assembled near one mount, and six tribes gathered near the other. Center stage, where it belonged, was the ark containing the covenant between God and man. The entire nation waited for this moment, as the Levites projected reverence, stationing the ark — the last item to leave the dry Jordan riverbed. With the altar hefted together, they smoothed it with plaster. Soon the Levites set fire to the sacrifices, and all the people marveled. The sweet aroma wafted up to the heavens. This was communion between God and His people as they worshiped at the oracle place.

Then they wrote — and wrote and wrote. On the plastered stones they inscribed with plain letters a copy of the law of Moses, adding the catalog of curses from Deuteronomy 27.

> Then Joshua built an altar unto the LORD God of Israel in mount Ebal, as Moses the servant of the LORD commanded the children of Israel, as it is written in the book of the law of Moses, an altar of whole stones, over which no man hath lift up any iron: and they offered thereon burnt offerings unto the LORD, and sacrificed peace offerings. And he wrote there upon the stones a copy of the law of Moses, which he wrote in the presence of the children of Israel. (Joshua 8:30–32)

With all the people assembled in earshot of Joshua, he spoke the ultimate blessing — words of Jehovah:

> And afterward he read all the words of the law, the blessings and cursings, according to all that is written in the book of the law. There was not a word of all that Moses commanded, which Joshua read not before all the congregation of Israel, with the women, and the little ones, and the strangers that were conversant among them. (Joshua 8:34–35)

The ark with the stone tablets, the whole law of Moses, and the journal of curses for disobedience — made quite a journey. The oracle place was no longer crossing the Red Sea, below Mount Sinai, or marching through the Edom desert. As the LORD assembled His words along the wilderness trek, each time the Israelites took another step toward the Promised Land, the oracle place moved with them. For the time such as then, Shechem is the place — the oracle place — where God spoke the mighty, unchanging words of His law to His precious people.

Oracle: A Holy Place

After reading 1 Kings 7–8, take a brief journey with your imagination.

Ascend from the east through the Kidron Valley to the City of Jerusalem. Once inside the city walls, and as you walk the beautiful avenue, you see a durable plateau of hewn and sawn solid rock, and thereupon a foundation, which took many months to build. Upon that sure platform is the most magnificent building ever constructed, jacketed in the purest of gold. Leading into the building is a great porch with grand entry doors, all covered over in pure gold. Guarding the porch and costly buildings are two brilliant brass pillars. These two columns are so important, the LORD names them Boaz (in His strength) and Jachin (He will establish). Surrounding the sides and end of the beautiful building are rooms of several sizes, each one teeming with pure gold, no section left wanting.

As you stand on the porch and view the inside of the holy place, you're overwhelmed at the sight of surfaces covered with pure gold and no space spared. Prevented from entering, you view the larger room (covered with pure gold) and in it are the tables and instruments used for worship, all fine brass, and pure gold. Standing in front of the giant doors leading into the holy place and astride the huge named pillars, your eyes lock onto the striking beauty of the **MOST HOLY PLACE**.

In view is a magnificent giant box — square on all sides. Every surface is precisely the same dimensions as its attached neighbors. Gold wraps every space and covers every surface of the splendid box. Each side of the box measures approximately thirty-five feet by thirty-five feet, making it thirty-five feet in height. They built each side of cedar wood. They do not allow tooling at its permanent place and there are no stones found nearby. Before this box is a partition of chains made of pure gold. The gold box has doors made of olive wood, which are foldable. Into the doors, they carved cherubims and palm trees.

When first built, the box contains nothing, but now the most distinct objects known to man occupy the glorious box. This holiest of all places rests behind the porch and doors of the grand house, amid the room greater in dimensions than the box itself. In the midst of the gold box are two giant identical cherubs standing over seventeen feet in height. The cherubs have two wings, one stretched out to touch one wall and the other stretched to touch the wingtip of the other cherub, each wing nearly nine feet long.

In the midst of the gold box, where the wings of the cherubs touch, is the place where the ark of God rests. This is the place — the oracle's place. There is no place like this place. It contains the ark of God, hosting the mercy seat. Inside the ark is the second set of stone tablets, written by God's finger in the oracle-place upon Mount Sinai. This place contains the words of God. There, upon the mercy seat, the Creator meets with the high priest once per year to grant mercy and accept the sacrificial blood of a spotless lamb, forbearing the sins of His people, until the Eternal Lamb of God takes away the sin of the world.

In the ark's belly, at the center of the oracle, is I AM's prime statutes:

> And all the elders of Israel came, and the priests took up the ark. And they brought up the ark of the LORD, and the tabernacle of the congregation, and all the holy vessels that were in the tabernacle, even those did the priests and the Levites bring up. And the priests brought in the ark of the covenant of the LORD unto his place, into the oracle of the house, to the most holy place, even under the wings of the cherubims. For the cherubims spread forth their two wings over the place of the ark, and the cherubims covered the ark and the staves thereof above. (1 Kings 8:3–4, 6–7)

With your tour nearing an end, awe and fear overcome your person, as does comfort, knowing that God's *words* rest safely within seven layers of shielding, each with its own specific purpose, each overseen by the High and Lofty One. I AM outfits the environment where the precious cargo of the ark remains free from decay, defended from the danger foisted by disobedient creatures.

God's word calls this place the **MOST HOLY PLACE**. I'm certain our limited understanding of holiness fails to fully appreciate how holy is this oracle where God will bring mercy and message. While magnificent — because of its cedar construction, fine artistry, finishing with gold, and outfitting with bright brass accouterments — this place is holy because it hosts HOLINESS Himself.

Muse for a moment on this: God honors His *words* above His name!

Every instrument, each wall, every room, each stone, all the materials, and the many emplacements had one focus — the oracle where God gives answers. He answers the query of mercy, the question of salvation, and the examination of every matter affecting mankind. It is amid the oracle where once per year the high priest asked Jehovah corporately, "Will you accept this offering for the sins of the people?" and Jehovah answered, "Yes!" and accepted the offering. There in the oracle — the centrum of the center of Jehovah's central mountain — in the presence of God's *words*, the prime question of man's needs received an answer. Thankfully, we no longer need a special building, as Jesus Christ fulfilled every law, blotting out every ordinance and nailing them to His cross.

Jehovah is immeasurably serious about every aspect of ensuring His *words* are untarnished from every notion of decay. The oracle of today is the Bible-place, where we go to get the answers.

Why do many people so easily cast aside His Scripture?

Oracle: A Reference Point

As with many big cities around the world, Chicago has many significant and famous points of interest. In the Windy City are the Cloud Gate, the Magnificent Mile, the Wrigley Building, Union Station, St. James Chapel, Lincoln Square, and an array of spectacular firehouses. The Skydeck Chicago sits near the top of the Willis Tower, the tallest structure in Chicago. From this deck, one sees far and wide. There are no mountains in Chicago and many people frequently use the Willis Tower to orient their location within the city and its surrounding area. Traveling through life, each person needs reference points to ensure proper directional control and avoid risk or injury.

Reading the Bible, we find the oracle is also a reference point; an anchor; the "true north." The oracle is the unbreakable kingpin from which all alignment and measurement calculate, and this concerns the physical and the spiritual. The oracle is a compass — a harbor lighthouse to illuminate the way!

The oracle's location highlights where they built the chambers and sundry walls.

> And against the wall of the house he built chambers round about, against the walls of the house round about, both of the temple and of the oracle: and he made chambers round about. (1 Kings 6:5)

The altar's position and orientation are relative to the oracle.

> And the whole house he overlaid with gold, until he had finished all the house: also the whole altar that was by the oracle he overlaid with gold. (1 Kings 6:22)

Within the dimensions of the oracle, they positioned the guardians with the walls and center-most point of the holy room as the reference.

> And he set the cherubims within the inner house: and they stretched forth the wings of the cherubims, so that the wing of the one touched the one wall, and the wing of the other cherub touched the other wall; and their wings touched one another in the midst of the house. (1 Kings 6:27)

The tables, altar, and candlesticks in the holy place orient relative to the face of the oracle.

> And Solomon made all the vessels that pertained unto the house of the LORD: the altar of gold, and the table of gold, whereupon the shewbread was, And the candlesticks of pure gold, five on the right side, and five on the left, before the oracle, with the flowers, and the lamps, and the tongs of gold, And the bowls, and the snuffers, and the basons, and the spoons, and the censers of pure gold; and the hinges of gold, both for the doors of the inner house, the most holy place, and for the doors of the house, to wit, of the temple. (1 Kings 7:48–50)

The staves for carrying the ark of God rested in the holy place, in view of the oracle.

> And they drew out the staves, that the ends of the staves were seen out in the holy place before the oracle, and they were not seen without: and there they are unto this day. (1 Kings 8:8)

The oracle place shields the ark.

> And the priests brought in the ark of the covenant of the LORD unto his place, into the oracle of the house, to the most holy place, even under the wings of the cherubims. (1 Kings 8:6)

> For the cherubims spread forth their wings over the place of the ark, and the cherubims covered the ark and the staves thereof above. (2 Chronicles 5:8)

Consider again King David. He knew precisely where prayers were answered: "Hear the voice of my supplications, when I cry unto thee, when I lift up my hands toward thy holy oracle" (Psalm 28:2). King David recalled when the LORD met with Moses at beautiful Sinai: "The chariots of God are twenty thousand, even thousands of angels: the Lord is among them, as in Sinai, in the holy place" (Psalm 68:17).

Oracle — the all-provisioned place where God's words dwell. Today, we can hold the oracle of God in our hand, read it on the tablet, or send it around the world instantaneously. The Scripture text is the place where the *words* of God dwell, but there is yet one place where God expects His words to find a home.

Meditate here: "The word is nigh thee, even in thy mouth, and in thy heart: that is, the word of faith, which we preach; that if thou shalt confess with thy mouth the Lord Jesus, and shalt believe in thine heart that God hath raised him from the dead, thou shalt be saved" (Romans 10:8–9).

Can we doubt for one moment that God's word is the lively violin bow playing beautiful music upon the strings of the heart?

> For the word of God is quick, and powerful, and sharper than any twoedged sword, piercing even to the dividing asunder of soul

and spirit, and of the joints and marrow, and is a discerner of the thoughts and intents of the heart. (Hebrews 4:12)

Your heart matters significantly to the LORD and you must maintain its safekeeping, for it affects everything you do, and everything you do affects the heart.

> Keep thy heart with all diligence; for out of it are the issues of life. (Proverbs 4:23)

> Create in me a clean heart, O God; and renew a right spirit within me. (Psalm 51:10)

We should make every effort to preserve, protect, and defend the heart. It must remain the place where we welcome the words of God. Still and all, as Jeremiah noted in 15:16, it seems God's word must become our joy and rejoicing — His oracle — housed within the heart and mind of each individual.

Oracle: A Reference Document

Holding Deacon Stephen against his will, they forced him through a mock trial by the politically motivated high priest. They falsely accused him, excoriated him for his faith and preaching, and a short time later stoned him until dead. Stephen's last sermon is a brief narrative of Hebrew history, beginning with Abraham, through Moses, the temple of Solomon, and ending with the prophets. Throughout Acts 6–7, he highlights the deliverance contributed by the Just One. And he indicts the fathers (and by extension the current listeners) who ejected Moses from their company, turned their hearts back to Egypt, and desired Aaron to craft an idol of gold.

We read of Stephen being, "full of faith and power" and doing great wonders and miracles among the people (Acts 6:8). The Holy Ghost filled him. In his humble and yielding state, at the end of this life, Stephen was more lively than on any other of his days.

All his acts stemmed from obedience to the Author of his faith. Stephen summarizes in his Acts 7 narrative all the key points he learned from the reliable reference document — the lively oracles of Scripture — handed down from the time of Moses through many centuries.

Stephen references Moses this way:

> This is he, that was in the church in the wilderness with the angel which spake to him in the mount Sina, and with our fathers: who received the lively oracles to give unto us: to whom our fathers would not obey, but thrust him from them, and in their hearts turned back again into Egypt, saying unto Aaron, Make us gods to go before us: for as for this Moses, which brought us out of the land of Egypt, we wot not what is become of him. (Acts 7:38–40)

Effectively, a few simple questions come to mind: from where did Stephen learn these centuries-old historical facts? From where could he relay the story of the fathers and tabernacle in the wilderness? From where did he learn about the golden calf, Moses killing the Egyptian, and Jacob who begat the twelve patriarchs? These are of course rhetorical questions, and the answers are patent — Stephen learned these things from the oracle — the holy place where the words of God dwelled, which are the lively Scriptures copied and distributed over and over through the ages since the prime writing. His turn of phrase came by the Holy Ghost's movement, not happenstance or even serendipity.

Oracle: A Preaching Place

Apostle Paul, when preaching to the Romans, reinforces the doctrine stating the Jews are the first custodians of the oracles, with the initial advantage: "What advantage then hath the Jew? or what profit is there of circumcision? Much every way: chiefly, because that unto them were committed the oracles of God" (Romans 3:1–2). The Jews, of course, abdicated their advantage.

Without getting lost in the weeds, one of the core doctrines taught from Romans 3 is just how necessary the law is for us to understand our condition. None are good, not even one. At the chapter ending, it becomes quite clear the perfect law of liberty in this New Testament has its foundation in the law of the Old. It teaches we are no longer temporarily pardoned by keeping the law (the oracle), but permanent pardon comes by faith learned from the law (the oracle).

> Therefore we conclude that a man is justified by faith without the deeds of the law. Is he the God of the Jews only? is he not also of the Gentiles? Yes, of the Gentiles also: seeing it is one God, which shall justify the circumcision by faith, and uncircumcision through faith. Do we then make void the law through faith? God forbid: yea, we establish the law. (Romans 3:28–31)

Consider: to *establish* in this context means to make the law stand fixed; firm like the Rock of Gibraltar. It continues safe and sound, standing unharmed, ready and prepared. Distinctly, if the words of God deteriorate, we cannot rely upon them for salvation or any other aspect of life. What misery we face if the Bible is unreliable.

In the church assembly, public speaking must follow the model (or manner) found in the oracle.

> If any man speak, let him speak as the oracles of God; if any man minister, let him do it as of the ability which God giveth: that God in all things may be glorified through Jesus Christ, to whom be praise and dominion for ever and ever. Amen. (1 Peter 4:11)

Oracle: Choicest of Places

I'm certain we can only slightly grasp how important Jehovah considers His words — even magnified above His name. The oracle is the choicest of places imaginable on Earth, because of the plenary and eternal nature of God's words.

Mount Moriah: a choice place for Abraham. A cleft in the rock: a choice place for Moses. Marching into the promised land: a choice place for Joshua. The desert and the ark: choice places for Noah. A fish and a faraway city: choice places for Jonah. The River Chebar: a choice place for Prophet Daniel and Prophet Ezekiel. Prison: several times a choice place for Prophet Jeremiah. The road to Damascus: a choice place for Saul. The cave at Adullam: a choice place for King David and his rag-tag band of followers. These venues, and countless more, are peerless dwellings, where God's distinguished words are the reason for preeminence. In these places, God spoke to these people.

For the soul of today, the choice place is the Bible text.

This planet is the biggest of the choicest places we can imagine where the words of God dwell. When you consider, "the earth is the LORD'S, and the fulness thereof; the world, and they that dwell therein" (Psalm 24:1), we agree Earth's purpose is to host the word of God first, and by extension the whole of human creation, which has as its genesis those Wonderful Words of Life. This is the choice place where He started His most precious creation — people. This planet is a choice place where the Word became flesh and dwelled among us: being full of grace and truth, intending to give His life for ours, and spill His blood to heal the sin wound.

The entirety of earthly existence is formed and maintained by the word of God toward a certain end.

> For this they willingly are ignorant of, that by the word of God the heavens were of old, and the earth standing out of the water and in the water: whereby the world that then was, being overflowed with water, perished: but the heavens and the earth, which are now, by the same word are kept in store, reserved unto fire against the day of judgment and perdition of ungodly men. (2 Peter 3:5–7)

Benhadad, king of Syria, knew the exact place to get the healing for his sickness: "And the king said unto Hazael, Take a present in thine hand, and go, meet the man of God, and enquire of the LORD by him, saying, Shall I recover of this disease?" (2 Kings 8:8). He knew the words of God had the answer (but he probably did not like the answer).

Repeatedly we see it is always the words of the LORD which make the place of unequaled quality. Places which house the words of God may possess great beauty and magnificent construction, but housing the *words* in those locations makes each place the *choice place*.

Notably, God determines the location where He intercourses His words with mankind. Sometimes the LORD directs His messengers to go to a particular location to deliver His words. The choice place (the oracle), does transition from one setting or locale to another, sometimes geographic and sometimes human.

There is a certain sophisticated connection between the man of God and the oracle of God, where, like Ahithophel, sometimes they are inseparable or speak as one.

Oracle: Location, Location, Location

This is the saying usually applied to the purchase of land or real estate. The demand and fervor about houses all comes down to a location. Families and businesses want the "choicest" location. If you think about it, David put the altar at the choicest location. Obeying Jehovah's specific instructions, David bought this choice plot of land in Jerusalem, later used to establish the oracle place where Solomon would build God's house.

Today, worship of the Creator doesn't stop in temples made by man, but so much more requires spirit and truth. Sure, it's important for us to assemble in buildings, so we can focus on ministering, and for practical purposes. However, buildings and land are not the prime concern. We gain truth from the oracle of today — the text of the printed Bible, the smart app, or any other medium where we find the words of God. Truth from Scripture is effective when it finds its location in the heart. We cannot begin to count how many people have housed the words of God in countless locations and circumstances over the many centuries.

The most important *location*, Solomon records, is the heart — the central interconnection between thinking and communion with God.

> My son, forget not my law; but let thine heart keep my commandments: for length of days, and long life, and peace, shall they add to thee. Let not mercy and truth forsake thee: bind them about thy neck; write them upon the table of thine heart: so shalt thou find favour and good understanding in the sight of God and man. Trust in the LORD with all thine heart; and lean not unto thine own understanding. (Proverbs 3:1–5)

From Ezekiel we learn, "Son of man, all my words that I shall speak unto thee receive in thine heart, and hear with thine ears" (Ezekiel 3:10).

Forsaking our own righteousness for salvation, we must rely upon the words of faith.

> The word is nigh thee, even in thy mouth, and in thy heart: that is, the word of faith, which we preach; that if thou shalt confess with thy mouth the Lord Jesus, and shalt believe in thine heart that God hath raised him from the dead, thou shalt be saved. For with the heart man believeth unto righteousness; and with the mouth confession is made unto salvation. For the scripture saith, Whosoever believeth on him shall not be ashamed. (Romans 10:8–11)

King Josiah went to the correct location, making ready his heart and the heart of all the people, as they inculcated the lively oracles into their society.

> And the king went up into the house of the LORD, and all the men of Judah, and the inhabitants of Jerusalem, and the priests, and the Levites, and all the people, great and small: and he read in their ears all the words of the book of the covenant that was found in the house of the LORD. And the king stood in his place, and made a covenant before the LORD, to walk after the LORD, and to keep his commandments, and his testimonies, and his statutes, with all his heart, and with all his soul, to perform the words of the covenant which are written in this book. (2 Chronicles 34:30–31)

Lively Oracles

It is no accident that the lively oracles we hold in our hands and read at any moment comprise the exact *words* the LORD chose for our spiritual enrichment. We must decrease and He must increase. We must conform to Him. His Word and His words — without decay — are the truth which brings eternal life.

> Verily, verily, I say unto you, He that heareth my word, and believeth on him that sent me, hath everlasting life, and shall not come into condemnation; but is passed from death unto life. (John 5:24)

It is the spirit that quickeneth; the flesh profiteth nothing: the words that I speak unto you, they are spirit, and they are life. (John 6:63)

Then Simon Peter answered him, Lord, to whom shall we go? thou hast the words of eternal life. (John 6:68)

That which was from the beginning, which we have heard, which we have seen with our eyes, which we have looked upon, and our hands have handled, of the Word of life; (for the life was manifested, and we have seen it, and bear witness, and shew unto you that eternal life, which was with the Father, and was manifested unto us;) that which we have seen and heard declare we unto you, that ye also may have fellowship with us: and truly our fellowship is with the Father, and with his Son Jesus Christ. (1 John 1:1–3)

The Lord gave the word: great was the company of those that published it. (Psalm 68:11)

The apex of wisdom and the highest expression of truth hail from God's written words — the intentionally safeguarded and divinely inspired Scriptures.

It's all about the words from The Word.

"For a day in thy courts is better than a thousand. I had rather be a doorkeeper in the house of my God, than to dwell in the tents of wickedness" (Psalm 84:10).

Chapter Seven

Purposely Stitched

It may not be easy, but I implore you to be in a quiet place and unclutter your thoughts before you continue reading this chapter. Ask the LORD to prepare your mind to receive knowledge and give you wisdom.

> PURPOSE, a noun; that which a person sets before himself as an object to be reached or accomplished; the end or aim to which the view is directed in any plan, measure, or exertion; intention; design.[1]

Now that you're settled, I ask you to focus your contemplations on these next very important moments. As you read on, paint a picture in your mind.

Imagine you are a privileged spectator of the creation events described in the Genesis record. You arrive early to your outlook station — an interminable, vast void. You enjoy no reference point, no perspective. Surrounding your person is emptiness — neither thing nor substance nor sound. As you think and look, and listen and attempt to feel — the unending absence of all things overcomes your being. With all your might, you muster your perceptions to catch some iota of sensory information — but there is no corresponding

---

1. Assembled from Noah Webster's American Dictionary of the English Language, 1828, as found at https://webstersdictionary1828.com/Dictionary/purpose

sensation. Void. Your sensory faculties realize only vacancy. All of your senses combine to produce the most profound awareness of utter nothingness.

In an instant so small and precise, that collective human scientific ability cannot measure it — the words of God begin the beginning. God creates the heavens and the earth, hanging the stars in the sky. Planet Earth is without form and void, and darkness covers the face of it — a darkness so unilluminated the human mind cannot conjure a concept of its emptiness of light. This is not the absence of light as in a cave, but the boundless, overflowing absence of light just before God commands light into existence!

No light, and then light. Light, like the beginning itself, comes into existence at God's command in a moment of time so infinitesimally small that earthly languages are incapable of describing its lack of length! Wondrous and beautiful and perfect rays of illuminating glory from the Creator God out of His eternal station. Light did not exist — but Jehovah God pronounced it into existence. The light pierces the darkness with an abrupt suddenness which confounds every one of your thoughts. You could not see: now you can. The light is good and the Creator divides the light from the darkness, calling one Day and the other Night.

No day nor night, and instantly both day and night. No time and then time starts its one and only (albeit lengthy) epoch. Instantaneously, you perceive a change in this marvelous new creation, named Earth, as the Holy Spirit moves upon the surface of the waters. **God said**.

For the rest of this day and during the next five twenty-four-hour periods, the perfect handiwork of the Creator captivates your entire being. In each day and at every step, the Eternal One uses His language — His words — to create this precious and spotless planet and all the surrounding universe. Everything is in place with perfect proportions, according to God's words.

God called. God created and moved. He divided and made. The LORD saw and blessed. And as the dawn of the seventh day glistens upon the horizon, God rests. By words, God furnishes all creation.

As if the entire planet is the set of a providentially choreographed play, God makes every piece, and in its correct form. God has spoken creation into existence — colossal handiwork from nothing. It is all word perfect. His sovereignty has summoned the elements sufficient for His creation, with no leftovers, and certainly nothing amiss. All the cast members of Planet Earth are in place, the scripts are ready, and the greatest show on earth is about to begin.

There is no sin here, and on Earth, there are no blemishes or blights. Your senses have witnessed the Almighty Wondrous Creator as He assembled all matter and made man from dust, simply by His utterance. Matthew Henry says, "he made the world with great exactness; it was a framed work, in every thing duly adapted and disposed to answer its end, and to express the perfections of the Creator."

At every juncture, the Genesis record shows God saw His creation and called it good. **God said.**

Perhaps King David considered just as you have pondered.

> For the word of the LORD is right; and all his works are done in truth. He loveth righteousness and judgment: the earth is full of the goodness of the LORD. By the word of the LORD were the heavens made; and all the host of them by the breath of his mouth. He gathereth the waters of the sea together as an heap: he layeth up the depth in storehouses. Let all the earth fear the LORD: let all the inhabitants of the world stand in awe of him. For he spake, and it was done; he commanded, and it stood fast. (Psalm 33:4–9)

This friend of God passionately describes the LORD Jehovah's greatness and might in Psalm 104, highlighting how He unfurled the curtain of Heaven and laid down the earth's foundations. "Through faith we understand that the worlds were framed by the word of God, so that things which are seen were not made of things which do appear" (Hebrews 11:3). The Prophet Isaiah closes his journal by declaring the greatness and ability of the LORD — when God himself says Heaven is His throne and Planet Earth is His footstool (Isaiah 66:1). Apostle John writes: "All things were made by him; and without him was not any thing made that was made" (John 1:3). We must advance Apostle Peter's truth-proof: Jehovah's words keep the footstool in store until the dreadful judgment and inescapable perdition of ungodly men (2 Peter 3:5–7).

Stop for a moment and consider the Creator, who set before Himself an organized and meticulous aim. We cannot measure His mighty work and we cannot replicate His creation plan. Expressing God's work and wonder by our own words is shortsighted. His energies are without fault, measured only by His choosing. His motives are pure, far beyond our sense of pureness.

To understand God, we must rely on the creative wonders revealed in Scripture. From God's book we learn about the making of matter and the fitting of time at the start of the beginning. When the LORD speaks, He declares His purpose from beginning to ending (Isaiah 46:9–11).

Can any man cast a shadow upon God's resolve to execute His plan? Job's record states, "Shall mortal man be more just than God? shall a man be purer than his maker?" (Job 4:17). Ethan the Ezrahite educates us: "For who in the heaven can be compared unto the LORD? who among the sons of the mighty can be likened unto the LORD?" (Psalm 89:6). Apostle Paul describes the existence of everything this way: "For of him, and through him, and to him, are all things: to whom be glory for ever. Amen" (Romans 11:36).

The Record

Christians and others understand, by reading the Bible, to resolve the sin matter and gain salvation by grace, one must have an understanding in his mind. We understand both sin and salvation according to the Bible text. Growing in faith, virtue, and the other building blocks of grace (2 Peter 1) comes by reading and applying the text record — the standard. Wonderfully, the Holy Ghost used the Apostle John to write a large cohort of the Scriptures and in his respondent sections of the text, there are two bookends about the record of the LORD Jesus Christ.

At the starting bookend, John writes of John the Baptist, saying,

> And John bare record, saying, I saw the Spirit descending from heaven like a dove, and it abode upon him. (John 1:32)

Near the closing bookend, John writes of the triune Godhead, saying,

> This is he that came by water and blood, even Jesus Christ; not by water only, but by water and blood. And it is the Spirit that beareth witness, because the Spirit is truth. For there are three that bear record in heaven, the Father, the Word, and the Holy Ghost: and these three are one. And there are three that bear witness in earth, the Spirit, and the water, and the blood: and these three agree in one. (1 John 5:6–8)

John's bookend verses teach us precisely of the Heavenly Word — He who came to earth to bear the written record. The Bible is the record extending from the persons of God about Himself and His dealings with humankind. The Heavenly Father knew He could not rely upon man to transmit His words orally. He knew His words, to survive man's handling, require writing as they transfer from one generation to the next. Over time, we see increased use of the holy men and scribes, as they record into written language the words which God says. From His eternity, Jesus Christ is the Word of life, handled and heard, being held forth for all to see (Philippians 2; 1 John 1; and 2 Peter 1).

As a result, the warp and weft threads of inspiration and preservation promote His purpose in every aspect, ensuring Jesus Christ can be "manifest in the flesh, justified in the Spirit, seen of angels, preached unto the Gentiles, believed on in the world, received up into glory" (1 Timothy 3:16). Jesus Christ came not to abolish the law, but to fulfill it. From His perspective, halting the Scriptures from decay had a reasonable goal — the restoration of defective (but redeemable) people whom He so loved.

Immutability

In our daily lives, when so many things are in entropy and upheaval, the Bible is the primary, never-changing record we can rely on. The oceans and rivers; the forests and mountains; and the cities and beaches — they change. Societies of every century have altered their forms of governing themselves (or replaced the government with chaos). Technology, while helpful, has driven modern societies into a volatile and unsteady turmoil. Political discourse, whether you think it is good or bad — has entropy as its prime directive, so the controlling party can remain one step ahead of the opposition.

We all, I dare say, are beguiled by alteration or frequent reform. Like it or not, humans decay and diminish. Red blood cells, which conclude their life only some three months after their invention, must be replaced with new. Organs and tissues fail, requiring surgery, which is not always successful. The human condition is one of physical and spiritual failure, and certain eternal death without Christ.

We cannot appraise God with our definitions. He is a Spirit, and He dwelled among us in the flesh. He is. His character and nature are without fault. His existence possesses no limits, neither by many dimensions nor physical properties. As humans, we are exposed to immense danger if the Saviour is vacillating.

The purposely stitched Scriptures remain without decay to show God's unalterableness. He does not change.

> For I am the LORD, **I change not.** (Malachi 3:6, emphasis added)

> Jesus Christ **the same yesterday, and to day, and for ever.** (Hebrews 13:8, emphasis added)

The psalmist writes about God, who endures, remains the same, and has no end.

> Of old hast thou laid the foundation of the earth: and the heavens are the work of thy hands. They shall perish, but thou shalt endure: yea, all of them shall wax old like a garment; as a vesture shalt thou change them, and they shall be changed: but thou art the same, and thy years shall have no end. (Psalm 102:25–27)

Whether in the womb, the cradle, or the synagogue; on the cross or in the grave; on the Damascus Road or on the Isle of Patmos — He is the same! In all ages, in every way — He remains invariable and without even a trace of turning (James 1:17). And by Apostle John in his first chapter, we see in our beginning, (or shall I say creation's beginning), HIS WORD WAS! Isaiah wrote: "The grass withereth, the flower fadeth: but the word of our God shall stand for ever." (Isaiah 40:8).

Neither the LORD nor His words possess any diminishing.

Armor

God prevents the decay of the purposely stitched Scriptures to equip the saint with armor. Is not the Christian's life a journey with at least occasional warfare? Do you have any enemies? You certainly have at least one (1 Peter 5:8). Christians are required to be good soldiers of Jesus Christ and to put on spiritual armor (2 Timothy 2:3–4; Ephesians 6).

Immediately upon salvation, the Holy Ghost grants the new Christian access to an armory of tools which aid him in the daily battle. From where does he learn about righteousness? How shall he stand against the fiery darts of the wicked devil? What agency can he depend upon for defense against the powerful rulers of darkness? How will he stand when the evil day comes? How will he put on the divine armor? In these, God sent no telegram or tweet. When donning the armor of God, the Christian must read the instruction manual. In there, he reads exactly how and why to outfit himself with Bible armor.

Among the Bible writers — Apostle Paul stands out as the prime recorder of God's instructions regarding the putting-on of His protective armor. The written Scriptures in Ephesians 6 give us the solution. Paul's charge produces the Christian's defense against the worst things which surround us. The Christian is to put on every piece of God's armor, to protect himself from the wiles of the devil, recognizing his battle is not against the flesh, but against powers and rulers of darkness. The Christian is to be strong by relying upon the power of Jehovah's might. He must stand strong, having the loins girt about with truth.

He must put on the breastplate of righteousness, and prepare his feet to carry the Gospel of peace. Above all, he must take up the shield of faith to prevent the fiery darts of the wicked from reaching his person. As the need for either defense or offense will arise, he must strap on the helmet of salvation. Every component of armor the Christian wears stands ready in his daily life by the "sword of the Spirit, which is the word of God" (Ephesians 6:17).

Reading God's indefectible Bible builds around you a cocoon of unparalleled protection, keeping you safe and your hope in Christ lively (1 Peter 1).

Glorious

Jehovah protects His purposely stitched Scriptures from decay so we may behold His glory. Ponder for just a moment or two this question: how can I perceive the nature or character of God? The answer: His word is the testimony of His nature. We can behold the glory marshaled to the only One begotten of the Father, and no other (John 1:14).

God's plan brings salvation to the sinful man, and the Bible record tells us: "Who being the brightness of his glory, and the express image of his person, and upholding all things by the word of his power, when he had by himself purged our sins, sat down on the right hand of the Majesty on high" (Hebrews 1:3).

Imagine the flourishing brightness of the LORD Jesus! He is full of splendor and luster! Earth's moon walks in the sun's brightness, but Jesus Christ is thousands of thousands of rays more illuminated. His brightness far surpasses the sum of all the assembled stars. In fact, He is the giver of light to all. Apostle John saw "no temple therein: for the LORD God Almighty and the Lamb are the temple of it. And the city had no need of the sun, neither of the moon, to shine in it: for the glory of God did lighten it, and the Lamb is the light thereof" (Revelation 21:22–23). By God's words, we acquire knowledge of the glorious LORD Jesus Christ who lights up the New Jerusalem.

In our hands, we can hold the completed canon of Scripture text, as received from the apostles and prophets. It is glorious when we read in our language the words of the Heavenly Father. From the Scriptures (Matthew 6 for starters), we read God is to be worshiped and hallowed. From the Bible we read: His will is to be done on Earth; He gives the daily bread; and He forgives our debts. By His words, we avoid temptation and gain deliverance from evil!

From His recorded text, we read of the glory in the cloud; the glory appearing in the tabernacle, under Moses's oversight. His glory teemed at the river with Ezekiel and on the plane. By the book of Isaiah, we read God glorified His people, Israel. Through the written words from eternity, we read of Jonah and a great revival. By the Bible record, we see Solomon yielding before Jehovah, who shows pleasure with the temple building. By Scripture, we read of Daniel who worshiped his God thrice every day. Apostle John records the LORD Jesus praying to the Heavenly Father about the glory brought about since the foundation of the world.

By the recorded Heavenly journals, we muse alongside King David when he proclaims in Psalm 19:1, "The heavens declare the glory of God; and the firmament sheweth his handywork." Splendidly, King David exclaimed to his son Solomon in Psalm 72:19, "And blessed be his glorious name for ever: and let the whole earth be filled with his glory; Amen, and Amen."

The Bible text reveals the hope of glory, unmasks the mystery, and teaches all wisdom toward the perfecting of the Christian.

> Whereof I am made a minister, according to the dispensation of God which is given to me for you, to fulfil the word of God; even the mystery which hath been hid from ages and from generations, but now is made manifest to his saints: to whom God would make known what is the riches of the glory of this mystery among the Gentiles; which is Christ in you, the hope of glory: whom we preach, warning every man, and teaching every man in all wisdom; that we may present every man perfect in Christ

Jesus: whereunto I also labour, striving according to his working, which worketh in me mightily. (Colossians 1:25–29)

The narratives in the collected Scripture which reveal God's glory are indeed boundless. Section by section and writer by writer, we read in the text about His glory. His reliable written journal points us to the cross of Christ. Simply put, His Word of Life convinces us of wrongdoing, defines the stars and heavens, and is a Light unto our path. His word is the avenue of eternity brought to our home by language. It is the alpha and the omega.

Epic Epochs

Many times in the Bible, we find the text describing a large period, commonly referred to as an epoch. An epoch is a particular period of history, especially a period which is beyond ordinary (or, might I say, epic). Epochs are associated with an event or series of events, and while some epochs have closed, some epochs remain open, and yet other epochs have yet to start. We typically define the start and end of an epoch by its events and circumstances. The Great Awakening and the Great Migration are just two examples. Epochs do not have a predefined length of time, but usually span years or centuries.

The Bible record covers time from its creation to its end, and all its constituents. We call this the creation epoch, or Earth epoch. The epochs found in the Bible are many. Some time periods are grander than others in their utility regarding the good or bad conduct of people. Notably, we shall examine just a few of these imperial spans, illustrating how the words of God exist before, during, and after the period described in the following examples:

Epic Epoch One: Apostle Peter writes of the whole epoch of Earth, and its residents' circumstances, from beginning to end. In his namesake second epistle, the entire third chapter describes how Earth's epoch started — and what its end will be. As he lays a foundation, he admonishes the reader of the things previously spoken by the prophets, and those commandments put forth by the apostles of the LORD Jesus Christ. He warns them of the last days, when there shall be selfish lust-filled scoffers who belittle the second coming of Christ. He asserts those doubters will boldly claim nothing has changed for hundreds of years — and therefore nothing will change, casting doubt upon the return of the LORD. Peter shows us these atheists are willingly ignorant of the truth: for by the word of God, the heavens existed, and the earth stood in and out of the water, as man aggressively carried on with his filthy behavior (2 Peter 3).

Peter then exclaims how the pre-catastrophe world perished by floodwaters and even though the earth has changed, the same word of God kept it in store (reserved it), eventually being subject to the judgment and perdition of ungodly men. Peter reminds the reader how God is not willing for any person to perish, but is desiring for all to claim repentance. Assuredly, Peter writes about the day of the LORD which comes suddenly, but not unexpectedly (for the Bible warns us repeatedly).

Having reiterated the warnings by the written words, that the heavens and Earth will dissolve and melt because of wickedness, he encourages the reader to believe the promises found in the written words and to look for the New Heavens and the New Earth. Above all, the coming judgment should galvanize the Christian to communicate the Gospel of Peace to everyone they encounter. God's words are eternal and have no ends, as the LORD Jesus stated in Luke 21:33, "Heaven and earth shall pass away: but my words shall not pass away."

Further on, to reinforce his authority, Peter buttresses his epistle to several epistles of the Apostle Paul, who also wrote of all the things Peter has noted. Throughout this snapshot of the history of the world and humanity, the center of focus is always the words. Over and over, Peter takes the reader to the words: *words* spoken before by the holy prophets; *words* which framed the pre-flood world; and *words* which reserve the current world until its end.

By citing the multiple examples of known facts of human history, Peter illustrates the prime purpose by which God stitches and preserves Scripture — the long-suffering salvation through Christ (2 Peter 3:9). Throughout the first canon, God's message to men always includes His desire for them to repair a broken relationship or continue an existing good relationship. The former things were closed when the LORD Jesus, by His life and ministry, provided an everlasting avenue for the Christian's lasting relationship with the Heavenly Father. Repair and restoration.

Epic Epoch Two: We read about a stunning turning point in Israelite history in the Exodus 32 record. This turning point accompanies a deep spiritual impact. The Israelites sinned a great sin when making the golden calf, and Moses judged them by the word of the LORD. But Moses also made a way of escape by ascending the mount to petition the LORD about forgiving their sin (peradventure). As a nation, they would soon cross the river and journey into the promised land. For now, God dealt harshly with their sin, bringing upon them a plague, because they made an idolatrous clump of gold.

Despite their predilection for disobedience, it was there on the mount where Moses made a very bold claim: petitioning Jehovah to remove him from the book of the living if the Hebrews did not receive forgiveness. If God does not forgive their sin, then he (Moses) should be subject to the plague as the others, even though he did not take part in crafting the golden blob. With resounding clarity, Jehovah confirmed those who committed this idolatrous endeavor were subject to death, being blotted out of the book of the living.

Obviously, Jehovah excluded Moses from the imminent punishment. Not all the Hebrews were involved in making the calf. If so, God may very well have concluded the Hebrew nation entirely and stopped their story there. Still and all, God is about mercy. He was not finished with the Israelites, nor is He finished with the rest of mankind (including you and me). At this point in Exodus 32, much of the story has yet to be written into the canon of Scripture — and God knows this. God already knew (and has already illustrated in earlier Scriptures) — man will go against Him, time after time again. Therefore, to establish His righteousness in written form, He moved upon Moses to record these words in the Pentateuch as a banner of warning against the filthy works of man, and as a marquee which points to righteousness.

Epic Epoch Three: Deuteronomy 31 is in a tiny class of Bible chapters which reveal several epochs, all related one to another — and all based upon the words of God. There are at least four epochs detailed in this single chapter. First, we read the epoch of Moses will soon end, being one-hundred-twenty years. Next we see the LORD shall go before the Hebrew people, clearing the way as Joshua leads them into the Promised Land, launching a new epoch. Further, at the end of every seven-year epoch, they shall read the law into the hearing of the people. And last, God will kindle His anger against the nation of Israel, at a future epoch, because they will prostitute themselves with other gods.

The penetrating indictment compels multiple generations to hear the song! Judgment will happen at some distant time. But running parallel to the thread of judgment are the threads of mercy and protection: "And the LORD, he it is that doth go before thee; he will be with thee, he will not fail thee, neither forsake thee: fear not, neither be dismayed" (Deuteronomy 31:8). Do you see the words describing the LORD's reliability?

As Moses finishes writing the law and all these words, we see the singular purpose: that the nation of Israel and their children and the strangers among them may learn the *words*, may fear the LORD, and do all the *words* of the law (verses 11–13). Like all other conversations between God and His prophets, the aim is to promote people to do all these words. It is marvelous and humbling when God condescends to man's low estate. He used human language to communicate His desire to promote a good relationship with Him by hearing and doing those precious words.

Epic Epoch Four: Isaiah's journal overflows with marvelous prophecies, and his twenty-ninth chapter is no less stirring as he described the woeful condition of Israel. Because of their rejection of God's words, the nation of Israel became like a ship with a broken rudder, unable to navigate the treacherous waters of its enemies. Without a doubt, the LORD of hosts visited Ariel (people of Israel) with thunder, earthquake, great noise, storm, tempest, and the flame of devouring fire (verse 6). They are not temporarily drunk with wine, but with the extended doldrums of spirit brought on by their lengthy rejection of God's words. (With all my might, I have tried to make this the essence of this book — to help people return to a love for God's words.)

So fallen into mischief is Ariel, God poured out a deep sleep upon them. A thick layer of volcanic ash blankets Israel's prophets, rulers, and seers, who are therefore useless. In fact, Ariel is so far removed from the spiritual connection with his Creator, the nation dismissed the visions and dreams from Jehovah like some book written in a long-lost language which is no longer understood. They reach deep to hide their godless works from God Himself. So long and distant is their heart from Jehovah, they can barely muster enough energy to move their lips in pretense of honor toward Him. They are *atheist*. Remarkably, Lebanon shall bear fruit again when the LORD Jesus conducts His ministry!

> Is it not yet a very little while, and Lebanon shall be turned into a fruitful field, and the fruitful field shall be esteemed as a forest? And in that day shall the deaf hear the words of the book, and the eyes of the blind shall see out of obscurity, and out of darkness. The meek also shall increase their joy in the LORD, and the poor among men shall rejoice in the Holy One of Israel. (Isaiah 29:17–19)

Even though it was a long way off, the LORD Jesus will fulfill this prophecy. John the Baptist put the question of sovereignty to the LORD Jesus, who responded with the fulfillment:

> Jesus answered and said unto them, Go and shew John again those things which ye do hear and see: the blind receive their sight, and the lame walk, the lepers are cleansed, and the deaf hear, the dead are raised up, and the poor have the gospel preached to them. And blessed is he, whosoever shall not be offended in me. (Matthew 11:4–6)

Two chapters later, Jesus specifically noted the fulfillment of Isaiah's prophecy:

> Therefore speak I to them in parables: because they seeing see not; and hearing they hear not, neither do they understand. And in them is fulfilled the prophecy of Esaias, which saith, By hearing ye shall hear, and shall not understand; and seeing ye shall see, and shall not perceive: for this people's heart is waxed gross, and their ears are dull of hearing, and their eyes they have closed; lest at any time they should see with their eyes, and hear with their ears, and should understand with their heart, and should be converted, and I should heal them. (Matthew 13:13–15)

Added to this, in Mark 7 the LORD Jesus condemned the hypocrites who honor only with their lips but never their hearts. Connected to this, we find Apostle Paul in Acts 28:25–27 quotes this same text from Isaiah 29. Jehovah had promised some eight centuries before Christ's ministry "to do a marvelous work among this people, even a marvelous work and a wonder" (Isaiah 29:14), and now the marvelous work and wonder had arrived. This event shows the purpose by which God had stitched Isaiah's record and defended it from decay, even during some of the darkest times of Israel's self-indulgence and wasteful living. With the LORD Jesus and at least two of His apostles recording the reference in the New Testament, we once again see His aim is the merciful salvation of all people. It is by words He brings salvation.

Scripture: the purposely stitched fabric of books and records of the spoken and otherwise delivered words from the Heavenly station. The words are the powerful hammer which breaks up the fallow ground of the heart. They are the quick writ piercing both soul and spirit, dividing them asunder. With scalpel-like precision, the lively words of God separate the joints and marrow, and discern every thought and intent of the heart.

> Will it be said that the Scripture cannot be destitute of power? Is it not powerful, by its divine energy, "to cast down in the human heart every high thing that exalteth itself against the knowledge of God?" Is it not "a hammer breaking the rock in pieces?" Is it not "a two-edged sword, piercing to the dividing asunder the joints and marrow?" Yes; it is all this; but only for those who hear it, and who expect to gain something from it. And how can it be all this for those who despise it, and do not believe that it comes from

God? Without reverence, there can be no attention; and without attention, no means of being touched; and without all this, there can be no faith, no communion possible with God, no efficacy in the blood of the cross, no salvation, no life.²

Thy word is true from the beginning: and every one of thy righteous judgments endureth for ever. (Psalm 119:160)

He hath remembered his covenant for ever, the word which he commanded to a thousand generations. (Psalm 105:8)

Have not I written to thee excellent things in counsels and knowledge, that I might make thee know the certainty of the words of truth; that thou mightest answer the words of truth to them that send unto thee? (Proverbs 22:20–21)

Each paragraph; every chapter; all volumes of God's inspired and preserved word fabric reveal His reasonable objectives. Whichever the subject, whomever the focus, the Holy Ghost has a clear mission — communicate God's glorious plan of restoration for mankind. Faith comes by hearing the words of God. The greater volume of Scripture points directly or indirectly forward or backward to the cross of Jesus Christ, where He so willingly gave His life to levy upon His own account all the sins of mankind, for all of humanity's time. Page after page, the Holy Bible compels the reader to look to Jesus, the Author — and Finisher — of all faith. Section after section, the reader confronts his human frailty, and also receives the way of repair — which comes by calling upon the LORD Jesus Christ after hearing His precious words!

I want to know one thing, the way to Heaven: how to land safely on that happy shore. God himself has condescended to teach the way; for this very end, he came from Heaven. He has written it down in a book! Oh, give me that book! At any price, give me the book of God! — John Wesley

Chapter Eight

Systematics

IT IS CERTAIN: THE Universe is the most complex system imaginable. The Universe contains everything and everyone in Creation — it is the complete system of all existing things. Since God spoke all creation into existence by using His indefectible words, we are confident those words are more tightly woven into the universe itself than we can imagine. Jehovah protects His words from decay through a system of subsystems. Each constituent language is a system of letters and words, and phrases, employing various punctuations and markings and establishing a uniqueness for the society using the language. He designed a system of systems which support the publishing of His words as text.

Systematics

Respecting the assembly and conduct of any system, let us examine a prime principle of its construction. In a system, each member depends upon the other members of the union. This interdependency upon one another respects no demographics, volume, epoch, or other characteristics. The unified effort is sufficient for its purpose. Some members may never contact other members, but they are all assembled into an agreeable whole, where each member contributes a part to the entire mission. For the system to have unity, no single component may cause a breach with another member. With their unified bonds, the entire enterprise achieves a regular method or order as it fulfills a predefined goal. Systems produce repeatable results.

A system enlists constituent parts from a purposeful design and unites them into a single-minded effort or sequence. As energy (labor or action) comes upon the assembly, it begins its motion in concert with its makers' intent and according to the programmed instructions. The system continues operating because of lively energy.

Consider the locomotive. While immensely heavy and sturdy, its design and construction conform to exacting standards demanding careful balancing of its many parts. All the joints where one part meets another must be tight and abundantly lubricated to avoid friction. Most any system, complex or simple, strives to perform at its best, and this massive machine is no different — conducting itself at peak performance.

We build our lives around ordered systems, from the basics of washing our hands to driving a car to the most complex life-saving surgeries. Consider the first man: "And God said, Let us make man in our image, after our likeness" (Genesis 1:26). The Creator set about to design and engage a natural and beautiful system (albeit unbelievably complex) — humans. Each person has three parts — a body, a soul, and a spirit. In this fashion, we each systematically replicate the image of our Creator. Each human body, composed of trillions of cells all working in prescribed harmony, is an organically united system, whose purpose is life support. Each cell is alive and contributes its tiny effort to the general enterprise of life. The insect, animal, botanical, and microbial kingdoms (systems) follow suit.

Your body, a temporary dwelling for your soul and spirit, has but one aim — systematically supporting your lively worship of the Creator. Whatever your choice may be, do all to the glory of God! King Solomon arrived at a bitter but reasoned deduction: "Let us hear the conclusion of the whole matter: fear God, and keep his commandments: for this is the whole duty of man. For God shall bring every work into judgment, with every secret thing, whether it be good, or whether it be evil" (Ecclesiastes 12:13–14).

Each person's substance (essential whole) contains members. God wrote those members in His book, all of which were fashioned from nothing (Psalm 139:13–16).

The locomotive is a *system* of conveyance. A satellite is a *system* for communications and early warning. For cataloging and lending books, we use an ordered *system* named library. A university is a multi-tiered system of learning. Systems of order (laws and codes), are necessary for a civil society. *Systems* of function (such as social and educational programs) have as their purpose the betterment of society. A printing press is a reliable system for publishing messages. Regardless of complexity or simplicity; irrespective of the design; with no consideration for the many or few parts of a system — it has a primary purpose. Like a choreographed play, the essence of a *system* is to produce one or more outcomes by following a script.

A system must produce a reliable output, or it results in failure, or even fraud. Far more competently than any other, the Scriptures are the eternally planned recording of words, small letters, and pen marks. The Scriptures are a *system* of books and journals — and so much more. The Bible is a purposely collected system of written systems, each with its own epoch, geography and nature, and players. Most of the chosen penmen were not contemporary with one another, but all contributed to the unified message of God's words, some in one fashion and some in another. Some wrote relatively few words, while others wrote several books, but all had the same respect for the mission: recording God's words as Scripture!

Throughout the several ages, the Scripture collection aligned into a plenary (full, complete) system of constituent writings — all fully energized and precisely overseen by the Holy Ghost. Each page and section work in unison with the others to deliver a unified message. An honest analysis of the *word-system* of the Bible captivates the reader into heart-searching. It is the words of God which are quick and filled with power, and no other book can claim this posture. The Bible is the only supernatural book found on Planet Earth, and it is the incorruptible seed supernaturally producing eternal life.

Time and Times

Time is itself a system. Time plays a role in practically every known system. Like the lilies of the field, the timing of the custodial efforts of Bible preservation possesses a beauty with no rival, still and all greater than all of Solomon's glory. None but the supernatural God could coordinate the many people and countless materials and sustained efforts through the dangerous centuries to arrive at a collection of His words in one book, and with indisputable precision.

The Master of Scripture is like the conductor of a very large orchestra directing the many members as they advance through the musical piece, each with accurate timing, precisely striking their instrument to meet every note, creating the music pleasing to ear and heart. "Pleasant words are as a honeycomb, sweet to the soul, and health to the bones" (Proverbs 16:24). As His masterpiece continues, we behold beauty as He composes each preservation stanza to arrive at the final crescendo — the canon of Scripture.

> A man may admire a sun-dial, he may marvel at its use, and appreciate the cleverness of its design; he may be interested in its carved-work or wonder at the mosaics or other beauties which adorn its structure: but, if he holds a lamp in his hand or any other light emanating from himself or from this world, he can make it any hour he pleases, and he will never be able to tell the

time of day. Nothing but the light from God's sun in the Heavens can tell him that. So it is with the Word of God. The natural man may admire its structure, or be interested in its statements; he may study its geography, its history, yea, even its prophecy; but none of these things will reveal to him his relation to time and eternity.[1]

There are sixty seconds in one minute, sixty minutes in one hour, and twenty-four hours in one day. These precisely graduated durations are necessary and sufficient for conducting our lives. I can't imagine a person who does not rely on time, to the lesser or greater, as they go about their daily routines. How many clocks are in your home? Whether we enjoy passing the time, simply conform to its stern march, or aggressively push against it, time does not change its frequency or reliability. Time is not some accidental construct appearing one day on the continuum of nature. In fact, it is a struggle to describe time without referring to time.

The plans revealed in Scripture have always and will always occur on time and with no missteps. Time is a terrifically reliable constant which moves in one direction, irrespective of any human labor to the contrary — tick and tock, faithfully advancing and never retreating. In the practical sense of our daily lives, never does time change its pace or interval. Because He is time's owner, only the LORD can cause time to stand still or back up. Time is at the core of the salvation of every man.

> (For he saith, I have heard thee in a time accepted, and in the day of salvation have I succoured thee: behold, now is the accepted time; behold, now is the day of salvation). (2 Corinthians 6:2)

Life has at least one certain appointment.

> And as it is appointed unto men once to die, but after this the judgment. (Hebrews 9:27)

---

1. Excerpted from Figures of Speech Used in the Bible: Explained and Illustrated, E. W. Bullinger, D.D., Grapho Press Limited, London and Wealdstone, 1898

> So Christ was once offered to bear the sins of many; and unto them that look for him shall he appear the second time without sin unto salvation. (Hebrews 9:28)

As the divine appointments of the warp thread and the purposeful scheduling of the weft thread weave together the tapestry of the Bible text, they forestall even the slightest alteration. From planting to plucking; weeping to laughing; from mourning to dancing; rending to sewing; from hating and war to charity and peace — "To every thing there is a season, and a time to every purpose under the heaven" (Ecclesiastes 3:1); and, "He hath made every thing beautiful in his time: also he hath set the world in their heart, so that no man can find out the work that God maketh from the beginning to the end" (Ecclesiastes 3:11).

Collected Components

The Bible shows there are so many materials and so many components on which God records His words through the ages, it's practically impossible to catalog them. Sometimes in large amounts, and sometimes in small volumes, we see God's words found on animal skins, stones, dirt, books, scrolls, and a Roman crucifix. Hosted on the tabernacle, the ark, the temple, the sky, the altar, and doorposts — are the words of God. Even a fish and a donkey contained the words. The most important material where Scripture rests is the heart of people. The Heavenly script is about the words, regardless where they are located.

Ponder again the pencil. Just think about the components and effort needed to create and assemble this marvelous gadget. It's not a complex device, by any measure. Most consider it rather plain, or give it no thought. And yet, manufacturing this basic writing implement requires precisely measured materials and specific procedures. And don't forget the many machines needed to prepare and cut the wood, mix the paint, stamp out the ferrules, press the planks, and extrude the erasers. Last but not least, there are packaging, shipping, distribution, receiving, stocking, and sales. All this — and innumerable people around the globe, all contributing their small part to the unified effort to produce the most basic writing widget.

On a scale even more vast, and through nearly two millennia, the chosen penmen inscribed the Heavenly words upon sundry materials. The effort started with Moses and moved on to Job, Habakkuk, Apostle Paul, and included so many other inspired men along the way, finishing with Apostle John. From Jerusalem and Judea and Samaria; to Mesopotamia, Assyria, and Asia; to Italy, Greece, Spain, Ephesus, Patmos, the Dead Sea, and throughout the many common or offbeat places in between. So many materials, so many people, so much effort and preparation!

All these components are the individual portions making up the Scriptural whole. The harmonized Heavenly words condescended from God to sinful humankind over hundreds of millions of minutes.

Mankind cannot, and only the Holy Ghost can, affect the collection and assembly of all the sections into the beautiful system of the received Bible.

Testament

I presume you're familiar with the two main sections of the Bible, commonly known as the Old Testament and the New Testament. These are also called the first and second covenants. The word canon refers to the collection of books in each, being the first and second canons. Typically, we refer to the first canon as the law and the prophets (or just the law), and the second canon is the more sure word. Together, they are the canon of Scripture.

The Scriptural record declares:

> For where a testament is, there must also of necessity be the death of the testator. For a testament is of force after men are dead: otherwise it is of no strength at all while the testator liveth. (Hebrews 9:16–17)

A testament (or sworn affidavit) is a written, authentic record of the actions and evidence of a legal matter. With Scripture, the testimony begins with the start of the beginning and continues through the last unit of time, when the Christians shall transition to the New Jerusalem. The Scriptures are wholly about the testator — Jesus Christ. In the Hebrews' letter (and the others), we read of His selfless act of dying for all people groups, despite their atheist rejection of Him as Saviour (Hebrews 9).

In law, a testament is a solemn, authentic instrument for the distribution of estate properties and assets after death. To be valid, the will requires witness signatories and notarizing (authentication) while the estate owner (testator) is of a sound mind. It is the law which prescribes when and in what fashion the estate matters are willed. Publishing of testaments is commonplace, and in developed societies, a local government records office often holds the last-will-and-testament for safekeeping.

The Bible text declares the establishment of facts proceeding from God. Observe: the whole of Psalm 119 refers to the law, precepts, commandments, statutes, judgments, truth, and so forth. The largest psalm contains the word "testimonies" twenty-three times. Psalm 119 is a testimony of the lively effects of the Scriptures themselves, summarized in verse thirty-one: "I have stuck unto thy testimonies: O LORD, put me not to shame."

The chosen writers, the common people, and the sundry characters who lived during the many epic accounts in the Bible are the witnesses to the authenticity of the testimony (or testament). The Bible's testimonial evidence, stipulated as multiple irrefutable facts, proves their experiences. Just as a "last will" takes more than moments to record, neither were God's words collected in a moment, and neither should they have been. We should be quite thankful God's book is not a "flash in the pan."

Systematic Publishing

Regarding the assembly process employed for the safekeeping of the collected Scriptures, let us explore further.

God did not fabricate His words, like some marketing plan or sales pitch. And I wholly dismiss any notion which assigns it as fantastical, proclaiming some deceitful men contrived it "from whole cloth." As well, I dismiss the notion of some who say the words from God suddenly appeared (like so many other religious books), as if mystically hidden until some magic act revealed them to the world. Latter-day "prophets" did not conjure up God's magnificent words during dubious mountain-top sabbaticals or camping trips in the desert.

God is no conspirator! The Holy Ghost oversaw the intentional and intricate actions to record, copy, collect, and assemble the written texts into the whole Bible. From the beginning, His purpose included the systematic preservation of His words. It is not possible to catalog the numbers of people, myriads of methods and events, and the multiplied centuries of effort, which were reliably compiled into the received text.

The phrase "Thus saith the LORD" and its variants, establishes the evidence: God spoke. With the holy man consumed by the close Voice of spoken words through the Spirit of the Word, the heard words became written words. I say this is systematic because it is the reliable method repeatedly engaged by the Holy Ghost. Some of the human agents recorded the words themselves directly, and others with the help of a scribe.

Let us review a section from the noble prophet Jeremiah. The focal point is Jeremiah 31 when the LORD is instructing His prophet to catalog all the words spoken to him. These are words of judgment against Judah and Israel, and the intended result is repentance and restoration. This section wonderfully illustrates God's repeatable process when firstly God speaks to Jeremiah, who then hears the words, followed by him speaking those words verbatim to Baruch, at which point Baruch hears the words, writes the words into a roll of a book, and finally recites the words (from the book roll) to others, and so forth.

Place yourself in this trustee's place for a moment. As a ready witness to Jeremiah's inspiration by the Holy Ghost, he records the Heavenly words transmitted through the mouth of Jeremiah. Can you see it? Baruch, by direction from Jeremiah, reads the book roll aloud in the LORD's house. He later reads it again in the high court, at the new gate of the LORD's house — in the ears of all the people! Still and again he reads the roll of the text to the other scribes and princes. In this, we see the shaping of the process for publishing the Scriptures. Jeremiah and his companions speak, hear, write, and copy the precious words. Then they speak, hear, and write copies again. So forth and so on, the systematic process repeats. Words published.

Systematic Rescue

When Jehovah God assessed the wickedness of pre-flood humanity, He measured it as great and pronounced man's heart was only evil continually. Humans are messy.

As the heart of God grieved because of man's corruption and violence which tore against His marvelous creation, He concluded the solution was global cleansing — effectively a reset of practically everything. He judged the earth as corrupt. The punishment: Earth would flood, all land-based flesh would die, and the breath of life would recede from every creature. But Noah, a just man who walked with God, found grace in God's sight (Genesis 6).

For more than a century, the lifeguards of humanity, Noah and his family, labored to build the rescue boat, the blueprints for which Noah received directly from the Heavenly Architect. The greater plans included detailed descriptions of the materials, foods, and stuff which his family needed to collect. Jehovah would bring the animals which survive the imminent calamity. Throughout the epoch of preparation, with God's mercy still available, Noah preached repentance, but not one person outside his family petitioned God for rescue from the impending doom.

Examine the enormous judgment and punishment ensuing after the last epoch of the pre-flood era. The LORD repented for making man upon the earth. Whoa! God's heart wrestled with agony and sadness at what man had achieved toward debauchery. For the first time in the planet's history, rain fell. The great deluge consumed every section of ground on the face of the planet. As He squeezed Planet Earth, the water and muck which poured forth buried all land-based life, much of the living seas, and the hills. The mighty, powerful barrage of materials consumed all land. And following this was the final consuming, where all birds, animals, and creeping things — and every man — ceased all life activities (save those in the lifeboat of God). For humans, God's unique and beloved creature — all but eight souls perished into eternity as the breath of life fled their bodies.

> And all flesh died that moved upon the earth, both of fowl, and of cattle, and of beast, and of every creeping thing that creepeth upon the earth, and every man: all in whose nostrils was the breath of life, of all that was in the dry land, died. And every living substance was destroyed which was upon the face of the ground, both man, and cattle, and the creeping things, and the fowl of the heaven; and they were destroyed from the earth: and Noah only remained alive, and they that were with him in the ark. (Genesis 7:21–23)

The grace Noah found kept him and his family safe from the illimitable wrath poured out upon every other person who rejected God's rescue plan.

Consider: God transformed the entire planet into a system for preservation, which for a time erased the evils and wickedness of His most beloved creature. To fend off the attacks from one creature against all the others, He intervened with global defensive protections, which the whole of humanity could not withstand. He could have just started over, but He chose grace and mercy!

Corporately, humanity did not deserve any rescue. With a carefully crafted plan for Noah and seven other souls to be saved, He gives precise measurements and plans for the giant boat. Noah's family collected, carried, and cut the wood. They likely hired subcontractors to help with several tasks, among which were the designing and fitting, and building and pitching. There were sufficient supplies on the ark to care for all the inhabitants for many months, and well beyond the subsiding rains.

The complexity of this undertaking is almost indescribable. There is no example to follow. All of mankind of all ages united in one collective effort could not accomplish what God did before, during, and after the cataclysmic flood. He dictated the instructions; He provided the wood and the supplies; He brought the animals; He shut the door; He brought the rain and floods; He dispatched the rain; He receded the waters; and, He brought the peace dove. Every step of the way and for any of Noah's foreseeable future, Jehovah set out to rescue His creation.

Noah and his family were entirely incapable of achieving any of these milestones on their own. It required the performance of God in their lives. Because of the grace given to Admiral Noah, you exist today. Because of God's grace, you and I can know the Holy Ghost. I can write, and you can read!

The story of the global flood is likely the most told story of any age. When you think about it, the inundating barrage is the re-beginning — the second opportunity. Now that's mercy! Most wonderfully, we can read of man's restart in the pages of the Bible, which precisely and accurately records the systematic rescuing of humanity!

Systematic Preaching

Enter Phillip the Evangelist. With the church at Jerusalem in havoc, Saul of Tarsus went about committing many people to prison, and scattering those not captured and beaten. In the Acts of the Evangelists, we find Philip traveling from Jerusalem down to the city of Samaria (about a distance of thirty-five miles). At Samaria, Philip preached Christ: he conducted miracles — casting out devils, reversing palsies, and healing the lame and blind. While he convinced the people of the Gospel, many reclined their belief on the LORD Jesus Christ. Even the sorcerer Simon believed and got baptized! The preachers preached and testified, seeing many Samaritan residents converted before they returned to Jerusalem.

As the story expands, an angel of God commissioned Philip to trek the corridor leading to Gaza. The purpose: to meet up with Queen Candace's eunuch. As Philip ran to meet the chariot, he heard the eunuch (a Gentile) speaking the words from the Isaiah record. The words perplexed the eunuch. Philip preached the same message he preached to the Samaritans, the Gospel of the LORD Jesus Christ. He began with the Isaiah record and expounded the Scriptures. As they traveled on, the eunuch desired to be baptized. For certainty, Philip queried the eunuch, "Do you believe in your heart?" and the eunuch responded with the clearest testimony of Christian confidence: "I believe that Jesus Christ is the Son of God" (Acts 8:37).

After stepping down from the chariot and entering the water, the Apostle Philip dunked the eunuch. Ascending from the water, the Spirit of God caught away Philip.

Salvation came to the eunuch because this evangelist followed the established gospel framework: **Scripture — Hearing — Faith**.

Repeatedly in the book of Acts we read of the preaching of the Scriptures converting the hearts of the hearers. It is appropriate to highlight Philip because it reveals the systematics of preaching. Philip repeatedly preached the same written message, with the same method commissioned by Jesus, which reliably produced the same results.

> And Jesus came and spake unto them, saying, All power is given unto me in heaven and in earth. Go ye therefore, and teach all nations, baptizing them in the name of the Father, and of the Son, and of the Holy Ghost: teaching them to observe all things whatsoever I have commanded you: and, lo, I am with you alway, even unto the end of the world. Amen. (Matthew 28:18–20)

Over and over, the apostles and disciples took the written Scriptures to the listeners, preached from those Scriptures, and the Holy Spirit performed the operation on their souls, conducting them into salvation. From the words of Scripture come hearing and from hearing those words comes faith, whence comes grace, truth, and eternal life.

Systematic Faith

The man named Gamaliel is a big shot law professor whom Saul studied under. Gamaliel probably had access to (or even possessed) many volumes of Scripture text. As a doctor of the law, he likely studied both the texts of the first canon writings and the Hebrew traditions handed down through the centuries. Today we describe him as a subject expert. That said, being a Pharisee, it's likely he adhered more to the traditions of the Jewish fathers than to the established law of Moses and the prophets. (Notably, the LORD

Jesus condemned this double-tongued nonsense in Matthew 15:2–9 and most of Matthew 23.)

With zeal, Saul of Tarsus absorbs much from Gamaliel. After all, he had a reputation to uphold and a duty to carry out the law (especially against these Jesus-following heretics). The question extends: which text did Saul study in Gamaliel's classroom? Both history and the Bible record the patent answer: he studied the first canon — the law, the prophets, the lamentations, and the psalms and proverbs.

After conversion and calling, Paul the Apostle (a prolific writer and very busy missionary), went hither and yon planting churches on two continents, which we understand from Scripture. His faith is among the greatest of Bible characters. Rarely could a sermon pass which does not mention the faith of this converted persecutor, who humbly claimed two titles: the least of the apostles and chiefest of sinners (1 Corinthians 15:9 and 1 Timothy 1:15). Paul preached directly to the most common of men and to the highest of officeholders. Not among the first Apostles, Paul describes himself as a Pharisee, being the son of a Pharisee and trained in the law at the feet of Professor Gamaliel. He was both Jew and Roman. Among the many aspects of Paul's life, we must consider the texts he studied. It is interesting that before his conversion he *wrestled against* the Scriptures, but after the Damascus Road regeneration, he quickly became a dynamic *promoter* of the Scriptures.

You'll notice in Acts 13:15 the attendants finished reading the Scriptures in the synagogue, and then the recently commissioned Paul (Saul) beckoned with his hands. Building upon the foundation Stephen, Phillip, and Peter had laid previously, his Acts 13 sermon became the linchpin of salvation for the Gentiles. As Paul summarized the key points of Hebrew history, it's very clear he learned these facts (evidence) from studying the written text of God's words. Paul quoted several sections of the law and even referenced the prophets. Paul preached the written word, handed down to him from ages past; transmitted at the hand of the holy men, the scribes, and the stewards at the synagogues. Saul (Paul) and Barnabas preached in many synagogues, and each location likely had at least one copy of the assembled Old Testament.

I imagine Persecutor Saul studied history, the law, and the prophets, in a sophisticated, systematic fashion. He originally meant his learning for evil upon the non-followers of the orthodox ways, but now means his learning for the publishing of the Gospel of Jesus Christ. His mistakes of the past, before meeting Jesus on the Damascus Road, were useful to his listeners then, and are useful today as examples, rather than shame. Paul continued the same method of preaching the Gospel as he received.

> For I delivered unto you first of all that which I also received, how that Christ died for our sins according to the scriptures; and that he was buried, and that he rose again the third day according to the scriptures. (1 Corinthians 15:3–4)

Later in prison, the Apostle Paul implores Pastor Timothy to bring "the books, but especially the parchments" (2 Timothy 4:13). Wow! My imagination springs awake when I consider Apostle Paul may have requested the exact volumes he studied from his days as a Pharisee. And, he may very well have desired parchment so he could copy those words for distribution to others.

In Apostle Paul's letter to the Christian church in Rome , we read of a broken-hearted Apostle Paul who desired for Israel to be rescued from their unbelief and wickedness. This coincided with his description of the ignorance of his own nation. They lacked knowledge, working to establish their own righteousness. In his Roman discourse, he instructed the listeners of Christ (who is the end of all the law) and quoted Moses for support. And still more, Paul supported his arguments using the Old Testament, citing various Scriptures some twenty-six times, nine of which are from Deuteronomy. Paul referenced the texts recorded by Moses some millennia and a half before; and here, like so many other times, he preached the written words from God. Paul was not relaying a fireside story or some fanciful homely. Paul's heart broke for his people to be rescued and restored!

All the words he recited, regardless of their form of transmission, are the same words of faith we read today! The intentional preservation of God's words is the vehicle which makes possible the Holy Ghost's work in the heart. The breath of Life who brought man into existence, in the beginning, is the same breath of Life who brings man into restored fellowship with the Creator. By the safekeeping of the Scriptures, we can read Apostle Paul's outline of the systematics of faith — first to hear the word of God, then to believe the word of God, then to repent in response to the word of God, and finally to call upon the name of the LORD Jesus for forgiveness. The Bible words come to us in various forms: paper, electronics, speech, preaching, and so forth. The medium changes — but the words endure!

Systematic Fulfillment

The LORD Jesus prayed, and He prayed repeatedly. He gave us a systematic model for prayer in Matthew 6 and Luke 11. We can follow His model, and not be vainly repetitious, which violates what Jesus taught. In Matthew's account, the LORD Jesus uses the phrase "after this manner." Webster defines manner as a way of performing; a custom, or habitual practice. The LORD Jesus instructs us to pray in a certain manner with consistency and vigor. Our prayer life should have regularity without vanity.

Let us examine one time when the LORD Jesus prayed. Once the supper ended, He finished a farewell sermon to His disciples, and continued His preparation to become the Lamb slain for the entire world. We find His intercessory words for His disciples recorded in John 17. In these words, the Prince of Peace engaged His Father with petitions, focusing on giving eternal life. Throughout the intentionally safeguarded account of the prayer, we read of the LORD Jesus stepping carefully and perfectly through the components of His work to make salvation and restored fellowship possible.

Amid this majestic prayer of the LORD Jesus, He models the transmittal of the words from Heaven to the recipients of His grace and mercy.

> Now they have known that all things whatsoever thou hast given me are of thee. For I have given unto them the words which thou gavest me; and they have received them, and have known surely that I came out from thee, and they have believed that thou didst send me. (John 17:7–8)

Notice the Father gives the words to the Son, who gives them to His followers, and they receive them! Those words, starting from the Heavenly Father, are a thread stitched into hearts of hearers. By receiving those words, believers inform themselves of the authenticity of what Jesus has been telling them: the Father sent Him. Tactfully, we see the weft thread of guardianship stitching together each of the inspired constituent members of the plan of salvation. Remember, the Scriptures are supernatural in every dimension and detail.

Global Consequences

Revisiting the Acts 13 chronicles, we read a series of events which literally reformed the moorings of history. Prior to this, very few humans knew of the event about to occur. We read here a marvelous endowment from the Holy Ghost as the newly converted Saul and certain other prophets and teachers were ministering to the LORD in the church at Antioch. As they fasted and worshipped, the Holy Ghost said, "Separate me Barnabas and Saul for the work whereunto I have called them" (Acts 13:2). After commissioning, Saul and Barnabas began their first missionary trip, which became an unrivaled pivot point in world events. Later in this same chapter, Paul proclaimed his commission to reach the Gentiles, "And when the Gentiles heard this, they were glad, and glorified the word of the Lord: and as many as were ordained to eternal life believed. And the word of the Lord was published throughout all the region" (Acts 13:48–49).

Notice carefully, the Gentiles did not praise Paul or Barnabas. No! They glorified the words of the LORD. And then we read the words of God were published throughout the large region. Over and over, copy after copy, they sent the words of Scripture forth into many places throughout the region.

As Paul and Barnabas traveled from place to place, preaching the Gospel, a sorcerer stirred up by the Jews interrupted them. Also, they suffered persecution by the chief men of the city, and they received much contradiction and blasphemy as they read publicly the law and the prophets. Imagine being punished for publicly reading the **public law**! Twice, almost the entire city came together to hear the words of God. The story shows a localized civil conflagration between believers and scoffers, but many gladly believed, yet others rejected and remained bitter and self-willed.

As Paul reads the Scriptures to those before him, he summarized the entire matter in the person of Jesus Christ: the mighty uncorrupted One who brought them salvation. Seven times he speaks of Jesus being raised and his quotations from the Scripture text span multiple centuries, and include Abraham, Moses, the judges, Samuel, Saul of Kish, King David (twice by name), Nathan, Isaiah, Habakkuk, and John the Baptist. In a succinct and accurate fashion, this well-educated former Pharisee delivered to their ears the fundamental heritage of Jewish patriarchs and their key role in the prophecy of the Messiah. Paul rightly excerpted the very harness and reins of Jewish traditions to advance the clear and present Gospel of the LORD Jesus Christ. Through his precious Acts 13 sermons, Apostle Paul quoted Psalm 2:7, Psalm 16:10, Isaiah 49:6, Isaiah 55:3, and Habakkuk 1:5. How marvelous is the Holy Ghost!

By now, you may ask: "How is Apostle Paul equipped to quote, read, reference, and preach the Scriptures? Where did he get this information?" Acts 13 upsets the apple cart! The promises and plans of eternal restoration include the Gentiles! Multiple contemporary prophets simultaneously hear the Holy Ghost speaking. Throughout their journeys, many bad actors foisted every imaginable evil against these messengers of the Gospel. And yet, Paul and Barnabas checked and balanced all their actions upon the existence and publishing of the written word of God. (Paul's reminder in 2 Corinthians 2:17 highlights the many unbelievers who distort the sanctity of Heavenly words.)

They perhaps had copies in their possession or used the copies found in the synagogues. Further, Paul's declaration (certification) of the words he preaches are boldly stated in Galatians 1:11–18.

If we remove the notion of written scripture from Acts 13, we end up with only punctuation — essentially nothing. We could say the same about almost any other section of the Bible. Again, we see both the warp thread and weft thread weave tightly together to form a brilliant tapestry of Scripture, beautifully illustrated by the publishing throughout the region. Preaching the written words of God to both Jews and Gentiles ushered in earth-shaking outcomes on a global scale.

Spoken, then Written

Scripture is not of any clandestine interpretation (2 Peter 1:20). These two excerpts from Hebrews illustrate precisely the method of preservation of written words. He remains. His words remain.

> God, who at sundry times and in divers manners spake in time past unto the fathers by the prophets, hath in these last days spoken unto us by his Son, whom he hath appointed heir of all things, by whom also he made the worlds; who being the brightness of his glory, and the express image of his person, and upholding all things by the word of his power, when he had by himself purged our sins, sat down on the right hand of the Majesty on high; being made so much better than the angels, as he hath by inheritance obtained a more excellent name than they. (Hebrews 1:1–4)

> And, Thou, Lord, in the beginning hast laid the foundation of the earth; and the heavens are the works of thine hands: they shall perish; but thou remainest; and they all shall wax old as doth a garment; and as a vesture shalt thou fold them up, and they shall be changed: but thou art the same, and thy years shall not fail. (Hebrews 1:10–12)

In this chapter, I show various forms of the systems found in Scripture. The essence of a system is a purpose (or goal) and I have shown that systems should produce a specific outcome. To the LORD, there is no more important matter than the restoration of the souls of children, women, and men into a state of new life in Christ. The rescue of people is intentional, because He loves them. By boundless love, He willingly offered Himself with cause. Jesus Christ fulfilled the systematic safekeeping of Earth, people, and His words.

> Therefore I esteem all thy precepts concerning all things to be right; and I hate every false way. (Psalm 119:128)

In the Gospel account from Apostle Luke, the living Word quotes the written word and systematically completes the fulfillment of those words.

> Then he took unto him the twelve, and said unto them, Behold, we go up to Jerusalem, and all things that are written by the prophets concerning the Son of man shall be accomplished. For he shall be delivered unto the Gentiles, and shall be mocked, and spitefully entreated, and spitted on: and they shall scourge him, and put him to death: and the third day he shall rise again. (Luke 18:31–33)

A Final Word on Order

Order is necessary for the conduct of your life and mine. Even our breathing and eye-blinking and walking are orderly. Thank you, LORD, for the orderly performance of my heart pump! Keeping the Scriptures safe follows an orderly manner, not an accidental stroke of luck!

> And Moses came and told the people all the words of the LORD, and all the judgments: and all the people answered with one voice, and said, All the words which the LORD hath said will we do. And Moses wrote all the words of the LORD, and rose up early in the morning, and builded an altar under the hill, and twelve pillars, according to the twelve tribes of Israel. (Exodus 24:3–4)

> Let all things be done decently and in order. (1 Corinthians 14:40)

The Psalmist desired: "Order my steps in thy word: and let not any iniquity have dominion over me" (Psalm 119:133). Worshiping the LORD demands order: "And thou shalt bring in the table, and set in order the things that are to be set in order upon it; and thou shalt bring in the candlestick, and light the lamps thereof" (Exodus 40:4). "And Hezekiah appointed the courses of the priests and the Levites after their courses, every man according to his service, the priests and Levites for burnt offerings and for peace offerings, to minister, and to give thanks, and to praise in the gates of the tents of the LORD" (2 Chronicles 31:2).

A quick examination of Leviticus 24 shows abundant order in the tabernacle and a prescribed manner of law. Later, in the same fashion, Solomon's magnificent temple gleamed of order in all the service and sacrifice.

> And he appointed, according to the order of David his father, the courses of the priests to their service, and the Levites to their charges, to praise and minister before the priests, as the duty of every day required: the porters also by their courses at every gate: for so had David the man of God commanded. (2 Chronicles 8:14)

Solomon also describes timely order in all of life in Ecclesiastes 3. The creation all around us continues its prescribed order.

Throughout Planet Earth's young life, the LORD always keeps His words safe, not leaving them to untethered human gamble. Jesus Christ sacrificed Himself, so we can be freed from the awful effects of sin. Every step He took was purposeful; every event was an orderly fulfillment of His words.

The Bible was not given for our information but for our transformation — D. L. Moody

Chapter Nine

Now and Later

SPEAK. USE WORDS.

Words arrest the conscience when receiving harsh news. By words, engineers exhibit magnificent machines, sparking our imagination. Words bless and heal. They curse and sever. Words have meaning. The smallest unit of language is the mightiest. These seem to be such simple declarations, but with penetrating results.

The Creator has wonderfully blessed mankind with the ability to communicate through languages. Sure, animals communicate at rudimentary levels. But it is man which assembles the grandeur of speech, and beauty of writing, which permeates every aspect of life itself. Without spoken and written transformations in languages, interaction with others quickly gets close to impossible. I do not dismiss the sign languages, Braille, or any other verbal or written language — all have a purpose.

Noah Webster defined the word speak as *to express thoughts by words*. When we consider the immeasurable utility of words, the heart overflows with wonderment, absorbing the beauty. When speaking, words are collections of sounds and tones. When writing, words build from letters and symbols. Spoken words transform into written words, and written words transform into spoken words, both by employing human cognition. Words make possible what you're doing right at this moment.

Speech: a thought in the mind triggers the orderly blending of chemicals, and physical and electrical actions transmitted through tissues and organs, to produce an utterance of articulated sounds. This connection of brain, mind, body, and spirit, (while often taken for granted), culminates in the wonderful act of speech. It happens practically instantaneously as a person's thoughts ignite nerves to carry an electrical signal to muscles. Through artistic comprehension, we hear the spoken words and then write words into recognizable pictures — an array of alphabet letters and language symbols. Each of the alphabet letters is a distinct character representing certain sounds in the language.

It is indeed marvelous how the typeface or font may differ from writing to writing, but the representative letter, with its unique shape and particular markings, expresses the same signature sound. Regional dialects and other properties do influence languages. However, century after century, the sound and meaning of a letter or symbol change very little, or not at all. And even today we can study languages which have long ago halted from regular use. The beauty and usefulness of languages come from the nuances of word formations, and accents and punctuations. Words are mighty!

Time and time again, with words written on innumerable types of media, the letter is recognizable through sight and thought. The assembling of letters into syllables, into words, into sentences — all work to convince our minds of thought and our brains of understanding. Mathematics comprises mostly numbers and very special symbols — but words and phrases, and sentences describe math concepts, both simple and complex. Not coincidentally, the very-long-term consistency of alphabets in sundry languages plays an integral role in the providential preservation of written Scripture.

The Creator uniquely endowed mankind with the innate capacity to use language — spoken, written, and otherwise assembled words. He did not grant the animal kingdom this same privilege. Further, when in Genesis 11, God confounded the languages at Babel, He ensured His words remained without decay from the assaults of men elevating themselves above God. Remarkably, Jehovah granted both mercy and grace to future humans by dividing and mixing one language into many. Protective retention of His words remained a primary goal, so future humans might read and hear the Bible.

The Creator uses words to express creation into existence. The first recording of God's words is of His speech, noted in Genesis 1:3. When the LORD Jesus completed His sacrifice, He used words: "It is finished" (John 19:30). As the mighty Voice of God stepped out of eternity and transmitted its way through holy men, those men eventually deposited God's words onto the media of written Scripture through the use of language.

The LORD beautifully conversed with the child (and later, prophet), Samuel. Initially perplexed, Samuel eventually recognized the Voice and said, "Speak; for thy servant heareth" (1 Samuel 3:10). The record shows the LORD's revelation to the man Samuel by words and language: "And the LORD appeared again in Shiloh: for the LORD revealed himself to Samuel in Shiloh by the word of the LORD" (1 Samuel 3:21). It is amazing how the LORD revealed Himself not by picture or fantastical event, but by His words.

In most instances, the LORD **speaks** His words. Occasionally, He **writes** the words directly onto a specific medium, even on buildings, oceans, and the heart of man. Sometimes God delivers His words through dreams and visions. By the weft thread, God perfectly and permanently kept unassailable the Heavenly warp thread of His words, weaving them tightly on the language loom of Scripture. The Bible is about, by, concerning, and extending from the Heavenly Creator. All the properties and nuances of Scripture are the beautiful benefits of the language. Scripture is without decay.

Durable Parchment

Owing to its namesake ancient Pergamon, the making of parchment starts with the skin of the animal, which is usually a sheep, calf, or goat. After soaking in water to remove dirt and blood, they remove the hair. Sometimes they use fermented vegetable "liquor" or lime. During the treatment and drying process, skin collagen rearranges but does not alter chemically. This results in a smooth and hard material that is also very sensitive to changes in humidity.[1]

People have written on prepared animal skins for millennia, hailing back to the Assyrians, Babylonians, Egyptians, and of course the Hebrew people. Even earlier, people wrote upon animal skins, but a new, more thorough method of cleaning, stretching, and scraping made possible the use of both sides of a manuscript leaf, leading to the supplanting of the rolled manuscript by the bound book (or, codex). Parchment was often the media of choice for early Islamic texts. Processing of a hide into parchment has undergone a tremendous evolution based on time and location. It is claimed that Moses wrote the first Torah Scroll on the un-split cow-hide called gevil. Parchment is still the only medium used by traditional religious Jews for Torah scrolls and is produced by large companies in Israel. For those uses, only

---

1. Derived from Parchment-making, Michele Brown, Cornell University Library Conservation, from https://blogs.cornell.edu/culconservation/2015/04/03/parchment-making

the hides of kosher animals are permitted. Since there are many requirements for it to be fit for religious use, the liming is usually processed under the supervision of a qualified Rabbi.[2]

For a long time, many considered parchment a durable medium on which to write text, handing it down to many generations. Time has shown that it does not last as long as we would like it to. Sometimes, the custodians erased the parchment and reused it for another text. Think of it as the Etch-A-Sketch of the day, but it is called palimpsest parchment.

Recitation

To recite is to repeat words using a voice. A recital is a rehearsal; a repetition of those words, relating especially to testimony. Recitals are typically told in a narrative fashion and declare the many details of a series of events or tell us about a person, place, or thing. Within the confines of Scripture, each of the holy men is the agent of recital. As you read the Bible text, with every experience, when the holy man recites and writes the words from God, there is purpose and precision.

What wonderful sights to see in Acts 1–3. These Galileans communicated the Gospel to all within earshot, without respect to ethnicity or nationality, or any other demographic. The Gospel was then — and is today — for everyone! We could title The Acts of the Apostles as The Speech of the Evangelists, or better yet The Speech of the Holy Ghost, for so much of the text describes the message of God brought through speaking. The *recital* of the Scriptures is the motivating directive of their mission; their acts. Their *works* were all about the *words* (preaching the message) of the Gospel of Jesus Christ. They obeyed His certified commission, teaching the Scriptures to everyone they encountered; and propelled the message of the Good News to the farthest reaches of the planet. Praise God!

As the Acts of the Apostles unfold, it begins with the evangelists speaking the words granted by the gift of the Holy Spirit. They practiced a speech which the assembled crowds (from many other cultures) heard and understood. Those disciples of Christ spoke various languages, while the audience heard in their native language. The Holy Ghost moved among all the attendees,

---

2. Derived from the article Parchment, Wikipedia, from https://en.wikipedia.org/wiki/Parchment

giving them gifts — the tools necessary to hear and understand the Gospel. To the Apostles, He gave the gift of *speaking* the words. To the many hearers, He gave the gift of *hearing* the words.

Throughout, we see the Holy Ghost *filling* the disciples, giving them *utterance*. With intent, He **marvelously translated** their *words* into the primary language of each listener. Regardless of where they were from, they **heard** in their own language the wonderful works of God!

Whether by speech or by letter, there can be no doubt the words of God moved through these preachers into the hearts of many listeners. The grand Acts 2 assemblies were *recitals* of the spoken and written message of the Gospel. The record of those here-and-now evangelistic *recitals* on the day of Pentecost was vital to the expansion of the Gospel into many earthly locations and future generations.

Extended Times

Recognizing that every small mark, tiny letter, and word has a purpose, let's discover some examples by which the holy men recorded the recited words from the LORD at a later time. By this I mean the spoken words and the written words were not contemporary. If chance prevailed over the writings, the LORD is a cruel creator, subject to whim and yielding to powers beyond His triune Godhead. Preposterous!

In so many passages, we read of the holy men being stopped to listen — to hear the thundering Voice. Whether an angel, prophet, whirlwind, or another instrument delivered it — every moment of inspiration had an immediate purpose and an eternal mission, stitching together the weft thread and warp thread of the text. Thankfully, the LORD is not susceptible to deception or the crafty devices of humans. In His perfect way, He chose for His words to be *reserved* for all generations by the method of human language writing.

Let us now examine several long epochs which existed between the time the Holy Ghost spoke to (or through) the holy man — and he then wrote those words. These examples will show God's oversight for safely keeping His word unblemished, not left to chance. God charged each of the writing agents with duties as an escrow officer for the stewardship of the most precious estate — His words.

The text shows us seasons of time may separate some events, even when they relate, and are perhaps consecutive — sometimes an extended season. More often than not, when the Holy Ghost moved, the agent wrote right away.

Sometimes he wrote those words later. Perhaps this occurred more often than we realize while assembling the canon during some sixteen centuries. I aim to show you this: the work of preservation provided the bulwark for the defense and welfare of God's words.

Does the timeframe matter? Know this: during the interim period between speech and hearing, and then writing — the words are, by God's safeguarding, kept without decay. If, for example, Isaiah did not write for several years after being inspired, who kept Isaiah safe? They had no **spare** Isaiah.

Let us not forsake a simple Bible deduction: the Scriptures are wholly a work of, and by, God. He is *invincible*. Thus, His words are *impervious* to any decay. The Bible is the collective message from God, deemed necessary for salvation, and sufficient for the behavior of His favorite creatures.

Long After the Unbridled Cataclysm

Genesis. God spoke to Adam and Cain, Noah, and others, and to a beguiling creature known as the serpent. We have in our grasp a witness-sworn affidavit, proving it was Jehovah speaking to these men. We can parse a copy of these conversations — written by the man Moses. He recorded the Pentateuch some nine centuries after the flood. Since the flood all but obliterated Earth, we conclude that the writings of Prophet Moses signify the preservation of God's words in the most complex way.

This recital of the holy man, Moses, tells in precise and clear detail the order of events from the start of the beginning until his death. Nothing vital is missing. There are no links missing from the Holy Ghost's chain of custody. The recital is complete with no part dislodged.

In many of the Scripture agents coming after Moses, we read references and quotes from the Pentateuch. In superb syntax, we read about Noah finding grace in the eyes of the LORD and having multiple conversations with the Creator. Whether Noah wrote the instructions for building the ship, or just committed them to memory, Moses later recorded the exact design details and the construction procedures for building the rescue ship. He received the instructions nine hundred years after the flood, by inspiration.

In Matthew 24, the LORD Jesus explains His return by the example of Noah's life and days. The epoch between Moses and the LORD Jesus Christ is approximately thirteen million hours. And during the entire span, the Holy Ghost carefully shepherded the words of God — without decay.

The Days of Noah

Continuing the example, Moses wrote the accounts of Noah's interactions with God. His account includes the events both before and after the cataclysmic flood. In his chronicle, he journals Noah's labors in building the ark, awaiting the assembly of animals, and taking various keystone steps. It is easy to see they could not influence the deluge of water.

After the rains ceased, the LORD sent a wind to push the waters off the land, to the point of equilibrium. The ark rested. Several months later, the tops of mountains poked through, and eventually, as the waters continued to recede, the dove dispatched by Noah found an olive tree and returned with a sample. The very first of brand new firsts now descended upon the ark and Noah's family.

> And it came to pass in the six hundredth and first year, in the first month, the first day of the month, the waters were dried up from off the earth: and Noah removed the covering of the ark, and looked, and, behold, the face of the ground was dry. (Genesis 8:13)

As God spoke to Noah shortly thereafter, He commanded him and his family to exit the ark, bringing all the animals with them. Noah and his family obeyed the commission to replenish the earth. What follows was an act of magnificent worship to the Saviour, and the Bible says His promises to protect Planet Earth continue to this day.

> And the LORD smelled a sweet savour; and the LORD said in his heart, I will not again curse the ground any more for man's sake; for the imagination of man's heart is evil from his youth; neither will I again smite any more every thing living, as I have done. While the earth remaineth, seedtime and harvest, and cold and heat, and summer and winter, and day and night shall not cease. (Genesis 8:21–22)

Did you see it? The LORD spoke in His heart! Forever and always the LORD will remember His covenant with all flesh. He will never again destroy the earth with a flood of water and He sets the rainbow as a token of promise.

He delivers the promise to Noah, and nine centuries later to Moses, by the inspired recital. Just imagine being Moses as God recounts what He said to Noah all those years prior! God *keeps* His word!

Said in the Heart

It's likely you have said something in your heart. A thought in your brain triggered a profound emotional response or a deep conviction, which you quietly kept to yourself, preventing the thought from expressing itself in verbal or written form. We keep things like this quiet to prevent an embarrassing situation, or perhaps to prevent spiritual injury to another, or to keep a promise to a friend. Sometimes we stay hushed in our words, such that a deep belief galvanizes our soul. Occasionally, we mute ourselves to commune with our Creator.

Hannah was Samuel's mother, a righteous woman married to a righteous man. Being childless, succumbing to the bitterness in her spirit, she vowed to Jehovah.

> O LORD of hosts, if thou wilt indeed look on the affliction of thine handmaid, and remember me, and not forget thine handmaid, but wilt give unto thine handmaid a man child, then I will give him unto the LORD all the days of his life, and there shall no razor come upon his head. (1 Samuel 1:11)

God honored her deep commitment, and Samuel soon arrived. During her hushed communion on the temple grounds, she moved her lips and Eli thought of her as being drunken. Taken aback, Hannah answered,

> No, my lord, I am a woman of a sorrowful spirit: I have drunk neither wine nor strong drink, but have poured out my soul before the LORD. (1 Samuel 1:15)

While her lips moved, Eli did not hear her voice. However, Scripture tells us she **spoke in her heart** — and God heard her. This snippet of Scripture shows the tender sensitivity of the LORD to His saints. Another may just be His attention to detail. Or perhaps this excerpt shows the LORD's compassion for those dedicated to His service while in an emotional upheaval.

Some amount of time passes, and eventually Samuel or a scribe commits this event into the Scriptural record. To know this story, someone had to hear it and write it down. It's possible they wrote in the journals kept near the altar, under the watchful eye of the Levite conservators. Regardless, Jehovah made provisions to keep this story safe until its inclusion in the canon.

The Volume of Job

Someday, as the saint walks along the gilded avenues of the pearly white city, he may encounter the man Job. Just imagine living in eternity, no longer bound by these dimensions, and speaking with Job; to ask him questions; understand his thinking; learn of his great sorrows from man and great comforts from the LORD!

Job was a man bound by suffering. By and by, we shall understand the whole of Job's experiences and trials.

The content of His namesake book is unique among all the other Bible books, with its origins mysterious. The text reveals little about the times and locations of Job's world, and the reasonable estimation is that the book of Job is one of the earliest recorded sections of the Bible. Some estimate Job's epoch on Planet Earth as around 2,200 years before Christ, making him contemporary with Abraham. Also, the first and last chapters reveal Job lived long enough to sire ten children, and it shows his children grew old enough to have their own homes. Further, after his catastrophic loss of all his family and possessions, he lived yet long enough to father ten more children and collect massive amounts more wealth. In the end, Job lived another one-hundred-forty years after all the things written in the Bible text, and this longevity enabled him to know his children and grandchildren to the fourth generation.

Job's life illustrates multiple interactions and direct instructions from his Creator. Even to this day, Job is probably one of the most quoted of all writers in any era, of any literature. God spoke directly to Satan about His darling Job: "Hast thou considered my servant Job, that there is none like him in the earth, a perfect and an upright man, one that feareth God, and escheweth evil?" (Job 1:8).

In the Job journal, the style of writing is mostly in a third-party narrative fashion, such as by a scribe who heard the various conversations between Job and his contemporaries. There are over two-thousand words spoken directly by Jehovah to the main characters, with the largest section in the last chapters, where He magnificently speaks with Job out of the whirlwind (what a beautiful event). While the text describes the beginning conversation with Satan and ends with a picture of Job's last days, the bulk of the text is the back-and-forth conversations between Job, Eliphaz, Bildad, and Zophar.

We can read the Job record today because the LORD, issuing a perfect insurance policy, reserved the text without decay. Even Job himself longed, "Oh that my words were now written! oh that they were printed in a book! That they were graven with an iron pen and lead in the rock for ever!" (Job 19:23–24). It seems Job is more forward-thinking than we might imagine.

Announced Expression

Exodus 3 is the gateway to multiple chapters describing the dread suffered by the Egyptians and the liberty marshaled to the Hebrews by God. Early on, we find Moses tending the flocks belonging to his father-in-law, Jethro. At Mount Horeb, the angel of God appeared to him in a flame of fire out of the midst of a bush — but the bush was fireproof! Standing near, the Voice spoke from the midst of the bush, telling Moses to remove his shoes, as the place where he stood was holy ground.

Continuing, the LORD explained He is the God of Abraham, Isaac, and Jacob. He would soon deliver the Israelites from the Egyptians and lead them into the land of milk and honey. Moses knew the Israelites would query him: "Behold, when I come unto the children of Israel, and shall say unto them, The God of your fathers hath sent me unto you; and they shall say to me, What is his name? what shall I say unto them? And God said unto Moses, **I AM THAT I AM**: and he said, Thus shalt thou say unto the children of Israel, **I AM** hath sent me unto you" (Exodus 3:13–14, emphasis added). This brief passage establishes the most central Bible doctrine — Jehovah is preeminent.

Notice a very important detail: "And I will stretch out my hand, and smite Egypt with all my wonders which I will do in the midst thereof: and after that he will let you go" (Exodus 3:20).

As the Exodus chapters continue, the plagues against Pharaoh and Egypt are the theme. Pharaoh, of course, punished the Hebrews by demanding more bricks, but not providing straw. The details of Pharaoh's responses to the plagues are many. Throughout, we find God speaking to Moses, and in those conversations, He told Moses to repeat (recite) the words from God to Pharaoh. In the story, over and over, Moses told Pharaoh to set the Hebrew people free.

Day after day, plague after plague, Moses and Aaron delivered the messages from God. In Exodus 4:14–15, the LORD confirmed the delivery method of His words: from His mouth into Moses' mouth, into Aaron's ears and through his mouth, and into the ears of Pharaoh. The LORD supplied the message and sent the messengers.

After finally leaving Goshen, and with the Egyptians destroyed by God at the Red Sea, we fast forward to Exodus 20. Here, the LORD first gave the ten commandments, and in the next three chapters gave many judgments, establishing the core of His law for the people. When you get to Exodus 24, we find Moses had written all the words of the LORD, "and rose up early in the morning, and builded an altar under the hill, and twelve pillars, according to the twelve tribes of Israel" (Exodus 24:4).

The LORD told Moses and others He would establish this law. Moses had journaled everything in writing, and it was time to "set it in stone."

> Come up to me into the mount, and be there: and I will give thee tables of stone, and a law, and commandments which I have written; that thou mayest teach them. (Exodus 24:12)

As Moses was on the mountain for forty days, from Exodus 24 until the end of Exodus 32, the LORD gave many instructions about the tabernacle of worship, other commands, and the LORD even repented of His thoughts of evil against His people. We often watch in theater reenactments as the finger of God (Exodus 31:18) magically appears out of thin air and scribes blank stone tablets with the commandments while Moses is stunned. But this is not the total story.

Jehovah told Moses He had written the law and commandments. The record does not show whether God wrote them the day before, a year earlier, or even the previous decade. It's entirely possible God wrote the tables in Heaven, reserving them for this very event and day. After all, the LORD knew this day would arrive.

Now Moses had those precious stone tablets: "And Moses turned, and went down from the mount, and the two tables of the testimony were in his hand: the tables were written on both their sides; on the one side and on the other were they written. And the tables were the work of God, and the writing was the writing of God, graven upon the tables" (Exodus 32:15–16). Even after Moses broke the first set of tables, the LORD wrote new tablets the second time with His own finger. Near the end of the Exodus chronicle, Moses again wrote more words from God into the Pentateuch. Notably, Moses was not a competent speaker, but he sure could yield to the LORD in writing!

Many centuries later, the LORD Jesus referenced these prime commandments as He upbraided the Pharisees, correcting their weak understanding of the commandments they so claim to love (Matthew 22:36–40).

These circumstances show a time span (perhaps a great or immeasurable duration) from when God wrote the commandments to then announcing them to Moses, to then giving them to Moses as the trustee. And of course, God recited them a second time to clear up Moses' mishandling of the first set of stone tablets. The Great I AM indeed made a promise. He kept His promise, and He safeguarded His promise by instructing Moses to memorialize those events in books. Written text. Not liable to decay.

Purposely Waited

Under the kingdom of David (because of his obedience to the LORD), the nation of Israel enjoyed protection and rest from all its enemies. Ever since Jehovah brought them out of Egyptian bondage, He has not dwelled in a permanent house but has instead dwelled in tabernacles and tents. But now, King David wished to build the LORD a lasting house, and while Nathan initially granted King David permission to make the building, the LORD quickly corrected him. This was not God's plan, and Nathan and David must change course.

As King David prayed, he humbled himself and confessed his subordinate and unclean position before the LORD, who made him both servant and king. His soul was open before the LORD, as he exclaimed it is a small thing for the LORD to remember David's throne. And David reminded the LORD of His remembrance of David's house for a great while to come. Reading 2 Samuel 7:19, we see the LORD "spoke" (past tense) of David's house for a long while "to come" (future tense). This timeline extends from bookend to bookend.

For many centuries and in many geographies and through so many administrations, not one time has Jehovah dwelled in a permanent house! Rhetorically, not one time has He queried His people, "Why build ye not me an house of cedar?" (2 Samuel 7:7).

This King David had just heard Nathan recite the word of the LORD from the night before. In short order, God repaired King David's doctrine and dream: David, I called you from the sheepcote. I've been with you wherever you have gone. And David, I have cut off your enemies, and I have made your name great upon the Earth! I will make a house for you and bless you beyond imagination. David, once you are sleeping with your fathers, I will establish your kingdom forever! Yes, I will preserve you! But David, you will not build my house, and I will assign this grace to your son, whose kingdom I will establish forever, dovetailing with yours.

As we read of David's continued prayer, he complied with the LORD's promise and gained a renewed understanding of his position in the LORD. King David showed both the letter and the spirit of the LORD's working amongst His people as he recognized: "For thy word's sake, and according to thine own heart, hast thou done all these great things, to make thy servant know them" (2 Samuel 7:21). Notice that God's actions benefit His words. It was clear to David: his son Solomon would fulfill his dream sometime later. David had shed too much blood, and Solomon would receive the commission to build the house. However, King David played a vital role in the entire enterprise, as he would be the first recipient of the temple plans.

In 1 Chronicles 28, the Spirit of God impressed King David with the pattern of every aspect of the temple. The LORD's detailed plans extended from the courts to the instruments; the tables to the basins and fleshhooks; from the altar to the cherubims and the chariots. Jehovah withheld no detail.

Fast forward to the time when King David delivered the plans and protocols to Prince Solomon. He tells his son: "All this, said David, the LORD made me understand in writing by his hand upon me, even all the works of this pattern" (1 Chronicles 28:19).

Do you see what God did? He wrote by His own hand into David's understanding — of every detail and design of the temple. From who else could he receive perfect blueprints for the temple, but from the Temple Owner?

King David declared:

> Solomon my son is young and tender, and the house that is to be builded for the LORD must be exceeding magnifical, of fame and of glory throughout all countries: I will therefore now make preparation for it. So David prepared abundantly before his death. (1 Chronicles 22:5)

Remember: the holy name of the LORD was to be hosted in and on and about this permanent house. The central point of the temple building was the promotion and action of worship. The whole of Planet Earth would soon know of the magnificent place where God meets with people.

As the sourcebook continues early in 2 Chronicles, it had been nearly five decades since King David received the blueprints. David had since died, and the temple construction consumed two decades, but is finished. They positioned all the accouterments; the priests and people were spiritually prepared; and the smoke of God filled the house where His name dwells. United worship began.

King Solomon offered one thousand burnt offerings on the brazen altar at the tabernacle, and the LORD was well pleased. He then appeared to Solomon during the night, asking what he needed. Thankfully, Solomon asked for wisdom, not stuff or power. The LORD bountifully granted wisdom, along with material blessing beyond measure.

> Wisdom and knowledge is granted unto thee; and I will give thee riches, and wealth, and honour, such as none of the kings have had that have been before thee, neither shall there any after thee have the like. (2 Chronicles 1:12)

Six chapters and a lot of years later, with the temple building completed, being mindful of his great responsibility, Solomon petitioned Jehovah to verify the word committed to his father, David. As he prayed, he expected God would fulfill the promise: putting His name on this temple.

> Now when Solomon had made an end of praying, the fire came down from heaven, and consumed the burnt offering and the sacrifices; and the glory of the LORD filled the house. And the priests could not enter into the house of the LORD, because the glory of the LORD had filled the LORD'S house. And when all the children of Israel saw how the fire came down, and the glory of the LORD upon the house, they bowed themselves with their faces to the ground upon the pavement, and worshipped, and praised the LORD, saying, For he is good; for his mercy endureth for ever. Then the king and all the people offered sacrifices before the LORD. (2 Chronicles 7:1–4)

The LORD Jehovah, high and lifted in His glory, contentedly approved of this building.

> For now have I chosen and sanctified this house, that my name may be there for ever: and mine eyes and mine heart shall be there perpetually. (2 Chronicles 7:16)

The LORD intentionally waited multiplied centuries to establish a durable house where His name dwelled and His oracle stood firm. He could have made this happen at any other time, but in all his glory, He chose this time, this king, these priests, and these people. Jehovah knew the day approached when His temple would transform from a building into the hearts of people, by salvation in Jesus Christ.

What beauty to see the name of the LORD perpetually expressed through this temple made by hands! In this we see His name written into the physical building materials of the magnificent temple. Just imagine how marvelous is the writing of His Name upon the souls of Christians! The promise started with the inspiration of King David some fifty years before, and now God fulfilled His promise to inscribe His name into the temple. Promised, written, and delivered, and all without decay.

The Journaled History

To chronicle is to write an account of events, describing what happened and when it happened, and the account is ordered by time.

The whole series of six books from Samuel, Kings, and Chronicles are often collectively referred to as first through sixth Kings, and in Scripture, they have several references, including the book of the chronicles of the kings which is usually assigned to the kings of Judah or the kings of Israel.

In 1 Chronicles 27, we find Joab numbering the people and recording the numbers in the chronicles of King David. It was not permissible to do the numbering, but that's not my main point. This Scripture and others found in the six books of the kings show an established method for keeping records of the various happenings in society.

We find another example of journaling in 1 Kings 11. Because of Solomon's sin, Israel split into two tribes, plus the Levites (Judah in the south), and the other ten tribes (Israel in the north). We know from reading the Kings and Chronicles records, each group kept separate journals (ledgers or logbooks) of the events happening in their societies. Theirs was a drastic division:

> Wherefore the king hearkened not unto the people; for the cause was from the LORD, that he might perform his saying, which the LORD spake by Ahijah the Shilonite unto Jeroboam the son of Nebat. So when all Israel saw that the king hearkened not unto them, the people answered the king, saying, What portion have we in David? neither have we inheritance in the son of Jesse: to your tents, O Israel: now see to thine own house, David. So Israel departed unto their tents. But as for the children of Israel which dwelt in the cities of Judah, Rehoboam reigned over them. (1 Kings 12:15–17)

Further, three times in Esther is a series of events written in the books of the kings of Media and Persia. Logged in Esther's early entries is the hanging of two foul fellows (Esther 2). In the next, we find the king disturbed and unable to sleep — so he called for the scrolled record to be read, whereupon he changed his edict about Mordecai, giving him great honor, and instead hanging Haman on the gallows (Esther 6). Third, the last sentences of Esther record how King Ahasuerus laid a tribute upon the land and the isles of the sea and "all the acts of his power and of his might, and the declaration of the greatness of Mordecai, whereunto the king advanced him, are they not written in the book of the chronicles of the kings of Media and Persia?" (Esther 10:2).

These are just a few of the examples where we read of various chronicles (or journals) being maintained. Isn't it wonderful how the LORD oversaw the maintenance of all these words, so we could read them today?

Hebrew Bloodline

Beautifully recorded in 1 Chronicles 1–9 are the genealogies from Adam through the sons of Benjamin and the rest of the Hebrew bloodline to that point. The details of the various officeholders and family heritages are some of the most detailed accounts in the Bible. The logging of this information is fundamental to understanding the Biblical worldview, the history of mankind, and certainly the salvation of all. This bloodline is a timeline.

The list is substantial, and includes mighty men, pre-Hebrew kings and princes, evil men and valiant men, concubines, scribes, craftsmen, warriors, captives — and so many more vocations. Throughout the historical narrative, we read of the family trees, the many skirmishes, the castles and coasts —

and so many people and venues. Fortunately, we read about their obedience. Sadly, we discover their rebellions. Chapter nine summarizes the whole.

> So all Israel were reckoned by genealogies; and, behold, they were written in the book of the kings of Israel and Judah, who were carried away to Babylon for their transgression. (1 Chronicles 9:1)

So many reports and explanations can be born out of just this section of Scripture. The myriad details provide a timeline, narrative, and historical evidence of the lineage, beginning the course with the first Adam. The picture almost paints itself. In this lengthy recount of multiplied centuries of human history, the writers describe it all in the past tense. It's possible they lived during those events, and wrote after those things occurred.

However, given the summary nature of the writings, it seems likely the writers learned of most of these facts through handed-down tradition or from other writings. Some of the text seems written many years after the events occurred. It is certain the Holy Ghost oversaw all the written narratives.

Isn't it wonderful how the LORD protected all these words, so we could read them today?

Recited Aforetime, Written Later

Even a casual reading through both the first and second testaments reveals the patience of the LORD interacting with His people. We often want instant satisfaction. Our petulance blinds us to the genuine majesty and penetrating work of the Bible. Meditating on the words and studying the beautiful language strengthens Christian faith. The lively words written on the pages will penetrate and affect our souls like no other text on Earth.

The paper or electronic Bible we hold in our hands represents the text of God's *words* and in our language. Through those words, we can get a glimpse of eternity. Neither the printed book nor the e-tablet possess magical abilities. However, when we read the *words*, the Holy Spirit bears witness with our spirit and does the work only He can do (Romans 8:16).

Many years ago, I purchased a one-half folio sheet from a first-edition of the 1611 King James Bible (Barker printing). Ezekiel's forty-fifth chapter is on one side and most of the opposing page, with chapter forty-six finishing the latter. The words on the four-century-aged page and the words in my 2020 printing of the AV 1769 edition are the same. While the English alphabet expanded by a few letters since the early 17th century, this additional precision aided the accuracy of the language, and strengthened the English language's position in the matter of preservation. The four-century old language, the two-century aged language, and the 2020 language produce the same understanding in my mind. There is no material difference when pronouncing the old letter "f" as the sound of "s" today. The paper will someday cease, but the words shall not pass away (Mark 13:31).

In this chapter, I outline several examples of Scriptural text written a long time after God spoke the words, and the holy man hears, and then recites, those words. So much more has gone into the marshaling and safe harboring of God's word than we might imagine; more than we can write into books. Caution requires we not take for granted or easily dismiss the abundant work of Jehovah to preserve His Scripture before, during, and after man's term of existence.

It is so easy today to pick up a Bible or use a smart app to read it digitally, without giving one moment of thought how it arrived in our hands. In each society, and as individuals, we must abandon the "instant satisfaction" mind-set and put on the whole armor of God. When we read the Bible, let us follow the example of Moses and Samuel, and Apostles Paul and John — be **in the Spirit**. The never-crumbling tapestry of Scripture text will protect your mind and cleanse your person if you allow it.

"He hath remembered his covenant for ever, the word which he commanded to a thousand generations" (Psalm 105:8).

Chapter Ten

By God's Finger

ETERNITY. THIS IS THE place where God dwells. His existence is always in eternity. Indeed, the Scriptures teach us He is at all times present in all places and in all dimensions. He does not alter nor does He deflect. The Bible tells us Heaven is His throne, and Planet Earth is His footstool.

As Prophet Isaiah famously wrote,

> For thus saith the high and lofty One that inhabiteth eternity, whose name is Holy; I dwell in the high and holy place, with him also that is of a contrite and humble spirit, to revive the spirit of the humble, and to revive the heart of the contrite ones. (Isaiah 57:15)

The psalmist wrote,

> The LORD looketh from heaven; he beholdeth all the sons of men. From the place of his habitation he looketh upon all the inhabitants of the earth. (Psalm 33:13–14)

> The glory of the LORD shall endure for ever: the LORD shall rejoice in his works. He looketh on the earth, and it trembleth: he toucheth the hills, and they smoke. (Psalm 104:31–32)

The Chronicles record the LORD's presence simultaneously in eternity and in the temple.

> Now when Solomon had made an end of praying, the fire came down from heaven, and consumed the burnt offering and the sacrifices; and the glory of the LORD filled the house. And the priests could not enter into the house of the LORD, because the glory of the LORD had filled the LORD'S house. (2 Chronicles 7:1–2)

And the journal of preaching in the Acts of the Evangelists proclaims,

> God that made the world and all things therein, seeing that he is LORD of heaven and earth, dwelleth not in temples made with hands. (Acts 17:24)

Mortal men cannot measure the perfection of God's Word! As we behold the glory of his handiwork in the reserving ability of the weft thread of Scripture, there are several magnificent times when the LORD Himself wrote, rather than moving His Spirit upon the chosen man to write. There are places where only God can do the writing; places where the Creator has sole authority to inscribe the words, and man remains just an observer — not an active participant.

When in heaven, the Christian may be awestruck as they listen to the chosen writers speak of being moved upon by the Holy Ghost; relaying the experience. Of the billions of humans created by God, it is by comparison a tiny number of holy men, especially called to host the inspiratory ministry of the Holy Ghost.

Now, take a moment to imagine how captivated you will be when hearing why the LORD registered some words with His own hand!

Woven Durability

A loom is a mechanical device which produces cloth, fabrics, or tapestry by the action of weaving. The basic operating principle of the loom is to hold the warp threads steady and tensioned while the weaver inserts the weft thread between the alternating warp threads. This crisscrossing effect gives the fabric strength and durability. Weavers often use various dyed threads for both warp and weft threads, allowing the weaver to bring patterns and colors alive into the beauty of their creation. While today weavers accomplish most weaving with high-speed, computer-controlled machine looms, the principle of interweaving the warp and weft threads remains fundamental to producing fabric, tapestry, or rug.

Another not-so-well-known weaving technique produces art. While less popular today, in the past, the weaving of silk threads on a loom to produce portraits found great popularity, especially in Europe. The French excelled at this skill in the 18th and 19th centuries. While not the first to build a programmable loom, Frenchman Joseph-Marie Jacquard perfected the design by others and brought full automation to the mechanics of the loom. In the early nineteenth century, thousands of Jacquard-type looms followed his template for construction. The Jacquard loom operates with a brain of sorts, which contains instructions telling the machine how and where and when to move each thread.

With near perfection, the loom operated by the Jacquard machinery is faster, more reliable, and much more accurate to the specifications of the weaver. This mechanical marvel employs a train of punched cards. On the cards, an open space (punched hole) moves the machine (and thus the thread) one way, and a closed space (not punched) moves the thread another way, or prevents its movement.

Jacquard's punched-card loom is the fundamental model of modern looms, and many other machine types, including printing presses and lathes. His on-and-off switch method is also exemplary of linear and parallel computers. Early business computers operated using the punched card method and the US Government calculated the 1890 census on machines operated by a punched-card mechanism.

Jacquard's invention is *precise* and *accurate*. The expert artist Michel-Marie Carquillat used a Jacquard-type loom of his design in 1831, producing a most beautiful portrait. Under commission by the city of Lyon, France, he copied a painted portrait of Jacquard into an identical duplicate — woven with fine silk thread. When completed, this woven portrait was so exquisite, the silk canvas weave method quickly set itself apart from all other pictographic recording methods.

With any art or artifice, one purpose of the creator is to preserve the artwork as long as possible for as many people as possible to behold its splendor. Silk portraits survive today, centuries after their weaving on a Jacquard-type looms, where artists precisely arranged simple warp and weft threads into complex and unrivaled elegance.

Similarly, throughout the centuries, the LORD assembled the canon of Scripture, first with His oversight and planning, next by inspiring His chosen vessels, and then moving upon those men to carefully and proficiently write His words. Like upon a larger-than-life loom, the Saviour has tightly woven the word-threads into the fabric of Scripture.

Autographs and Manuscripts

To write an autograph document, a person uses a pen or pencil. Hailing from Greek and early Latin, this "self-writing" of documents are those written by the author of the content. A manuscript (abbreviated MS) was formerly a text document written by hand, not mechanically printed. However, when practical typewriting came into common use, the typewritten document is also now known as a manuscript. In the digital age, manuscripts (abbreviated MSS) refer to documents that are the printed version of the author's work. What sets a manuscript apart is not the subject, but the originality of the author's writing. Autographs are recognized by their words, far more than their medium.

Let us consider the handwriting autographed by the LORD and look at several examples.

Jehovah Delivers the Pattern

We have already seen God rehearsed to King David (and later Solomon) the design and arrangement of every facet of the temple. God specified each of the patterns — the whole body of architectural specifics. The Holy Ghost moved upon the king to recite the blueprints of the temple to king-appointee Solomon. These blueprints are "the pattern of all that he had by the spirit" (1 Chronicles 28:12).

In a particular fashion, God also confirmed through King David a sequence of events and selection protocols regarding the troops of the priests and Levites, and the prescription for the work of service to be carried out in God's house. The LORD gave exact measurements for all the vessels for the service of worship. Regarding all the gold and silver, He instructed exact weights and measures. He details the candlesticks, the lamps, the tables, the seas and basins and baths, as well as the fleshhooks, bowls, and cups — in multi-dimensional prototypes. In the grandest fashion, the Holy Ghost's movement indelibly printed the design and outfitting of every vessel, and all the instruments, upon the hearts of father and son.

And let us not dispatch with the altar of incense. Neither let us forsake the mercy seat, fixed upon the ark containing the tablets, with its guarding cherubims. Every item teeming with a jacket of the purest gold or the finest silver. The finest of brass also played a big role. Oh, how marvelous the time will be when we can listen to David and Solomon as they recite the patterns of the temple in the most accurate and complete picture! Solomon said later how critical it would be to keep to the exact patterns of the temple building, for the LORD would put His name upon the building!

Put yourself in King David's shoes for just a moment and consider the manner in which he received the patterns of the temple from the LORD.

> All this, said David, the LORD made me understand in writing by his hand upon me, even all the works of this pattern. (1 Chronicles 28:19)

As Eternity came down and glory filled the whole person of this friend of God, Heaven revealed the patterns in perfect precision when God wrote directly upon the heart of King David in His own writing and with His own hand. In all the magnificence we muster about the Creator, He abundantly gives us understanding about the mathematical *accuracy* and material *precision* of every aspect of the temple and its attendants — all recorded by His own hand.

His medium of choice: David's heart. Later, father David expressed the blueprints from his heart to his mouth and into the ears of son Solomon. God wrote on their heart-pages.

By Holy Ghost protection, every part of the rendering of the temple transmitted successfully, accurately, and wholly from God's heart to David's heart to Solomon's heart. One original, two copies. Here again, another marvelous construction project begins, thoroughly overseen, and completed according to God's words. They skipped no step. No board is out of place. Every crafted piece perfectly fits its purpose. Solomon's temple project so pleased God, He put His words and His name on the building! Only later by the writer are these precious words inscribed into book form, copied countless times, and ultimately canonized into the Scriptures we hold today.

Jehovah Writes Upon the Heart

> But this shall be the covenant that I will make with the house of Israel; after those days, saith the LORD, I will put my law in their inward parts, and write it in their hearts; and will be their God, and they shall be my people. (Jeremiah 31:33)

> This is the covenant that I will make with them after those days, saith the Lord, I will put my laws into their hearts, and in their minds will I write them; and their sins and iniquities will I remember no more. (Hebrews 10:16–17)

> The mouth of the righteous speaketh wisdom, and his tongue talketh of judgment. The law of his God is in his heart; none of his steps shall slide. (Psalm 37:30–31)

> I delight to do thy will, O my God: yea, thy law is within my heart. (Psalm 40:8)

> Keep my commandments, and live; and my law as the apple of thine eye. Bind them upon thy fingers, write them upon the table of thine heart. (Proverbs 7:2–3)

At this point in his administration, King Solomon had not yet plunged into the idolatry and lecherous behavior destined to destroy his relationship with the LORD. He learned God's commandments, which are written on the heart by seeking understanding — by seeking knowledge and wisdom.

We too, by reading and hearing, absorb into our minds the effective words from the Bible pages. The tangible words on the written page of the Bible speak to the intangible writings in the heart of every person. "Let the word of Christ dwell in you richly in all wisdom; teaching and admonishing one another in psalms and hymns and spiritual songs, singing with grace in your hearts to the Lord" (Colossians 3:16).

The writing of God's words upon the heart of the Christian rescues them from the awful effects of sin. The application of those words brings mercy, grace, and hope (and so much more)! Faith for salvation, and faith for everything in life, comes from hearing or reading the word of God, whether by natural or mechanical means.

Once the Holy Ghost seals the Christian at salvation, there is no unsealing by any form of might: "In whom ye also trusted, after that ye heard the word of truth, the gospel of your salvation: in whom also after that ye believed, ye were sealed with that holy Spirit of promise, which is the earnest of our inheritance until the redemption of the purchased possession, unto the praise of his glory" (Ephesians 1:13–14). Notice the Holy Ghost sealing (preserving) the individual by the words of God (word of truth) until the day of "redemption through his blood, the forgiveness of sins, according to the riches of his grace" (Ephesians 1:7). What could be a more powerful safeguard than being sealed by the Holy Ghost?

The Hebrews' letter reiterates the promise of the covenant established by God, which also clarifies how Christ purchased the new covenant. His purchase includes the forgiveness of our sins and the replacement of an unbelieving and rebellious heart with a new heart, convinced of faith and desiring to obey. The LORD Jesus abolished the frail, insufficient requirement of pouring the blood of a lamb onto the horns of the altar year after year. It is the LORD Jesus who converts the short-sighted, old method into the everlasting Gospel words written permanently upon the hearts of His children!

King David reveals a simple solution for keeping our lives safe from the awfulness of sin, which corrodes, decays, and pollutes the heart of man. Be careful Christian — sin so easily prevents the work of God in your life.

> With my whole heart have I sought thee: O let me not wander from thy commandments. Thy word have I hid in mine heart, that I might not sin against thee. (Psalm 119:10–11)

Jehovah Writes His Epistles

An epistle is a more formal letter, typically communicating solemn information to a distant person or group. In the Bible, we read of the Holy Ghost moving upon several of the apostles to write now-famous epistles to churches and pastors. In the Old Testament, there are many examples of epistles (specific letters) sent between various parties. Through the Apostle Paul, the Holy Ghost elevates the writing of an epistle to an intangible and spiritual level.

> Do we begin again to commend ourselves? or need we, as some others, epistles of commendation to you, or letters of commendation from you? Ye are our epistle written in our hearts, known and read of all men: forasmuch as ye are manifestly declared to be the epistle of Christ ministered by us, written not with ink, but with the Spirit of the living God; not in tables of stone, but in fleshy tables of the heart. (2 Corinthians 3:1–3)

The Scriptures proclaim here and in other passages how the Holy Ghost writes the law of God upon the hearts of men and women. Paul and his company reject needing letters of recommendation from others to the Corinthian church. Called by God to carry His Gospel to the far reaches of the known world, these men had all the certification required. There is no greater academic degree than the one signed by the great Chancellor Himself. In fact, God wrote Paul's diploma for all to see in Acts 9! Paul turns the notion of an earthly résumé on its head, declaring a factual conviction: the Corinthian Christians are an all-sufficient certification!

God sealed (redeemed, saved) these Corinthians and preserved them from the ensuing wrath. It's like each person is an ambulating letter of Christ's ministry and saving grace. The precious Spirit of the Living God wrote their "life letters" upon soft and malleable tables of the heart, not with ink on parchment or with a chisel on stone tablets. His words, His media, His epistles.

The LORD Jesus is the Author and the Holy Ghost is the Finisher of faith. He wrote the book, He publishes the book, and He seals each person's faith-book. Just as the Corinthians and others of Paul's day, the Christian of today is a letter from Christ to all they encounter. Do not fold your letter and leave it hidden in the envelope of self-righteousness. We must all be about the Father's business of declaring His words to all around us. God's preserved words never return void.

Go ye therefore, and teach all nations, baptizing them in the name of the Father, and of the Son, and of the Holy Ghost: teaching them to observe all things whatsoever I have commanded you: and, lo, I am with you alway, even unto the end of the world. Amen. (Matthew 28:19–20)

So shall my word be that goeth forth out of my mouth: it shall not return unto me void, but it shall accomplish that which I please, and it shall prosper in the thing whereto I sent it. (Isaiah 55:11)

Troubling Visions and Jehovah's Open Books

We enter Daniel's seventh chapter. The word pictures are strikingly beautiful! The winds from the North, South, East, and West strive upon the great sea. Four different beasts come up from its midst. The fourth beast is more dreadful and far more terrible than the other three, and it has ten horns.

This is what Daniel dreamt during the first year of Belshazzar of Babylon, and God instructed him to write what he saw. These visions of Daniel, dispatched from Jehovah's Eternal library, are likely the most impactful of all prophecies, and certainly remain in the top ten, should it even be possible to grade such a marvel. Because of Daniel's obedience, we have before us the words of marvelous prophecy.

We read Daniel's summary account of the inspired dreams and received visions — as if giving us just a glimpse of the time passing during his dreams. As the books open, the Voice speaks: the judgment and punishment will pass upon the beasts and others. We see before us the thoroughly cleansed Daniel, watching, as the Son of man draws near the Ancient of days. He gains dominion and glory and a kingdom of all nations. It is Son's domain which shall not pass away! After all the terribleness, the Ancient of days will restore the kingdom to His Son and judgment to His saints. Wow! The pictures painted by the words are some of the most detailed seen in Scripture!

As the eighth chapter ensues, the visions continue, and Daniel sees a ram and a goat engaged in battle. In these visions, is a host of Heaven, a mighty prince, and a little horn who waxes great to the North, South, and East. The daily sacrifice is now gone. The sanctuary, the ram, the host of stars, and the truth — all cast down. As Daniel seeks an understanding, he is stunned as an appearance of a man stands before him. This man's voice, emanating from between the banks of the Ulai River, calls Gabriel and commands him to apprehend Daniel's understanding. Then, as if compelled, Daniel falls into a deep sleep, with Gabriel asking, "Do you understand?" — and the chief angel touches him and stands him upright!

Gabriel then explains the true visions and closes with this commandment: "And the vision of the evening and the morning which was told is true: wherefore shut thou up the vision; for it shall be for many days" (Daniel 8:26). Gabriel has already told Daniel his vision will take place at the appointed time of the end (Daniel 8:17). What Daniel's mind and soul are about to view is prophecy, which only he shall know (Daniel 8:19). Astonished, sick, and exhausted, he communicated both the summary to be written into the canon record and the resemblant message to be delivered to the Hebrews in Babylon, but they do not understand (Daniel 8:27).

In these two brief chapters of prophecy, we have seen in written form a summary of the visions experienced by Daniel. The Bible calls it a sum of the matters. Isn't it marvelous how the LORD Jesus and Apostle John will springboard from these prophecies many centuries later? When we reach the Heavenly palace, we will behold all things with clarity. Personally, I think this is just a taste of eternal beauty — a glimpse of the hope waiting for us in Heaven.

The Voice and His chief interpreter Gabriel granted these visions to Daniel from eternity, moved them into his person, and cemented the visions into his understanding. Not even one time in just the fifty-five verses do we see man's intellect, ability, or opinion intermeddle with God's work.

Of note, Daniel sees the books opened. These are the same books which Apostle John later writes about in the Revelation of Jesus Christ (Revelation 20:12). Termed as the books of works (or deeds), we see the dead being judged out of those things written in the books. It's also quite telling when the Apostle Paul, writing to the Corinthians, summarized the notion of fire which manifests and reveals every man's works (1 Corinthians 3:13–15). These books belong wholly to the realm of God, and man has no influence over the recordings in these books.

Neither John nor Paul was alive when Daniel saw and wrote these visions, but they read the account from the copies of the first covenant. Only the LORD could ensure the survival of the written Daniel records from Babylon, out to many cities on the continent, through the turmoil of the several centuries, likely onto the prison island with John, through continued decades of terribleness, and finally into the canon of Scripture, centuries later.

Daniel's visions are telling of the eventual revealing of every man's works — be they good or bad. God alone will someday judge our works and cast them as worthless wood, hay, or stubble, or He will include them in our account as valuable. His judgments stem from **His words — His truth**.

Just a few years before Daniel received the visions, a powerful king learned of open-book judgment the hard way:

> Now I Nebuchadnezzar praise and extol and honour the King of heaven, all whose works are truth, and his ways judgment: and those that walk in pride he is able to abase. (Daniel 4:37)

From eternity, through the intense dreams, confirmed by the Voice at the River, Gabriel verbally interprets the visions summarized by Daniel. We see just a glimpse for now. All this is sequestered until the end of time, when the Ancient of days will execute the instructions we see in those visions. Whoa! These sections of the first writings, carried through multiplied centuries, and ultimately on out into eternity again — remain unaffected by any potential decay.

Jehovah's Book

Idolatry is a horrible rejection of the authority of God. Idolatry comes in many forms and fashions and sometimes isn't just about material things. We visit again with Moses, as he attended the mountain meeting with Jehovah. We read of cowardly Aaron hastily rejecting God's sovereignty, fashioning a calf-idol of gold, and leading the Hebrews to worship clumps of metal while shamefully disrobed in their full nudity. Next, the Levites slaughtered three thousand Hebrews at the righteous command of Moses. When Moses pronounced judgment upon the people, he simultaneously sought the LORD in order to secure atonement for their great folly!

Moses said to Jehovah,

> Oh, this people have sinned a great sin, and have made them gods of gold. Yet now, if thou wilt forgive their sin--; and if not, blot me, I pray thee, out of thy book which thou hast written. (Exodus 32:31–32)

Jehovah said to Moses,

> Whosoever hath sinned against me, him will I blot out of my book. (Exodus 32:33)

Moses understood there is a book in Heaven, and in it are names. It is God's book; He owns it, maintains it, writes into the book or erases from the book, and has very strict journaling rules for the book.

Continuing, we see King David, surrounded by a myriad of haters, petitioning Jehovah's mighty action to have those detractors "blotted out of the book of the living, and not be written with the righteous" (Psalm 69:28). In the strongest of terms, the son of Jesse was asking the Owner to remove from the book those unworthy to maintain their membership in the book. Further, King David knew God harnessed him as a simple substance with no form, writing his existence (members, essential whole) into His book! Unfortunately, rejection of Christ means a person's name is not written in the Lamb's book of life.

In Daniel's prophecy, at the end time, amidst the worst trouble known in the history of man on earth, there will be a deliverance of the people found written in the book (Daniel 12:1).

And in a parallel prophecy, Isaiah wrote about those left in Zion (the future New Jerusalem) saying all those called holy are "every one that is written among the living in Jerusalem" (Isaiah 4:3).

To His disciples, the LORD Jesus said, "rejoice, because your names are written in heaven" (Luke 10:20).

To the Philippian fellow laborers, the Apostle Paul charged them to rejoice because their names are in the book of life (Philippians 4:3).

Six distinct times, the Revelation of Jesus Christ records that the book of life is the source of authority regarding who can, and who cannot, worship The Lamb! Only one certification matters at the time of the end — your name written in the book of life.

> And there shall in no wise enter into it any thing that defileth, neither whatsoever worketh abomination, or maketh a lie: but they which are written in the Lamb's book of life. (Revelation 21:27)

Perdition ensues for some: "And whosoever was not found written in the book of life was cast into the lake of fire" (Revelation 20:15).

Heaven records the members of the general assembly, which is the church of the Firstborn Son of God, just as if they have an entry in the public ledgers. There in Mount Sion, the city of the Living Head, in witness of an innumerable company of angels — God hosts the eternal register. It contains the names of the children and women and men who have trusted the LORD Jesus for their eternal destiny. With His own finger, the LORD writes their names forever!

There is no greater example of preserving your name than when Jehovah Himself writes it into His book!

Jehovah's Revealed Record

In jury instruction in most courts, the testimony of a single witness in a trial is acceptable as evidence — if the jury believes the witness. Corroboration is not required.

In contrast, when we consider the Holy Scriptures, it is self-evident that there is no greater witness than the Holy Ghost, for all of His testimonies are truth (regardless of our belief, disbelief, or opinion). Apostle John declares his vocation as he bears witness of God by both declaration and record, and by manifesting in his life the saving grace of Jesus Christ! "If we receive the witness of men, the witness of God is greater: for this is the witness of God which he hath testified of his Son" (1 John 5:9).

The Saviour has conducted beautiful work to bring His record to all of humanity on Planet Earth. The nexus between the heavenly origin and earthly destination of The Word Jesus Christ, God's words, and the words of Scripture are a tightly woven continuum which stands forever. A mere mortal man is incapable of pulling even one thread to unloose the eternal fabric.

Examine the beauty of the language and words written in 1 John. Almost the entire book serves as the testimonial record; an unyielding picture of the LORD Jehovah condescending from eternity to earthy man:

The word *message* appears twice in 1:5; 3:11. We find the word *record* thrice in 5:7, 10, and 11. The words *testify* and *testified* occur in 4:14; 5:9. The word *witness* reveals itself seven times in 1:2; 5:6, and 9–10.

Watch as the pattern of word-usage unfolds. Initially, we read about John testifying:

> This is he that came by water and blood, even Jesus Christ; not by water only, but by water and blood. And it is the Spirit that beareth witness, because the Spirit is truth. (1 John 5:6)

Next, we read of three persons, in Heaven — who declare and publish the record. These three persons: the Father, the Word, and the Holy Ghost, comprise the triune Godhead. While verse seven is speaking of their actions regarding the record, context matters. What is the record?

Then, in verse eight, we read about the three real persons of the triune Godhead:

> And there are three that bear witness in earth, the Spirit, and the water, and the blood: and these three agree in one. (1 John 5:8)

But again, context matters. What is the record?

On earth, the Holy Spirit is in perfect harmony with the water and blood of the LORD Jesus Christ. Each of the three persons of the Godhead has a unified mission, through the reconciling ministry of the LORD Jesus. We see already the witness of the Holy Ghost is far greater than the witness of men (1 John 5:9).

Scripture tells us those who dismiss belief upon the Son of God are liars — because of the rejection of the *record* of the Son given by the Father. It seems so obvious by verse ten that God settled His record in Heaven and on earth. His words are a continuum, and not compartmentalized. And yet, so many reject the simplest of faith. But as I stated, context matters. What is the record?

It is not until the eleventh verse where the definition of the *record* becomes clear. As the Holy Ghost inspires John to write, we learn:

> And this is the record, that God hath given to us eternal life, and this life is in his Son. (1 John 5:11)

If not for the junction of the heavenly record becoming Scripture, we cannot comprehend the triune Godhead, nor have any hope of salvation. It's all about the words.

Before the first breath of creation, God planned eternal life for His creatures. The Creator never intended for men and women to sin, but reality reveals the true circumstances. Despite the obvious consequences, Adam and Eve chose sin, and since we all hail from that first couple, they passed their sin to all humans. God's plan did not change. Man changed.

Jehovah ejected Adam and Eve from Eden's garden for fear they would eat of the tree of life in their sinful state. A single tree belongs to God — and God alone. He commands Adam and Eve to not touch it, else death ensues! We have read the story, and know how it ends. Man broke himself and does not have the solution to the problem — we come up short every time. We needed then and we need today a Saviour! "But God commendeth his love toward us, in that, while we were yet sinners, Christ died for us" (Romans 5:8). Someday we shall spiritually eat of the Tree of life, because of the work and ministry of the LORD Jesus Christ.

We were not there at Calvary when Jesus paid the full price, **but we have a written record** — He brought to us eternal redemption.

John testifies of the avenue whereby God the Father transmitted the eternal record through His Son and His Holy Ghost onto earth. There, the water and blood at the Roman crucifixion did the sealing. Thankfully, John yielded himself to be a holy man who God could inspire to write these precious words of salvation into **THE RECORD**, ensuring its liberation from the powers of human putrefaction.

God's Hand Writes

> And this is the writing that was written, MENE, MENE, TEKEL, UPHARSIN. This is the interpretation of the thing: MENE; God hath numbered thy kingdom, and finished it. TEKEL; Thou art weighed in the balances, and art found wanting. PERES; Thy kingdom is divided, and given to the Medes and Persians. (Daniel 5:25–28)

These are the famous words from the Prophet Daniel while interpreting the wall writings for Belshazzar, the son of Nebuchadnezzar. Above the astrologers and sycophant "wise guys" of the kingdom, Daniel could spell out all the details for Belshazzar — *because he submitted to God.* Just before decoding these words, Daniel pronounced the indictment and imminent judgment handed down from the Court of God.

> And thou his son, O Belshazzar, hast not humbled thine heart, though thou knewest all this; but hast lifted up thyself against the Lord of heaven; and they have brought the vessels of his house before thee, and thou, and thy lords, thy wives, and thy concubines, have drunk wine in them; and thou hast praised the gods of silver, and gold, of brass, iron, wood, and stone, which see not, nor hear, nor know: and the God in whose hand thy breath is, and whose are all thy ways, hast thou not glorified: then was the part of the hand sent from him; and this writing was written. (Daniel 5:22–24)

This hours-long event, starting with debauchery and ending with slaughter, was framed by words written on the palace wall. The very hand of God that gives Belshazzar breath to live; the God which he refuses to glorify — is writing his now-famous epitaph — and he watched it happen: "In the same hour came forth fingers of a man's hand, and wrote over against the candlestick upon the plaister of the wall of the king's palace: and the king saw the part of the hand that wrote" (Daniel 5:5). God revealed only part of His hand (Daniel 5:24).

Hours later, they slew him as Darius the Mede took over. This forecast against Belshazzar is on the shortlist of prophecies fulfilled with such haste. While some Bible prophecies have yet to be fulfilled, this prophecy matured only hours after being interpreted by Daniel.

Notably, Daniel got involved after the writing of the prophecy. I wonder if Daniel had an early warning about the Hand which wrote on the wall. Was he informed of the fulfilled pronouncement? Did he know about the imminent time of judgment? Just as in Exodus 8 and 31, and in Deuteronomy 9, **the LORD did the writing**. The palace walls and the text written thereon have long since passed into oblivion. Thankfully, we have today a reliable copy of the record of Daniel's interpretation, entrusted to the faithful prophet, who the Bible tells has no fault nor error.

Beautiful Words of Life

Throughout this chapter, I illustrate examples of Scripture recording an event where the LORD writes directly through His own actions. There are so many more.

I do not intend to reduce or limit God's movement as the genesis of inspiration and preservation for the whole of Scripture. All the words of the Holy Bible are God's words. Whether those words emanate from God, His angels, or man shows the marvelous interaction between the Creator and His creatures. Regardless, He owns them all, and we are just subscribers and borrowers. What a haughty imposter I should be, thinking I could double-guess the LORD. He is the Author; He is the copyright Owner; He is both Chief Editor and Master Publisher — and He is the protector.

The LORD uses human languages to transmit His words — because those words are about His creatures as much as they are about the Creator. Imagine how dreadful it would be to have God's words, but in a language only He understands. Preposterous! He is the grand caretaker of the book upon which faith finds a resting place. There is no qualitative difference between what God Himself wrote with His own hands, what He inspired the chosen men to write and speak, or what others contributed to the many conversations.

With God's words, there are no gradations, for with Him is no variableness, and not even a glimpse of unsteadiness (James 1:17). He may have used the personality and intellect of various men and women, but their employment remained submissive to the Holy Ghost. God chose specific people for a reason, just as He chose Elizabeth and Mary to bear John the Baptist and the LORD Jesus.

There are many nuances to Scripture and how it arrived into the canon. Certainly, my aim in this book is to increase your adoration for the written lively text. We must not consider the text a boring book in a plain wrapper with no substantial objectives. God's eternal words are eternity itself manifested in language and made plain to humanity. Marvelous. Wondrous. Beautiful. Language!

"Now go, write it before them in a table, and note it in a book, that it may be for the time to come for ever and ever" (Isaiah 30:8).

Chapter Eleven

Surviving Originals

It is written — In the book of the law of Moses.

It is written — In the volume of the book, about the LORD Jesus.

It is written — He shall give His angels charge concerning the LORD Jesus.

It is written — Of the Son of man, who must suffer many things.

It is written — The just shall live by faith.

It is written — There is none righteous, no, not one.

It is written.

When we read written language, we are mostly reading about past events, and sometimes future happenings (e.g., prophecy). Even current events are writings about things which happened in the recent past. Letters and words, along with optional punctuation are the essence of language. Those basic components are expressive of the events and people involved. The act of writing produces the thing written. Even though the phrase "it is written" occurs only a few times in the Old Testament, it prevails over fifty times in the new. From the New Testament quoting or paraphrasing the Old Testament we learn the notion of "chain reference." Let us explore this simple phrase, which literally transforms the life and eternal destiny of many people over the ages. In the New Testament, the writers relied on copies of the Old, often quoting or paraphrasing its portions, as the Holy Ghost directed them.

When Satan tempted Jesus, both Apostle Matthew and Apostle Luke recorded the story of rebuke upon the devilish serpent. The command is also a promise.

> But he answered and said, It is written, Man shall not live by bread alone, but by every word that proceedeth out of the mouth of God. (Matthew 4:4)

> Jesus said unto him, It is written again, Thou shalt not tempt the Lord thy God. (Matthew 4:7)

> Then saith Jesus unto him, Get thee hence, Satan: for it is written, Thou shalt worship the Lord thy God, and him only shalt thou serve. (Matthew 4:10)

But notice, Jesus stated **IT IS WRITTEN**! He means the writing does today exist, existed at that moment, existed when Moses scribed it, and existed well before then, hailing from the Eternal Library! He is likely quoting Deuteronomy 8:3, clarifying for each man to conduct his life according to the words of God. The LORD Jesus Christ did not need to prove to Himself the sufficiency of the written words — they were already **authentic evidentiary proof**. If the copy of Deuteronomy was good enough in those days, it is good enough for us.

Timothy was taught the *written* Scriptures from childhood. In those *written* Scriptures, he learned of Jesus Christ, and His death and burial. Timothy also learned how Jesus Christ rose again on the third day — according to the *written* Scriptures (1 Corinthians 15). Philip read to the eunuch from the *written* Scriptures (Acts 8). The LORD Jesus quoted and read from the *written* Scriptures in the synagogues and elsewhere. Peter, James, Stephen, and all the others preached from the *written* Scriptures. The Apostles marshaled their Holy Ghost ministry around the *written* Scriptures. The mighty prophets led decorous lives so God could use them to write the *written* Scriptures.

Tucked inside the Bible are the words the Creator chose for us to know. Not more. Not less. On every page and with every letter, God has given us His reliable *words*. Please dispatch from your thinking about human error, which commingles with the written text of God's words. If in error, then which part is false and which part is true? If some portion of the Bible has mistakes or blunders, who is the qualified authority to highlight those aberrations and make the corrections? Who is to decide which part stays and which part leaves? We simply trust the Creator's words are unimpeachable.

SCRIP'TURE, a noun, in its primary sense, a writing; any thing written; appropriately, and by way of distinction, the books of the Old and New Testament; the Bible. Compared with the knowledge which the Scriptures contain, every other subject of human inquiry is vanity and emptiness. (Adapted from various dictionaries in the public domain.)

In Hebrew: **scripture** (*kathab* and its constituents) is a written thing, such as manuscripts, records, or books, and may also be a register, edict, or royal decree.

In Greek: **scripture** (*graphe* and its constituents) is a holy writ, or a thing written, pertaining to the book itself, or its contents.

The Eaten Word

Alongside the river named Chebar dwelled a great company of captives. Taken against their will (but according to God's will) from their homeland, they were force-marched across the Arabian Peninsula to a strange place. The captives were serfs to a powerful king presiding over a ferocious kingdom. This is Babylon, and she was great (so much so that even the Egyptian army ran from her). At this Babylonian stream is where we find Ezekiel the priest, with his fellow captives. Just as prophesied and promised, they now dwelled under severe persecution; and this suffering is not unwarranted for their behavior.

If close by, we might just see Ezekiel with his focus rapt by the Holy Ghost. The Bible calls this act of God *inspiration*, and Ezekiel's experience is such an amazing example, it deserves expansion. As he saw the heavens open, visions from God of eternal things consumed him, leaving no doubt. Then the hand of the LORD pressed upon this great priest, and from the North came a whirlwind bringing a great cloud with fire folding in and wrapping upon itself, with its brightness everywhere!

He heard the noise of the wings of the four beasts, "like the noise of great waters, as the voice of the Almighty, the voice of speech, as the noise of an host: when they stood, they let down their wings. And there was a voice from the firmament that was over their heads, when they stood, and had let down their wings" (Ezekiel 1:24–25).

Then emerged a mighty hand, bringing a roll of a book to the priest. As the stalwart hand spread open the scroll, Ezekiel realized God wrote within and without, on both sides, with no space spared.

God set His roll before the prophet as a meal, and commanded him to eat the book and then speak its contents to the house of Israel. Just imagine for a moment how rare any writing is amid the captives. Ezekiel opened his mouth, and the LORD caused him to eat the roll of the book. How marvelous to imagine Ezekiel consuming a Heavenly book! A meal, sweet as honey, filled his gut, just like the psalmist proclaimed! (Psalm 119:103). The direction from Jehovah could not be more clear: "Son of man, go, get thee unto the house of Israel, and speak with my words unto them" (Ezekiel 3:4).

God delivered His mighty words via Ezekiel in a way unique only to the prophet, attaching his tongue to his palate. The prime writing was published safely into the belly of the priest. There, he harbored unblemished the precious words of God until needed at the precise moment. Ezekiel spoke those words in their entirety to the rebellious house of Israel. The original scroll is gone, never to be seen again, but we can read this marvelous account today.

Presses Preserving Value

The currency of the United States is printed by the Bureau of Engraving and Printing. Accomplishing the task of printing the currency involves highly skilled craftsmen, special equipment, and a combination of old-world printing techniques merged with cutting-edge modern technology. They work diligently to retain familiar characteristics that identify the currency notes as distinctly American currency. Starting with carefully selected metal, the printing plates are carefully engraved. Later, individual plastic molds are made from the master die and are assembled into one plate containing exact duplicates of the master die. The original engraved dies are stored and can be used again and again as needed.

After a long process to produce the printing plates, the final plates are coated for hardness. These plates contain the intaglio image, just deep enough to hold ink for printing the notes. United States currency "paper" is composed of 75% cotton and 25% linen, giving it a distinct look and feel. All notes utilize green ink on the backs. Faces, on the other hand, use black ink. These and the other inks appearing on US currency are specially formulated and blended by the Bureau.

As the notes are crafted through this delicate and precise process, the prime objective is the durability and safekeeping of the currency. It takes a long time to go from sketches to the final printing of notes as they come off the presses. Every step along the way is very carefully guarded, remains secure at all times, and is specifically followed so the currency will have a long "life" in general circulation.[1]

The King's Duty

Someday the Israelites would reach the promised land, and there set up a king to rule over them. The LORD said the king has one prime task: to put the law of God at the pinnacle of his administration. He must not be a harsh ruler, but a leader who develops God's people to have a fervent heart for their God. The simple instruction:

> And it shall be, when he sitteth upon the throne of his kingdom, that he shall write him a copy of this law in a book out of that which is before the priests the Levites: And it shall be with him, and he shall read therein all the days of his life: that he may learn to fear the LORD his God, to keep all the words of this law and these statutes, to do them: that his heart be not lifted up above his brethren, and that he turn not aside from the commandment, to the right hand, or to the left: to the end that he may prolong his days in his kingdom, he, and his children, in the midst of Israel. (Deuteronomy 17:18–20)

Over and over, God expected the king to read the law of God for his entire life. God's purpose: the king must keep a humble heart and obey the laws of God. This example of copying the Deuteronomy journal shows two things. First,

---

1. Adapted from How Money is Made, U.S. Bureau of Engraving and Printing, https://www.bep.gov/currency/how-money-is-made

the writings shepherded by the Levite priests required cautious handling, only manipulated when duplicating a transcript from the prime writing. Second, the identical facsimile is unrolled and rolled repeatedly, so they wear it out with abundant reading. God does not commission a king to keep His law if it dissolves over time with usage.

Surviving the Arid Excursion

Throughout the wilderness journey, God promised the Hebrews He would never forsake them. Like His promises for His words, He preserved the Hebrew nation. The journey's end on the other side of the Jordan River resulted in a grand homecoming. The people of God entered the land flowing with milk and honey, having left the bondage of Egypt a generation prior. He made the promise with *words*. On this first day, they had one simple job: a remembrance of the LORD.

Jehovah gave a clear commandment to remember. First, set up an altar of great stones and smooth them with plaster. Second, on the plastered surface, write the *words* of this law. Onto the daubed surface, from the scrolls stewarded by the scribes, the artisans inscribed plainly all the words of this law (Deuteronomy 27:3, 8). Various administration leaders stood upon Mount Gerazim for blessings and Mount Ebal for cursings, with the ark nearby. This etched-in-plaster copy of the copies of book rolls the Israelites carried on their journey is a marquee monument to the law of God and it served as a billboard reminder for the travelers.

At the passage trail, the artisans transformed the text from scrolls to muddied stones. Every person journeying through this rocky funnel saw the marquee and read the identical transcript of the law. The plastered copy held just as much jurisdiction as the roll copy, which held just as much authority as the prime writing from Moses. The medium itself does not attach sovereignty. It's all about the words.

On this marvelous day, Moses recorded the instructions for them to follow when transiting into God's Land of Promise. Joshua also obeyed those instructions, as the Hebrew nation departed one era, entering the next.

Finally, they Show the Copies

The city of AI was burned desolation and made into a heap of ashes forever. The former king of Ai was hung, and in the evening, they threw his carcass outside the city, and piled upon it a great heap of stones.

With brilliant victory comes great responsibility, which Joshua certainly understood. Like Moses before him, "Joshua built an altar unto the LORD God of Israel in mount Ebal, as Moses the servant of the LORD commanded the children of Israel, as it is written in the book of the law of Moses, an altar of whole stones, over which no man hath lift up any iron: and they offered thereon burnt offerings unto the LORD, and sacrificed peace offerings" (Joshua 8:30–31).

The altar was built according to Exodus law using no tools, just rocks pulled from the earth, with none of man's alterations. Joshua did not market his own agenda. In the presence of the Israelites, "he wrote there upon the stones a copy of the law of Moses" (Joshua 8:32). They instantiated a copy of the law, in plaster, on a new altar, which became the place for sacrifice. We see Joshua, mindful of his responsibility, reading to all in earshot "all the words of the law, the blessings and cursings, according to all this is written in the book of the law" (Joshua 8:34).

It has not been long since Moses read the whole of Deuteronomy to them. The Bible says Joshua followed suit, and did not skip one word. Through all the preceding wilderness events and many years, the scribes gave abundant attention to the accuracy and completeness of Jehovah's words, and maintained a running succession of copies — identical transcripts — from the prime writings.

By this time, the prime recording of the Pentateuch is at a zenith. It is certain: He protected the Israelites during their journey, and He most assuredly sustained His words.

> The LORD shall command the blessing upon thee in thy storehouses, and in all that thou settest thine hand unto; and he shall bless thee in the land which the LORD thy God giveth thee. (Deuteronomy 28:8)

And thou shalt not go aside from any of the words which I command thee this day, to the right hand, or to the left, to go after other gods to serve them. (Deuteronomy 28:14)

Written, Posted, and Read

Daniel set his face to seek God with fasting, and in sackcloth covered with ashes.

We have sinned. We have committed iniquity. Ours is a wicked rebellion against your precepts and judgments. We rejected the prophets — and confusion deforms our faces. Whether of Judah or Jerusalem; whether near or far off, my people have trespassed against the LORD. All of Israel has transgressed Your law, disobeyed, and departed. We drew the curse upon us, and we deserve it. Also, the oath in the law of Moses now bears down upon us, for we have sinned (Daniel 9).

Why did Daniel pray this way? Simple: he read the prophecies against the Hebrews. Daniel says, "In the first year of his reign I Daniel understood by books the number of the years, whereof the word of the LORD came to Jeremiah the prophet, that he would accomplish seventy years in the desolations of Jerusalem" (Daniel 9:2).

While Jeremiah remained in Jerusalem, over in Babylon, Daniel held a similar office. The prophet understood — by reading the copied books containing the word of the LORD delivered through Jeremiah. History reveals a continuous circuit of letters, decrees, and other writings posted back and forth between Judah and Babylon. In the Scriptures, there is evidence of the same (e.g., Ezra).

Further still, at the hand of Elasah and Gemariah, the prophet Jeremiah dictated a letter (Jeremiah 29). He addressed the letter to the elders of Jerusalem, the priests, the prophets, and all the residents, now held captive in Babylon by Nebuchadnezzar. The brief letter is primarily the instructions from Jehovah to settle into their new neighborhood, as they will live there for at least seventy years. He commanded them to build houses, raise families, and plant gardens — and to seek peace and pray for the cities they inhabit. Set up your society, is the injunction. Pray for your enemies, He demands.

In marvelous prose, Jeremiah delivered the promise of Jehovah to preserve His people. Even amid extremely troublesome times, Jehovah and His angels shepherded the captives (even if they did not know it). Actually, His burden is light, even in captivity: search for God with the whole heart. The LORD Jesus gave a similar message: "Come unto me, all ye that labour and are heavy laden, and I will give you rest. Take my yoke upon you, and learn of me; for I am meek and lowly in heart: and ye shall find rest unto your souls. For my yoke is easy, and my burden is light" (Matthew 11:28–30).

The Jeremiah 29 letter contains two promises. First, God has thoughts of peace, not evil, toward the captives; and, there is an expected end to the captivity. Second, the LORD will return the captives to Jerusalem from all the various places they disperse to (promised previously, such as in Jeremiah 12). Personally, I think some captives did not stray from God in Jerusalem, only later to be caught up in Nebuchadnezzar's net. Controlling these circumstances was not possible, distress rules the day, but the LORD "had their back."

After reading the letters from Shemaiah, Jeremiah responds with the words of the LORD in a letter back to the captives in Babylon, warning them to be guarded about Shemaiah, for he is a liar. God did not send Shemaiah, who has falsely warned the people against Jeremiah's prophecy and letters. "Therefore thus saith the LORD; Behold, I will punish Shemaiah the Nehelamite, and his seed: he shall not have a man to dwell among this people; neither shall he behold the good that I will do for my people, saith the LORD; because he hath taught rebellion against the LORD" (Jeremiah 29:32).

Step back from the details for just a moment and see the bigger picture. Jehovah could have chosen the easier method and moved upon one prophet in Babylon to deliver these messages. Instead, since the prophecy of their current condition started with Jeremiah, He continued with Jeremiah to write several letters. Being a well-known prophet of his day, Jeremiah had been preaching for many years, and with bona fide credentials.

Summing it up, Jeremiah 29 is a *record* of the **records** sent between Jerusalem and Babylon. The Pony Express of their day posted the books and letters (or facsimiles) into Babylon, Jerusalem, and other cities. It is there many people read those letters directly, or heard them read by a scribe. Thankfully, by God's oversight, these copied records survived without decay, joining the canon of Scripture.

The Record of the Copies

Ezra, being in the sixteenth descending generation from Aaron the priest, was a ready scribe in the law of Moses. His skills included expertise in the Hebrew language and the copying of Scripture. There is no question Ezra was a competent scribe. Earlier, we considered Ezra was possibly the primary custodian who assembled the first complete collection of the Scriptures existing during his time (and this he likely did after arriving back in the precious jewel of Jerusalem).

The theme of Ezra is the return of the Hebrews to Jerusalem to rebuild the temple and cleanse their tribes of wickedness. Much of his namesake book is a catalog of letters and decrees between various parties. The events start with Cyrus writing a proclamation to rebuild the temple in Jerusalem. With his deputy, Sheshbazzar, leading the captives back to the hill of Zion, Cyrus granted money for the purchase of Lebanese cedars from Tyre. (Imagine the journey across the Arabian Peninsula from Babylon to Jerusalem, which even today is a substantial feat.)

The record shows some fifty-thousand people and over eight-thousand working animals traveled with the troop from Babylon to Jerusalem, a journey which took four or more months to complete. This is, in actuality, a colossal construction company with an exclusive contract to repair one *very important building*.

The "people of the land" (probably squatters) showed their displeasure when the now-freed captives arrived back in Jerusalem. And they "weakened the hands of the people of Judah, and troubled them in building, and hired counselors against them, to frustrate their purpose, all the days of Cyrus king of Persia" (Ezra 4:4–5). With mighty, adversarial resentment of Judah, they banded together with practically every tribe in the region and separately dispatched two letters: one to Ahasuerus and another to Artaxerxes, both in Babylon. In the days of Artaxerxes, they wrote in the Syrian tongue to beseech the king to stop the rebuilding of the temple, lest his revenue diminishes, because the Jews "are come unto Jerusalem, building the rebellious and the bad city, and have set up the walls thereof, and joined the foundations" (Ezra 4:12).

In a unique way, these adversaries showed the Scriptural copy and archive process. From the story, we see they relied on the historical record found in the collected Scriptures. When this committee "taught" the king of the supposed dangers because of the Jews, they made false allegations, intent on manipulating the king's thinking. They claimed the Jews are rebellious and moving by sedition against his high throne. They implored King Artaxerxes to search the archives for the evidence. Those archives, within the realm of Babylon, contained details about the supposed "insurrections" in Jerusalem. Poignant thought: how did they know of these archives?

The records in Babylon most likely also contained the writings of Nebuchadnezzar (and his companions) and probably contained some (or all) copies of portions of the existing written Scripture at that point. The Babylonian, Median, and Persian kings employed many scribes. Remember too, in captivity are Jewish scribes, held in Babylon for multiple decades by this time. The job of scribe is an important and noble vocation (even in captivity), with the copying of Scripture as its prime directive.

Notice Rehum and Shimshai, in Ezra 4:23, receiving a copy of the letter from King Artaxerxes, which they carried across the Arabian Peninsula and it is then read near Jerusalem. Scripture shows they did not record some or all of the Ezra journal until a few years (at least) after this event because the building "ceased unto the second year of the reign of Darius king of Persia" (Ezra 4:24).

After a while Darius becomes king. This time Tatnai (the governor in Jerusalem) and Shetharboznai write to Babylon, attempting to convince the king a second time to stop the rebuilding of the temple. By the Scriptural story, it seems they were not entirely abrasive against the Hebrews, but certainly had some motive to stop the construction (or at least retard the efforts). The order came: cease rebuilding the temple. But the rebuilding never stopped, and in fact had sped up.

The copy of the letter contains a citation from the elders who managed the temple building.

> We are the servants of the God of heaven and earth, and build the house that was builded these many years ago, which a great king of Israel builded and set up. (Ezra 5:11, a reference to King Solomon)

Unquestionably, the Ezra Construction Company endeavored (though only partially succeeding) to rebuild the House of God into its prior glory during Solomon's administration.

In the letter, Tatnai requests Darius to search the archives for a copy of the decree which Cyrus made years earlier. Darius approves the request and a "search was made in the house of the rolls, where the treasures were laid up in Babylon. And there was found at Achmetha, in the palace that is in the province of the Medes, a roll, and therein was a record thus written." (Ezra 6:1–2).

Consider: the palace housed a special place containing the rolls of all the records and journals kept for the kingdom, and amid all those rolls, is the record of Cyrus's decree. Notice also, the rolls are neighbors to the treasury. It seems they closely guarded book rolls alongside the treasury because all those items are highly valuable and worthy of protection. When King Darius replies by letter, he decrees the building of the house shall continue, and Tatnai and Shetharboznai will not interfere; and his money and materiel be used to aid the rebuilding with no hindrance. He decrees further: anyone impeding the reconstruction is to hang with timber from the House of God. Fortunately, the Tatnai administration obeyed speedily.

With so many references to copies in the Ezra journal, its subtitle could be *The Catalog of the Copies*. And one of the major events in Hebrew history is the second wave, which leaves Babylon during the seventh year of Artaxerxes. We see the mighty movement of God in the account. "For Ezra had prepared his heart to seek the law of the LORD, and to do it, and to teach in Israel statutes and judgments" (Ezra 7:10). During this journey, the king writes a letter which Ezra carries with honor. This To Whom It May Concern letter essentially grants Ezra all the faculties and supplies necessary for the re-outfitting of the temple furniture and instruments.

Notably, the king's letter also emancipates any Jews who are "minded of their own freewill" (Ezra 7:13) to go with Ezra; he grants vast sums of money for the purchase of whatever is needed; he orders the treasurers to make whatever provisions are necessary. And, he decrees they will not levy toll, tribute, nor custom upon the priests, Levites, and others.

Ezra penned his most gracious response to the king:

> Blessed be the LORD God of our fathers, which hath put such a thing as this in the king's heart, to beautify the house of the LORD which is in Jerusalem: and hath extended mercy unto me before the king, and his counsellors, and before all the king's mighty princes. And I was strengthened as the hand of the LORD my God was upon me, and I gathered together out of Israel chief men to go up with me. (Ezra 7:27–28)

When Ezra beseeched Jehovah for forgiveness in his ninth chapter, assembled with him are "every one that trembled at the words of the God of Israel, because of the transgression of those that had been carried away" and Ezra "sat astonied until the evening sacrifice" (Ezra 9:4). They learned God's words by studying written copies of the Pentateuch, the Chronicles, the Psalms, and so forth.

Numerous

There are many accounts in Scripture referring to the copies. The LORD Jesus quoted the Scriptures and prophets many times. Jesus recited Scripture to the disciples as they traveled the road together after He arose from the grave. Several times we read of various people writing copies of God's words onto the frontlets, hearts, and hands of the Jews (with a great example in Deuteronomy 11). There are so many, its impossible to catalog them all. Here are just a few more:

1. Apollos spoke boldly in the synagogues in Acts, for "he mightily convinced the Jews, and that publickly, shewing by the scriptures that Jesus was Christ" (Acts 18:28).

2. Apostle Paul reasoned with the listeners from Scripture in Acts 17:2.

3. Hezekiah dispatched postal messengers in 2 Chronicles 30.

4. After spilling buckets and driving the money changers out of the temple, the LORD's disciples remembered the **written prophecy**: "The zeal of thine house hath eaten me up" (Psalm 69:9). Shortly thereafter, the LORD Jesus boldly stated a written prophecy of His resurrection (possibly drawn from Isaiah 53:5, Daniel 9:26, and Psalm 16:10). "When therefore he was risen from the dead, his disciples remembered that he had said this unto them; and they believed the scripture, and the word which Jesus had said" (John 2:22). Before and after the resurrection, the disciples had read these things in the written Scriptures (and believed the written text, and the Word Himself).

5. In Luke 4, the temple attendants handed a **copy** of the Isaiah (Esaias) **record** to Jesus.

6. In 2 Chronicles 17, Jehoshaphat dispatched his princes to teach the word of the LORD in all the cities surrounding Jerusalem, which they did with **copies of the book of the law**.

Originals and copies. Then more copies, and more copies. His words ARE WRITTEN.

The Bible contains the revelation of the will of God. It contains the history of the creation of the world, and of mankind; and afterward the history of one peculiar nation, certainly the most extraordinary nation that has ever appeared upon the earth. It contains a system of religion, and of morality, which we may examine upon its own merits, independent of the sanction it receives from being the Word of God; and it contains a numerous collection of books, written at different ages of the world, by different authors, which we may survey as curious monuments of antiquity, and as literary compositions. In whatever light we regard it, whether with reference to revelation, to literature, to history, or to morality — it is an invaluable and inexhaustible mine of knowledge and virtue — John Quincy Adams

Chapter Twelve

Enduring Originals

THE SO-NAMED ORIGINALS WERE replicas. In every instance, the inaugural words which form the written text of Scripture are those words spoken (and sometimes written) by God Himself, His special custodians, or the other chosen characters. The primary manuscript from the holy man is, in reality, a facsimile of the words moved upon him by the breath of Heaven. Any writings thereafter are duplicates, in whole or in part.

The Holy Ghost involved human agents as stewards (custodians), not owners. As the Holy Ghost moved upon the chosen servant, He breathed through them the exact language, syntax, and grammar of the words. Most times, after speaking to his audience, the choice servant wrote those words into the record. And there are sections of Scripture showing the writing and the receiving by others are not contemporary.

I like the way King Solomon puts it: "Let us hear the conclusion of the whole matter: Fear God, and keep his commandments: for this is the whole duty of man" (Ecclesiastes 12:13). Keeping those commandments is not only a duty for us, but a protection method. Did Solomon have any of the prime writings? Perhaps yes. Perhaps no. Regardless, Solomon concluded man's primary duty is to **keep God's commandments**. This statement from the wisest man begs the question: are those commandments available today?

Over the centuries, God moved men to assemble the Bible at assorted times and in diverse ways. He planned the enterprise and oversaw every nuance. Scripture is complete, and has continued its publication during several millennia. The text of the Bible is neither lacking nor redundantly ample. Scripture is fixed in Heaven: nothing more and nothing less.

We rightly say the holy men, the choice servants, and their scribes laid out those initial writings on physical media. My favorite "writing story" is the Prophet Jeremiah, and his scribe Baruch, when told to write in a book the things spoken to him by God. Others like the amazing man Job, the complex priest Ezekiel, and the wonderful Apostle John follow suit — recording into books what Jehovah (or His agents) showed them.

Sometimes we see God did the writing, such as when the LORD Jesus wrote on the ground, shortly before the accusers exited the scene. Or when God twice wrote the commandments upon the stone tablets with His own finger. The Bible also records scribes (and others), who attentively listen to conversations between the LORD and men, jotting down the statements, historical facts, or narratives into the text.

Further in, I will highlight some sections of Scripture which do not have any prime written text, but where the Bible records the events or statements. In some cases, follow-on or subsequent writings substituted for the prime writings. Our sureness of the Bible stands upon faith, because we did not witness the prime writings and have no other choice. The canon is complete, and it is certain none of us are holy men or their ready scribes.

Promoting Heart Movement

When you visit the U.S. National Archives to view the Declaration of Independence, you are viewing what you believe is the prime document, penned by Thomas Jefferson. In fact, what you are most likely viewing is a carefully crafted facsimile of the original document. For security reasons, the viewer never knows if it is the real one or an exact duplicate. The visitor relies by faith on the document being the real thing. By the way, even the case storing the document is a marvel of engineering excellence, providing protection well beyond common understanding.

Notice the power in these moving words:

> We hold these truths to be self-evident, that all men are created equal, that they are endowed by their Creator with certain unalienable Rights, that among these are Life, Liberty and the pursuit of Happiness. (Preamble to the Declaration of Independence)

You could simply read the Declaration from a book or the world wide web, or hear it read to you. No matter what form it comes as, and while the medium of the Jefferson writing is very interesting — it is the WORDS which move your heart, not the web page, paper or animal skin. The Declaration words survive, being copied verbatim countless times in English, and translated into many other languages. **The message from the words** remains intact because the words, copied and published, are intact.

It's all about the words.

> In the beginning was the Word, and the Word was with God, and the Word was God. (John 1:1)

> In the beginning God created the heaven and the earth. (Genesis 1:1)

Regardless of how you get the words of the Bible, the *words* cause the movement in your heart — not the method. (I am not dismissive of the method nor the means, for they too are important, but less so than the words.)

But how shall we rely upon the Bible text we hold in our hands today? Is the translated and copied text we study and memorize in our language the descendant of those first writings? What shall we do in the absence of the first writings? We have no choice but to rely — *by faith* — upon the content transmitted through the ages, by supernatural oversight. The LORD does not dismiss caring for the thing He magnifies **above His name**!

Throughout the text of Scripture, bound to every word, letter, and small mark, is an impenetrable jacket which shields against the forces of decay. This weft thread of preservation remains inextricably yoked with the God-breathed words of the text as they have transmitted from one medium to another, throughout the ages, out to every country and continent.

The Frozen Lady Survives

Beginning their workday on July 15, 1942, the aircrew probably did not consider how the day might end. These fellow aviators were piloting a squadron of two B-17 bombers and six P-38 fighters toward the British Isles in Operation Bolero. A strong blizzard forced them to land on the ice in Greenland. After nine harrowing days, rescuers safely retrieved the crews, but they abandoned their aircraft on the ice. It seems this is just a footnote in the annals of world-war-two history.

Over the decades, ice and snow slowly but surely entombed all the aircraft to a thickness of over two hundred feet. Great distances separated the planes, as natural forces moved them apart slowly. These durable planes and their intrepid pilots started out the mission like most others. Their plans, and their planes, changed course.

After over five decades, one of these planes eventually stands out as the representative hero of the others — Glacier Girl. Entombed below two-hundred-sixty-eight feet of ice, this recovery is anything but simple. Prodigious amounts of snowfall, which never melts, blanket the region of Greenland where the six P-38s and two B-17s fell abandoned. In 1980, the lost squadron lay buried, but the quest to extract an intact aircraft began.

After twelve years, thirteen expeditions, nearly a million dollars, and ground-penetrating radar, they found the aircraft. The explorers were anxious as they probed the icy depth. Then the probe found its mark. When returned to the surface, type 5660 hydraulic fluid coated the probe. Evidence: they found a P-38 Lightning. The final expedition cost $350,000, but Glacier Girl emerged from her icy tomb, and in fantastic condition. They estimated a complete restoration taking 18 months and costing $600,000. Five decades of ice and pressure had conserved Glacier Girl. Her guns, engines, and propellers, with not a bolt or rivet missing, also survived. They discovered much of the fabulous airplane was broken.

Virtually every piece of Glacier Girl got disassembled, with nothing left standing but the main wing spar. Working from a set of Lockheed plans borrowed from the Smithsonian Institution, the team stripped Glacier Girl to bare metal, and then treated, primed, and painted the many parts. As the restoration inched forward, the legend grew. The Kentucky hangar opened to anyone who wanted to stop by, and eventually 50,000 people a year were coming through.

On September 6, 2000, Glacier Girl came alive again. Over the many months, the team restored Glacier Girl with eighty percent of her original parts, at a cost of some $4 million. Finally, almost ten years after the airplane arrived in Middlesboro, she triumphed again, taking her second maiden flight. New life was hers. On October 26, 2002, her engines ran up, landing gear checked, a few fittings tightened, and with nary a high-speed taxi test, Glacier Girl roared into the skies over Kentucky.

Surrounding this frozen lady were immeasurable amounts of ice and snow. She had likely moved quite a distance from the emergency landing zone. Intrepid just barely describe how this original WW2 plane endured hardship and decades of harshness, emerging into our day by unmatched restoration. The engineers relied on the *words* and drawings from the duplicate blueprints. Now just think how much more reliable is the blueprint of Scripture as it restores and heals our spirit — by its *words*.

Prime Writings Broken

We visit again with Moses and the events at Mount Sinai.

> And the LORD repented of the evil which he thought to do unto his people. And Moses turned, and went down from the mount, and the two tables of the testimony were in his hand: the tables were written on both their sides; on the one side and on the other were they written. And the tables were the work of God, and the writing was the writing of God, graven upon the tables. (Exodus 32:14–16)

Jehovah was angry with Israel and warned Moses of their certain destruction, but Moses interceded on their behalf and the LORD repented of the evil. Marvelous mercy! After receiving the commandments of the LORD (engraved by Jehovah Himself), Moses descended the mountain with Joshua close by.

The Bible's account of what happens next is truly profound. Upon seeing the Hebrews have already broken the commandments, Moses shattered the tables. Over the next weeks, several events occurred which were vital to the preservation of Scripture. Moses meets with God, and in conversation, like two friends, they spoke one with another. By reiteration, as if to reinforce the commandments already given from Heaven, the LORD spoke many of the same words again through Moses.

Moses wrote all these words: "for after the tenor of these words I have made a covenant with thee and with Israel" (Exodus 34:27). By the use of the word tenor, we understand the intent of Jehovah. He established His covenant with His people by His words.

To fulfill His promise of not breaking this covenant, the Author, using His own finger, engraved a second set of tables, which are identical to the first, but are not the prime writings, per se. These *words*, not so much the stone tables, are necessary for the covenant with the Hebrew people (and really all of humankind). They also serve as the standard for correcting man's mistakes. He could not let shortsighted Moses interrupt His covenant agreement. The

Levites later placed the second set into the ark for safekeeping — sufficiently serving Jehovah's other purposes.

Since the second set is good enough for the LORD, it is certainly good enough for us. **Copies endure.**

Prime Writings Missing

Not only did the initial documents drop from our reach, but there are fine examples in the Bible showing some of the first manuscripts went missing shortly after writing.

In the latter ministry of Prophet Jeremiah, he wrote of all the evils to come upon Babylon. For years he's been prophesying and preaching the imminent calamity. By direction (inspiration) from Jehovah, he wrote in a book (or book roll).

> Thus saith the LORD of hosts; The broad walls of Babylon shall be utterly broken, and her high gates shall be burned with fire; and the people shall labour in vain, and the folk in the fire, and they shall be weary. (Jeremiah 51:58)

After writing, Jeremiah convinces Seraiah of something very interesting. He tells this quiet prince this: he will **see** and **read** the words — all the words. And when he finishes reading, he will confess to the LORD the revealed evil, and acknowledge Babylon's forthcoming utter desolation. Seraiah shall say Babylon will sink and shall not rise.

Last, to illustrate exactly what will happen to Babylon, Jeremiah gives explicit instructions from Jehovah: bind the book describing all the evils with a stone and discard it into the midst of the Euphrates River (where it will sink with no possibility of recovery). Jeremiah even rehearses the exact words which Seraiah shall repeat: "Thus shall Babylon sink, and shall not rise from the evil that I will bring upon her: and they shall be weary" (Jeremiah 51:64).

Therefore, Jeremiah's prophecy, read by a hushed prince, is the irretrievable prime writing, sunk to the bottom of the river. And yet, the weft thread of Scripture conserves the content of the book, and the record of its physical destruction. Jeremiah's subsequent writings were a *necessary* and *sufficient* replacement.

Prime Writings Consumed

Continuing with the stalwart Prophet Jeremiah, we find several opportunities when he summarized the prophecies. To each of the kings during Jeremiah's five-to-six-decade ministry, God presented the case against those kings, the indictments against the people of Israel and Judah for their sin, and the imminent siege and captivity.

For his preaching, punishment and jail come upon him multiple times, and ultimately, he finished life as a captive in Egypt. We read of God's judgment falling upon the Hebrew people, and yet it's clear the captivity and punishment is in their best interest. Thankfully, Jehovah's mercy is in direct concert with the condemnation. Amazingly, Jeremiah not only denounced the people for their behavior, but he also repeatedly invited them back to the LORD and gave them consolation. He clarified: salvation could be theirs.

In Jeremiah 36 is the record which Jeremiah will dictate not once, but twice and Baruch will scribe not one, but two book rolls. In the story, seven times God safeguards His words and defeats man's depraved attempts to dismiss those words! Jehovah intended from the beginning of the prophecies to induce repentance in the house of Judah: "that they may return every man from his evil way; that I may forgive their iniquity and their sin" (Jeremiah 36:3). For them, salvation is so close.

With Jeremiah shut up, it becomes Baruch's commission to publish the freshly written roll into the LORD's house and among all the people. It is essential to emphasize the technique which Jehovah employed to guarantee the endurance of His words: a) inspire Jeremiah; b) Jeremiah speaks those words verbatim; c) Baruch receives those words in his ears, absorbing them into his heart and mind; d) Baruch moves to write the spoken-heard-spoken-heard words into the book roll; and, e) Baruch reads the words aloud several times for the audiences to hear.

Interestingly, in the commandment from Jeremiah to Baruch (verse six), it seems the prophet knew months or even more than a year early that proclaiming a fast was coming soon. In the fast, people proceeded to their cities (verse nine). Baruch will eventually fulfill his commission to proclaim the *words* as people head for Jerusalem from their surrounding cities.

As the storyline continues, Michaiah hears from the book all the words of the LORD, and declares all those words to the council of scribes and princes. Baruch also reads the entire set of prophecies from the book.

As fear overwhelms these cowering court jesters, they query Baruch: "Tell us now, How didst thou write all these words at his mouth?" (Jeremiah 36:17) and he replies: "He pronounced all these words unto me with his mouth, and I wrote them with ink in the book" (Jeremiah 36:18). Reminder: Baruch wrote the words of God. Shortly thereafter, the fearful sycophants tell the king all the words. At his summons, Jehudi fetches the roll and reads it again to the king, with all the princes standing about. (That's twice the king has heard these words.) It did not take long for King Jehoiakim to reject God's words, such that he cut the roll with a knife and threw it into the fire. With no fear of God before their eyes, pride controlled them, and they did not repent!

I find it very telling how Elnathan, Delaiah, and Gemariah pleaded with the king to not burn the roll, but he dismissed them. Without a doubt, these scribes recognized the book-roll as the fresh writings of Jehovah's words, but fear of man, not the fear of God, overtook them.

Watch what happens next! Famously (or perhaps infamously), the dastardly Jehoiakim has burned the first copy of the book roll. Meanwhile, the LORD descends upon the careful Jeremiah to compose another. The Scriptures don't tell us directly, but since the LORD hid Jeremiah and Baruch, it's entirely likely no other person knew their geolocation. I wonder if they learned from Jehovah Himself about the fire destroying the first book roll. Jehovah does not surrender His will or His word to man's devices.

As the second prime writing replaces the first, it will include a grave judgment upon Jehoiakim, rejecting his heritage upon the throne of David, and punishing him, all his descendants, and his servants for their iniquity. And finally, as the story concludes, Baruch writes the replacement prime writing (also called a *true copy*), including many other words.

Wow! Encapsulated in a small package of just a few people and two book rolls, and spanning only a few months of time, is a short story illustrating the long epic tale of the repeated attacks against the words of God. And yet, by the mighty, holy hand of Jehovah, His word survives, not only for just a moment but for all generations — including this wonderful story in the Scripture canon.

Prime Writings Lost

Eureka! With much enthusiasm, Hilkiah the high priest brought the book of the law to Shaphan, the scribe, because they found it! The record of this event is 2 Kings 22–23.

Notably, the book of the law lay dormant for many years, representing the spiritual condition of Judah and Israel. Neglect of God's house and Jehovah's words became the rule — not the exception. They deserted the book of God as a dusty and forgotten scroll in the decrepit temple. Whether you consider it hidden, misplaced, ignored, or abandoned, there are three historic things about this book: someone wrote the book, the book is coated with dust, and this book is again on center stage.

Soon thereafter, "the king went up into the house of the LORD, and all the men of Judah and all the inhabitants of Jerusalem with him, and the priests, and the prophets, and all the people, both small and great: and he read in their ears all the words of the book of the covenant which was found in the house of the LORD" (2 Kings 23:2). While it seems reasonable to account that the reading of the book took some number of hours, the text does not suggest whether they read it all in one standing, took meal breaks, or just how long the reading lasted. (Personally, I think the words brought much joy while they waited patiently for the conclusion of the reading.)

Amazing! They knew exactly what they had when they saw it and read it. **Scripture is unmistakable**.

While this may have been the only copy known, it's simply not possible to determine (from the Scriptures or history) if the book Hilkiah found is the prime copy from the hand of Moses himself. It may have been just the Deuteronomy record, and many historians claim Shaphan read from Deuteronomy 28–29. Whether it contained all of God's text to that point; or, what exactly the book of the law contained, we must learn when we arrive in eternity. In the meantime, let's rely on faith.

This is a grand example of the indefectible nature of God's words. Man neglects the Scriptures, but the LORD Jehovah ensures their imperishable safekeeping despite the neglect. God waits patiently for the return of His people, and His words endure firmly to take their rightful, preeminent place in society. The leadership quickly realized what lay before them and took appropriate action to restore the Scriptures to the posture so deserved.

Oh, that leaders today, around the world, would heed this passage in Scripture — dusting off the Bible and reading it aloud for all to hear — restoring the *words* of God as the head of every society.

Prime Writings Compiled

Joel and Abiah were corrupt judges, soaking up bribes and filthy grafts. They corrupted Beersheba and the surrounding cities. The elders of Israel were fermenting and disrupted, and finally take matters to the high priest. Their demand for a king to judge them displeased Samuel (also a judge). To his surprise, when he took the matter to the Supreme Judge, the LORD told him to heed to their demands, and the LORD corrected Samuel: "for they have not rejected thee, but they have rejected me, that I should not reign over them" (1 Samuel 8:7).

Even after Samuel detailed exactly the manner of the king they will be subject to, the people refused to concur with his wisdom.

> And Samuel heard all the words of the people, and he rehearsed them in the ears of the LORD. And the LORD said to Samuel, Hearken unto their voice, and make them a king. And Samuel said unto the men of Israel, Go ye every man unto his city. (1 Samuel 8:21–22)

Despite all this upheaval, God appointed Saul, son of Kish, as king. The lead-up conversation between the LORD and Samuel was a wonderful instance of the holy man compiling the spoken words from God into a journal.

Notice the LORD spoke softly and quietly in Samuel's ear:

> Now the LORD had told Samuel in his ear a day before Saul came, saying, To morrow about this time I will send thee a man out of the land of Benjamin, and thou shalt anoint him to be captain over my people Israel, that he may save my people out of the hand of the Philistines: for I have looked upon my people, because their cry is come unto me. (1 Samuel 9:15–16)

Do you see the magnificence? Capture this thought: these are the words of God Himself, addressed to Samuel — in his ear. Samuel recognized the Voice of God, having heard it before. Further, right in the middle of the next sentence, there is a very important small mark. When you come across this rare punctuation in Scripture, think of the urgency, importance, and grandeur that comes with the occasion.

The very next day, the spoken prophecy occurred, as expected by Samuel: "And when Samuel saw Saul, the LORD said unto him, Behold the man whom I spake to thee of! this same shall reign over my people" (1 Samuel 9:17). Notice the exclamation and excitement! I think Jehovah intentionally made a bold pronouncement of the new king. But I also think the LORD spoke only to Samuel.

As Samuel began the installation of Saul as king, two more very important events occurred which directly inform the matter of text preservation. After the Holy Ghost indwelled Saul and he finished prophesying, and after he hid, the LORD revealed him as being among the "stuff." Just after the people shout for God to save their king, Samuel made a very important record of the events leading up to Saul being crowned. He includes in his journal the words the LORD spoke **into his ear**. Being in charge of the temple administration, Samuel oversaw meticulous records of all the events which occurred at the temple.

> Then Samuel told the people the manner of the kingdom, and wrote it in a book, and laid it up before the LORD. And Samuel sent all the people away, every man to his house. (1 Samuel 10:25)

This method of protecting all the written journals is familiar to Samuel by the example of Moses laying up the memorial book before the LORD. The conservator Levites held the book in safety, placing it before the LORD near the altar. Once again, we see the warp thread (being Samuel and Saul's inspiratory ministry), bound tightly with the weft thread of guardianship, all stitched into the fabric of Scripture text. There, by the altar, held fast in a place of protection, the Holy Ghost oversaw the book stewarded by His Levites. What could be safer?

The Scripture and its innate protection are like the negative film and positive print of a photograph. How fitting those words are like apples of gold in pictures of silver (Proverbs 25:11). In reality, these Samuel journals are diaries of the Scripture record.

Yes or No, Not Maybe

For centuries, thousands of archeologists and bibliologists, and preservation experts have conducted many Middle-east site explorations, but have not yet discovered the whereabouts of just one section of God's prime writings. None has surfaced. Even today's magnificent technology cannot find one iota of any "original document." Even if someone discovers a presumed prime writing, how will they know? Did the chicken or the egg come first?

Outside the pages of Scripture, there is no record of any human having seen or touched the supereminent writings. There is no earthly chain of custody, no human certifications, and no surviving eyewitnesses of this past five millennia. On this side of Heaven, none knows the whereabouts nor disposition of the inaugural writings of Scripture text.

Inspiration and preservation are neither partial nor unequal — nor are they unraveling. The weft thread of safety weaves inextricably with the warp thread of God's breath. If there is no guardianship of the penetrating breath of God upon all God's words, then inspiration has succumbed to the ash heap of fables and preservation is a useless myth.

Perhaps you now see why faith plays such an important role in our trust of the Solid Rock of Bible text.

Within the Scripture, there is a balm for every wound, a salve for every sore
— Charles Haddon Spurgeon

Chapter Thirteen

Conveyance

By now you have noticed Scripture is replete with ample self-evidence. God ensured the recording of His word and guaranteed the successful publishing to every generation. From the beginning of the Creation, through every nation and people inhabiting His planet; to the innumerable events in every society known in history; to the end of time itself on out into eternity, the *words* of God are the singular, reliable constant which anyone and everyone can recline the whole of their faith upon. The dreadful accusations from Satan do not surprise God, nor do the feeble perjuries from man blindside Him.

As Scripture shows, it is in keeping with His perfect nature, to take steps and employ many people, from myriad walks of life, and using a variety of mechanisms, and during centuries of events, upon multiple continents, spread across thousands of miles — to record and distribute the written text of His *words*. Sometimes, He even used people who didn't give Him the time of day.

I have called out many accounts in the Bible which illustrate the penning and copying of spoken words into scrolls, rolls, letters, stones, journals, books, and other materials. Throughout the development of the Scriptures, only those who initially penned or dictated the spoken words into writings can tell us the eventual disposition of those initial works.

There is neither a place nor a building where we see a collection of prime documents. If the prime writings were available today, people would worship the books — instead of the **AUTHOR** of the books.

Remember the rules of evidence and witnesses? Many societies, long ago, established those rules, which remain useful in modern litigation and criminal matters. In those rules, eyewitnesses are often paramount to the case. If an eyewitness is believable or corroborative, then the jury treats his testimony as truthful. What could be more impeccable than the eyewitness testimony of the inspired penmen? They were the first vessels to receive and convey the recited words and visions from the Holy One and then spoke or recorded those beautiful words. Those eyewitnesses of God's prime writings are supreme in their position, but not by human might. God breathed the words into and through them.

With this in mind, we confirm man's capacity to deduce the location or final disposition of those originally penned texts lessens with each passing minute. I believe we will never discover the prime texts this side of eternity, for the reasons already stated. Therefore, by submitting to the Holy Ghost, the Christian compels his faith farther and more abundantly as each day passes. Faith becomes more imperative and of greater value.

There is no light between the pillars of faith: hearing the word and practicing in the word.

> But whoso looketh into the perfect law of liberty, and continueth therein, he being not a forgetful hearer, but a doer of the work, this man shall be blessed in his deed. (James 1:25)

The veracity of the words remains indefectible: "Sanctify them through thy truth: thy word is truth" (John 17:17).

The sturdiness of the words of God increases in our minds as we grow and exercise our faith in those words. Indeed, the holy men and their writings have long since disappeared, but the results of their willingness as clean vessels continue with every published copy of God's words. Wonderfully, we can in practice hold the whole replicated depository and index in our hands, ready for reading, able for preaching, and both necessary and sufficient for all of life's events.

The written words are the precious silver treasure in the heart, which abolishes the human propensity to sin!

> Although we often hear and speak of the 'original manuscripts,' it is a remarkable fact that, of all these sacred writings, there is not one original manuscript — either of the Old or New Testament — now in existence, so far as is known. In some cases, when these precious documents became old, they were reverently buried by the Jews, who used reliable copies in their stead; others have been lost during the wars and persecutions by which God's ancient people have been from time to time op-

pressed. Even when the New Testament was written, the original documents of the Old seem to have been lost; so that when the whole Bible was first completed, it consisted of Hebrew copies of the Old Testament — together with a Greek translation of the Hebrew.[1]

Sydney Collett further highlights that early copies of the Greek New Testament have also disappeared, and, "Surely, however, in this we may see the wise providence of God, for had there been any of the original documents bearing the handwriting of Moses, David, Isaiah, Daniel, Paul, or John in existence now, so foolish is the human heart that they would almost certainly be regarded with superstition and worshiped, as was the brazen serpent in the days of Hezekiah (2 Kings 18:4), thus defeating one of the very objects for which they were given."[2]

In this twenty-first century, we have many indexes and references to aid the Bible student. There is more published today on the sureness and authenticity of Scripture than at any other time in human history. We have at our instant use the multiple lexicons, dictionaries, indexes, concordances, online search tools, databases, and many other ways to verify accuracy and precision in the copies of Scripture.

There is more discovered material evidence to convince people of God's existence and providence today — than ever before. There are actually *mountains* of archeological evidence which conclusively prove thousands upon thousands of Bible facts. Preserving the text is like a conveyor belt which reliably publishes the package of the inspired words to every place, people group, and time period. If the Bible, collected and handed down through the centuries, is not in a faultless state, all those who put their faith in it, are plunged into foolishness. Such deception leads to misery and dreadful death. Man crafts such deception, not God. Rhetorically I ask, as we near the end of this first volume: when did Jehovah stop defending His Word, leaving it subject to happenstance by fetid human hands?

---

1. Sidney Collett, The Scripture of Truth, Fifth Edition, pp. 13, S. W. Partridge & Co., 8 & 9 Paternoster Row, London, 1905, as found in the Library of the University of California, Los Angeles.

2. Sidney Collett, The Scripture of Truth, Fifth Edition, pp. 13, S. W. Partridge & Co., 8 & 9 Paternoster Row, London, 1905, as found in the Library of the University of California, Los Angeles.

Heard but Not Seen

While this example may seem tangential to picturing the act of preservation from an earthly view, I think it shows how words are preservable, whether for short or long periods. This example describes one method of conveyance for words.

Conveyance is the act of bearing, carrying, transporting, or transmitting something through a defined medium. It is to pass a thing from place to place, or person to person.

Whether we think Marconi, Tesla, or Maxwell "invented" the radio, the effort needed a team (albeit independently of each other). Each of these scientists' discoveries and technologies formed the foundation for harnessing radio waves to transmit voice, sound, song, and information. Other entrepreneurs contributed significantly. Marconi seems to be the first to transmit words over long distances via radio waves, without significant time delay. Fessenden, who worked for Thomas Edison, consistently successfully transmitted voices and music. His methods found many uses in WWI. And in the 1920s and 1930s, the public could harness the power of radio as the technology became less expensive and more prolific: The Golden Age of Radio.

Planetary Ubiquity

In 2023, billions of people around Planet Earth carry a radio which both transmits and receives — the cellular telephone. It uses radio waves to communicate with radio towers, which convert the signal into other forms and send it to the correct destination, often involving other radio towers. This all happens in fractional seconds, with a reliability unequaled in any other technology. These amazing and powerful "pocket radios" have reached lofty reliability such that life-saving measures and instant access to countless services (like banking and medical records) have become as dependable as the telephone dial tone itself, and as widespread as food and water.

The radio, invented more than a century ago, is probably the most-giant leap of communications ever made. However, man's invention simply harnessed the technology provided by God. Before the telegraph radio, people waited for long periods before hearing any news from family or friends. It's hard to determine which came first — the information demand egg or the radio supply chicken. As societies became more sophisticated, the need for more current and accurate information grew dramatically. Having a way to communicate in real-time fed their insatiable appetite for information. Radio continues to transform the entire world.

As radio technology developed more and more reliability with successive inventions, it contributed substantially to other technologies: transistor radios for car dashboards, telephones, telegraphs, microwave transmissions, remote controls, and televisions. Without communication, societies fade and cease. Without radio, modern societies could not communicate as they do now.

Notably, some of the earliest radio transmissions in the US came from preachers and church services, broadcasting the Gospel of Jesus Christ from the pages of Scripture to vast and distant audiences. Many people have grown in faith by literally hearing the words of God conveyed invisibly through the air from station to station. The Scriptures have found a comforting place in the hearts of many listeners through the medium of radio.

Cause

Regarding *preservation*, the cause has always been the same — the safekeeping, publishing, and distribution of the text of God's words. Regarding *inspiration*, the cause has always been the same, with its action being the breath of God as He transmits the words.

> A cause is that which produces or effects a result, often by use of energy and effort. A cause is a reason for an action. Noah Webster defines a cause as "that which impels into existence, or by its agency or operation produces what did not before exist; that by virtue of which any thing is done; that from which any thing proceeds, and without which it would not exist. The reason or motive that urges, moves, or impels the mind to act or decide.[3]

> Cause me to hear thy lovingkindness in the morning; for in thee do I trust: cause me to know the way wherein I should walk; for I lift up my soul unto thee. (Psalm 143:8)

---

3. Noah Webster, from his American Dictionary of the English Language, 1828, as found on https://webstersdictionary1828.com/Dictionary/cause

> Therefore, behold, I will this once cause them to know, I will cause them to know mine hand and my might; and they shall know that my name is The LORD. (Jeremiah 16:21)

> Turn us, O God of our salvation, and cause thine anger toward us to cease. (Psalm 85:4)

> Pilate therefore said unto him, Art thou a king then? Jesus answered, Thou sayest that I am a king. To this end was I born, and for this cause came I into the world, that I should bear witness unto the truth. Every one that is of the truth heareth my voice. (John 18:37)

Natural disasters *cause* property damage and loss of life. Internal combustion *causes* the engine to motivate the automobile. The breath of God *causes* life to begin. God causes rain on one city and causes no rain upon another. The LORD caused Ezekiel to eat the roll. Jehovah caused the waters of both the Red Sea and the Jordan River to separate.

Manner

A manner is the way something is done (achieved or effected). Manner is one's customary method of acting (or doing something); a sort, kind, or style. Noah Webster says, "a manner is a form; method; way of performing or executing. A manner may be a custom or habitual practice; a distinct mode."

> And when he had called unto him his twelve disciples, he gave them power against unclean spirits, to cast them out, and to heal all manner of sickness and all manner of disease. (Matthew 10:1)

And Jesus went about all Galilee, teaching in their synagogues, and preaching the gospel of the kingdom, and healing all manner of sickness and all manner of disease among the people. (Matthew 4:23)

What manner of man is this, that even the winds and the sea obey him! (Matthew 8:27)

And, behold, the courses of the priests and the Levites, even they shall be with thee for all the service of the house of God: and there shall be with thee for all manner of workmanship every willing skilful man, for any manner of service: also the princes and all the people will be wholly at thy commandment. (1 Chronicles 28:21)

Which also said, Ye men of Galilee, why stand ye gazing up into heaven? this same Jesus, which is taken up from you into heaven, shall so come in like manner as ye have seen him go into heaven. (Acts 1:11)

An artist has a particular *manner* by which they paint or sculpt. A writer's style is the *manner* by which they communicate via the written word. A surgeon follows a particular *manner* when applying the scalpel to mend and heal. Carpenters follow a *manner* of plan when constructing a house. Couriers deliver packages by following a prescribed manner. The pastry chef prepares his confectionary delights in a manner which produces smiles and wonderment.

The manner by which God moves *inspiration* through the chosen writers did indeed differ, for no two people are the same. For some, the chosen mode is face-to-face with Jehovah or the LORD Jesus. With others, the chosen form is through visions or dreams, such as with Isaiah, Amos, Peter, or John. For some, the chosen practice is indirect, receiving the messages through other people or various media.

The manner by which God conducts *preservation* differs from place to place, person to person, group to group, material to material, and from time period to time period. We know many of the manners by which God conveys the text through the centuries, but we do not know all, and some remain mysterious.

By conveyance, as relating to the Scriptures, it is the Holy Ghost who proactively engages the oversight of transporting those precious words to every aspect of creation for all time and beyond by a particular manner.

> Thou shalt keep them, O LORD, thou shalt preserve them from this generation for ever. (Psalm 12:7)

The words of the LORD stand like a rock undaunted and the lively text reaches beyond history and time!

> And the scripture, foreseeing that God would justify the heathen through faith, preached before the gospel unto Abraham, saying, In thee shall all nations be blessed. (Galatians 3:8)

As the Gospel of Jesus Christ blossoms to the Gentiles, after rejection by those Hebrews first entrusted with the oracles, Apostle Peter, "opened his mouth, and said, Of a truth I perceive that God is no respecter of persons: but in every nation he that feareth him, and worketh righteousness, is accepted with him. The word which God sent unto the children of Israel, preaching peace by Jesus Christ: (he is Lord of all:) that word, I say, ye know, which was published throughout all Judaea, and began from Galilee, after the baptism which John preached; how God anointed Jesus of Nazareth with the Holy Ghost and with power: who went about doing good, and healing all that were oppressed of the devil; for God was with him" (Acts 10:34–38).

Constituent Media

As you read through the Bible, you will encounter many varied and unique materials used to bring God's words to people. Some prevail more than others. There are so many. It's doubtful we can catalog them all. We should be very thankful for all the many various materials used by the LORD as His words moved through many societies, and from region to region. Being ever so careful with the transmission of His words, the LORD knows best how to diversify His portfolio.

Unique media are sometimes used to record judgments: "Gather unto me all the elders of your tribes, and your officers, that I may speak these words in their ears, and call heaven and earth to record against them" (Deuteronomy 31:28).

The words convey through many less-tangible materials.

> Therefore shall ye lay up these my words in your heart and in your soul, and bind them for a sign upon your hand, that they may be as frontlets between your eyes. And ye shall teach them your children, speaking of them when thou sittest in thine house, and when thou walkest by the way, when thou liest down, and when thou risest up. And thou shalt write them upon the door posts of thine house, and upon thy gates: that your days may be multiplied, and the days of your children, in the land which the LORD sware unto your fathers to give them, as the days of heaven upon the earth. (Deuteronomy 11:18–21)

The LORD revealed His cause through Moses: preserve the righteousness of the people and multiply their days. The injunction: inscribe the words onto every medium, everywhere, all the time, in every act of life, and in each sector of society. God's words are to be preeminent in all things.

In millennia past, the scribes and copiers hand wrote the words onto plant fibers, animal skins, plaster, stone, wood, and various other materials. Buying such materials often incurred substantial cost and was subject to limited availability. Today, we are privileged to read the Bible on the finest of papers, encased in the best covers. Also today, we can read those words on a variety of electronic devices, with every imaginable page color, size, typeface, and font. In fact, modern technology easily enables anyone to HEAR Scripture, as software reads the words. I am grateful.

Consider the engineering excellence built into papers, inks, printing presses, and binderies. All these marvelous inventions give us the ability today to hold in our hands the completed Bible — easy to read and portable — yet every bit as accurate a medium as those early employed by scribes in their necessary endeavors. The media used today, in their excellent presentation of the Scriptures, far surpass the materials of yesterday. By comparison, we easily conclude God's words, in physical form on Planet Earth, are safer now than at any point in history (as viewed by the human faculty). When the LORD sends forth His words, never do they fail or falter in their mission.

> So shall my word be that goeth forth out of my mouth: it shall not return unto me void, but it shall accomplish that which I please, and it shall prosper in the thing whereto I sent it. (Isaiah 55:11)

The LORD Jesus said His words are both spirit and life (John 6:63). The lively words of the Bible are today so easily attainable. Yet, it seems the easier it becomes to read the Scriptures, and the more available they are, the less interested people are to include them in their daily lives.

I have done my best to help you know this: we must put God's words back into first place in my society, and your society — *if we are to survive*.

Methods of Transmission

A method is a process by which we complete a task; a way of doing something; a means.

Jehovah Himself spoke the first words at the beginning and subsequent creation. **God said**. His manner of transmitting the very origins of all things is by speaking words. From His everlasting and powerful words, we know "all things were made by him; and without him was not any thing made that was made" (John 1:3), and by Him all things consist (Colossians 1:17).

From this beginning spring all other methods for dispatching the words of God throughout Planet Earth. It's not possible on this side of Heaven to discover how many times the words of God have reached into the Creation, prospering every time it transmits and every place it arrives.

The Scriptures reveal the many ways of conveying from one person to another, or from one time to the next. People spread abroad the Wonderful Words of Life! People in all walks of life read them, handed them down through family traditions, studied them, showed them, delivered them, heard them, and dreamed them. They envisioned them, wrote them in letters and posts, journaled them, housed them, scribed them on walls and altars, and of course — wrote them upon their hearts.

In almost countless places in the Bible text, we read of methods (ways, manners) employed by the LORD and many others, to conduct messages from one party to another; to carry out activities of life; to make transactions.

Joshua had a method of setting tribal boundaries.

> Give out from among you three men for each tribe: and I will send them, and they shall rise, and go through the land, and describe it according to the inheritance of them; and they shall come again to me. And they shall divide it into seven parts: Judah shall abide in their coast on the South, and the house of Joseph shall abide in their coasts on the North. Ye shall therefore describe the land into seven parts, and bring the description hither to me, that I may cast lots for you here before the LORD our God. (Joshua 18:4–6)

We have also seen in the LORD's temple there is a method of worship. In similar fashion, in the local church there is a prescribed method of worship: "Jesus saith unto her, Woman, believe me, the hour cometh, when ye shall neither in this mountain, nor yet at Jerusalem, worship the Father. Ye worship ye know not what: we know what we worship: for salvation is of the Jews. But the hour cometh, and now is, when the true worshippers shall worship the Father in spirit and in truth: for the Father seeketh such to worship him. God is a Spirit: and they that worship him must worship him in spirit and in truth" (John 4:21–24).

The Christian compels himself to have proper conduct before others (Philippians 1:27; Colossians 4:5–6; and, Galatians 5). The Bible shows a method of adding to faith (2 Peter 1). Throughout the Acts of the Apostles, we find the Holy Ghost ministering and engaging with people in a manner befitting His high office. In Titus 3:5, we see the Holy Ghost saving, washing, regenerating, and renewing!

God uses the right method, in the right way, at the right time, with the right people.

Salvation and faith are not in methods, but methods can help us travel the Christian journey faithfully. Following a method for the sake of completing a religious exercise is vain. Thankfully, there is no central church or government office for Christian conduct. Scripture is the one and only authority which prescribes for the Christian how to live his life. We are free to choose our own path, but we should choose the narrow path. Just as God has provided a method for transmitting and preserving His inspired words, we must carry out our worship, and conduct our daily lives, in a way which pleases the LORD — obedient to those *words*.

A Christian — one who seeks to be like Christ — shall follow the truth of the words of God, abandoning vanity and self-truth. God prescribes the method, and we simply must conform our ways to His satisfaction.

There are no gradations of *quality* to inspiration. It's all good. Inspiration is lively.

There are no gradations of *quality* to preservation. It's all decay-proof. Preservation is lively.

It's all about the words.

> All scripture is given by inspiration of God, and is profitable for doctrine, for reproof, for correction, for instruction in righteousness: that the man of God may be perfect, throughly furnished unto all good works. (2 Timothy 3:16–17)

> Thy word have I hid in mine heart, that I might not sin against thee (Psalm 119:11).

The Scriptures then being acknowledged to be so full and so perfect, how can we excuse ourselves of negligence, if we do not study them? of curiosity, if we be not content with them? — The Translators to the Reader, in the precious King James Bible

The End of Volume One

Afterword

It all started on a cold, rainy late-February night. After the Boy Scout district meeting in Santa Rosa, CA, Bryan and I waited for his mom to take us home. Before that night, we had only briefly discussed spiritual matters a few times. This night was different. Bryan gave me a clear description of what Jesus had done on the cross at Calvary. And with this, he explained how trusting Christ for salvation was an act of faith which required repentance and calling upon His name.

This conversation troubled me much in the following days. I accepted Bryan's invitation to attend church with his family.

Beginning February 27, 1983, I attended the Sunday services at First Baptist Church in Windsor, CA. Each Sunday, Bryan and I sat one pew closer to the front, and a little closer to the outside. On Sunday, March 20, the preacher made a clear presentation of the Gospel of Jesus Christ. He also carefully explained what Hell was all about — and who goes there. After the preaching, as the invitation started, I could feel my heart pounding. The Holy Ghost was moving upon me. I reckon now Bryan probably heard it too — because he asked me to go forward to get saved, and I quickly accepted. I knew what I needed, and I knew where to get the answer. This is the beginning of my Christian journey.

In a side prayer room, like so many before me, Pastor Larry Blythe showed me some Bible verses from Matthew, John, and Romans. Nobody had to tell me the Bible was reliable. In my simple state, knowing nothing of the Scriptures, it was by faith that the Bible was speaking to me. The words showed me as a sinner (which I knew), prompted me to confess my sin, repent, and ask Jesus Christ to save me. I asked and Jesus did save.

I now had a new life in Christ and later learned I had been born again. I can remember walking out of the prayer room, and speaking with the Senior Pastor. As we walked out of the church building, I could sense the change in my life. It was like I was walking 3 feet off the ground. He lifted the burden at

Calvary, and I was a new creature. Diligently searching the lively Scriptures makes it 100% certain with me — I am a reborn child of God!

This brings me to you. If you have never been born again, I implore you to keep reading.

Believing the Scriptures solve the sin problem in your life is the first step in trusting the LORD Jesus Christ for eternal salvation. He lived a sinless life. He gave His life freely to pay your sin debt in full. Where sin has captivated or distracted you, God's grace abounds and overflows so much more. God's grace heals the wounds from sin and despair. Even though you and I are sinful, there is a sufficient answer to the problem: the pages of Scripture, carefully protected from decay throughout the centuries — give the answer.

We find the Good News of Jesus Christ in the trustworthy Scriptures:

> For I delivered unto you first of all that which I also received, how that Christ died for our sins according to the scriptures; and that he was buried, and that he rose again the third day according to the scriptures: and that he was seen of Cephas, then of the twelve: after that, he was seen of above five hundred brethren at once; of whom the greater part remain unto this present, but some are fallen asleep. After that, he was seen of James; then of all the apostles. (1 Corinthians 15:3–7)

Because of the love of God, Jesus Christ gave His life to save anyone who asks — including you:

> For God so loved the world, that he gave his only begotten Son, that whosoever believeth in him should not perish, but have everlasting life. For God sent not his Son into the world to condemn the world; but that the world through him might be saved. He that believeth on him is not condemned: but he that believeth not is condemned already, because he hath not believed in the name of the only begotten Son of God. (John 3:16–18)

AFTERWORD

You are faulty and need rescuing. You cannot do this on your own:

> As it is written, There is none righteous, no, not one: there is none that understandeth, there is none that seeketh after God. They are all gone out of the way, they are together become unprofitable; there is none that doeth good, no, not one. Their throat is an open sepulchre; with their tongues they have used deceit; the poison of asps is under their lips: whose mouth is full of cursing and bitterness: their feet are swift to shed blood: destruction and misery are in their ways: and the way of peace have they not known: there is no fear of God before their eyes. (Romans 3:10–18)

> For the wages of sin is death; but the gift of God is eternal life through Jesus Christ our Lord. (Romans 6:23)

It is the name of the LORD Jesus that can save you:

> And it shall come to pass, that whosoever shall call on the name of the Lord shall be saved. (Acts 2:21)

> Neither is there salvation in any other: for there is none other name under heaven given among men, whereby we must be saved. (Acts 4:12)

God does all the work — you cannot:

> But God commendeth his love toward us, in that, while we were yet sinners, Christ died for us. (Romans 5:8)

> But what saith it? The word is nigh thee, even in thy mouth, and in thy heart: that is, the word of faith, which we preach;

> that if thou shalt confess with thy mouth the Lord Jesus, and shalt believe in thine heart that God hath raised him from the dead, thou shalt be saved. For with the heart man believeth unto righteousness; and with the mouth confession is made unto salvation. For the scripture saith, Whosoever believeth on him shall not be ashamed. (Romans 10:8-11)

Will you act by faith now?

Have you come to the end of yourself? Are you now rejecting your sin?

Is the Holy Ghost pounding your heart to call upon the LORD Jesus right now to save you?

> I tell you, Nay: but, except ye repent, ye shall all likewise perish. (Luke 13:5)

> For whosoever shall call upon the name of the Lord shall be saved. (Romans 10:13)

If you have been born again because of reading this book, please contact us via https://ridleyhousebooks.com or Calvary Baptist Church in American Canyon, California so we may rejoice with you, and help you further on your journey of Christian faith.

May the LORD eternally preserve you.

About the Author

James describes himself as both introvert and extrovert — a **hybrivert**. His varied vocations and many experiences give him a unique perspective on life's many challenges — and how to solve them.

James has over three decades of experience as an originating writer, producing hundreds of multi-volume documents, including white papers, procedures, manuals, and policies across a range of business, technical, and ministry disciplines. These days, he lends his expertise with unique e-discovery situations to large and medium organizations.

In 1978 James joined Boy Scout Troop 21 in Healdsburg, CA where he met lifelong friend Bryan. Through their friendship, James came to know Christ as a teen, and soon thereafter developed an affection for reading the Bible. Learning the English of Scripture substantially improved his reading skills and launched a lifelong journey of studying God's words. He is an active Sunday school teacher, policy adviser, has preached often, and continues to serve in various local church roles.

Responding to some turns in life and spiritual growth, he now propels his years of manuscript expertise and many experiences into writing books which help others. His great desire is to help people face difficult times in life, expand their knowledge and wisdom, and grow spiritually. James writes in several genres and is especially interested in writing which points others to the glorious Gospel of Jesus Christ.

Among his various skills, James served as a US Navy Hospital Corpsman and Surgical Technologist aboard USS *ENTERPRISE* where he led shipboard Bible studies, seeing men saved and baptized into local churches. He lives in the Napa Valley of California with his wife Tonya, where they are long-time members of Calvary Baptist Church, under the mentoring leadership of Pastor Marshall Stevens.

More information about James is available at ridleywriter.com.

A Note from the Author

THANK YOU FOR READING Without Decay. I trust it has blessed your life and demonstrated the reliability of the Scriptures.

I humbly ask for a few minutes to leave a review on my Amazon book page for Without Decay Volume One. Thank you very much for your time.

Also by James Ridley

Step aboard the USS ENTERPRISE and bear witness to the gripping true account of one Hospital Corpsman's extraordinary journey amidst the relentless demands of life at sea. When tragedy strikes with the sudden death of a fellow sailor, all eyes turn to him, accusing him of responsibility.

Falsely accused and grappling with betrayal, he finds himself isolated, navigating the stormy waters of suspicion and doubt, wondering if the truth will emerge. As the chaotic investigation intensified, he bounced like a pinball between despair and hope. When so many around him demanded his guilt, truth was only a convenience, and no human advocate was coming to his rescue.

Join him as he shares his journey from accusation to exoneration and shows how you too can sail out of the darkest storm into a safe harbor of rest by prayer.

Reference Index

Scripture References by Bible Book

GENESIS: 1:3 p. 118, 6 p. 106, 11 p. 118, 12:5 p. 39, 29:2 p. 68.

Exodus 2:11–15 p. 63, 3 p. 126, 3 p. 59, 8 p. 150, 20 p. 127, 24 p. 127, 31 p. 150, 31:18 p. 127, 32 p. 127, 32 p. 92.

Leviticus: 24 p. 116.

Deuteronomy: 9 p. 150, 11 p. 165, 16 p. 68, 27 p. 68, 27 p. 69, 27:3, 8 p. 158, 28–29 p. 175, 31 p. 93.

2 Samuel: 7:19 p. 128.

1 Kings: 7:10 p. 68, 7–8 p. 70, 11 p. 131.

2 Kings: 7:14 p. 181, 22–23 p. 174.

1 Chronicles: 27 p. 131, 28 p. 129.

2 Chronicles: 7:14 p. 52, 17 p. 165, 30 p. 165, 30:5–9 p. 57.

Esther: 2 p. 132.

Job: 32:8 p. 17.

Psalm: 1:2–3 p. 6, 2:7 p. 113, 16:10 p. 113, 19 p. 13, 19 p. 50, 33:4 p. 4, 104 p. 3, 104 p. 85, 119:89 p. 54, 119:160 p. 6, 121 p. 16, 138 p. 55, 139:13–16 p. 100.

Proverbs: 25:11 p. 177.

Ecclesiastes: 3 p. 116.

Isaiah: 29 p. 95, 46:9–11 p. 86, 49:6 p. 113, 53:5 p. 165, 55:3 p. 113, 66:1 p. 85.

Jeremiah: 15:16 p. 75, 29 p. 160, 31 p. 106, 32 p. 41, 36 p. 173.

Ezekiel: 26:1 p. 4, 29:17 p. 4, 31:1 p. 4, 32:1 p. 4.

Daniel: 5:24 p. 150, 8:17 p. 144, 8:19 p. 144, 8:27 p. 144, 9 p. 160, 9:26 p. 165, 12:1 p. 146.

Habakkuk: 1:5 p. 113.

Matthew 3:15 p. 7, 5:48 p. 61, 6 pp. 90, 111, 15:2–9 p. 110, 22:36–40 p. 128, 23 p. 110, 24 p. 122, 27:59–60 p. 69.

Mark: 7 p. 95, 13:31 p. 134.

Luke 1:70 p. 56, 4 p. 165, 8 p. 44, 11 p. 111.

John: 1 p. 41, 1:14 p. 89, 6:35, 48 p. 6, 17:17 p. Foreword, 18:10 p. 63, 19 p. 13, 21 p. 17.

Acts: 2 p. 121, 3:21 p. 56, 6–7 p. 75, 6:8 p. 75, 7 p. 76, 8 p. 154, 9 p. 142, 13 p. 46, 13:15 p. 110, 17;2 p. 165, 28:25–27 p. 95.

Romans: 3:12 p. 63, 5 p. 52, 10:13–15 p. 52, 15 p. 60.

1 Corinthians: 2:13 p. 56, 3:13–15 p. 144, 15 p. 154, 15:9 p. 110.

2 Corinthians: 2:17 p. 113, 4:18 p. 42.

Galatians: 1:11–18 p. 114, 5 p. 189.

Ephesians: 4 p. 14, 4:11–12 p. 56.

Philippians: 1 p. 14, 1:27 p. 189, 2 p. 87, 4:3 p. 146.

Colossians: 1:17 p. 188, 4:5–6 p. 189.

1 Timothy: 1:15 p. 110, 3:15 p. 14.

Titus: 3:5 p. 189.

Hebrews: 1:1–2 p. 56, 4:12 p. 16, 11:3 p. 44, 11:7 p. 42.

James: 1:17 p. 151.

1 Peter: 1 p. 89, 1:23 p. Foreword.

2 Peter: 1 pp. 86, 87, 189, 3 p. 91, 3:2 p. 56, 3:5–7 p. 85.

1 John: 1 p. 87, 1:2, 5 p. 147, 3:11 p. 147, 4:14 p. 147, 5:6–7, 9–11 p. 147.

Revelation: 2–3 p. 17, 20:12 p. 144.

Scriptures Quoted by Bible Book, Quotation Reference, and Page

Genesis: 1:1 p. 169, 1:26 p. 100, 7:21–23 p. 107, 7:4 p. 38, 8:13 p. 123, 8:21 - 8:22 p. 123.

Exodus: 3:13–14 p. 126, 3:20 p. 126, 20:11 p. 3, 24:12 p. 127, 24:3–4 p. 115, 24:4 p. 127, 32:14–16 p. 171, 32:15–16 p. 127, 32:31–32 p. 145, 32:33 p. 146, 34:27 p. 171, 40:4 p. 116, 40:4 p. 12.

Deuteronomy: 4:2 p. 58, 4:39–40 p. 58, 11:18–21 p. 187, 17:18–20 p. 157, 28:14 p. 159, 28:8 p. 159, 31:28 p. 187, 31:8 p. 93.

Joshua: 6:15 p. 27, 8:30–35 pp. 69, 159, 18:4–6 p. 189.

Judges: 20:16 p. 10.

1 Samuel: 1:11, 15 p. 124, 3:10, 21 p. 118, 8:21–22 p. 176, 9:15–17 p. 176, 10:25 p. 177, 17:45 p. 51, 17:49 p. 10.

2 Samuel: 7:7, 21 pp. 128, 129, 16:23 p. 66, 23:1–4 p. 56.

1 Kings: 6:5, 22, 27 p. 73, 7:23 p. 28, 7:48–50 p. 73, 8:3–4, 6–7 p. 71, 8:6, 8 p. 74, 9:3 p. 31, 12:15–17 p. 132.

2 Kings: 8:8 p. 78, 18:4 p. 181, 23:2 p. 175.

1 Chronicles: 9:1 p. 133, 22:5 p. 129, 28:12 p. 138, 28:19 pp. 129, 139, 28:21 p. 185.

2 Chronicles: 1:12 p. 130, 5:8 p. 74, 7:1–4, 16 pp. 130, 136, 7:16 p. 31, 8:14 p. 116, 31:2 p. 116, 34:30–31 p. 80.

Ezra: 4:4–5. 12 p. 162, 4:24 p. 163, 5:11 p. 163, 6:1–2 p. 163, 7:10, 13, 27–28 p. 164, 9:4 p. 164.

Esther: 10:2 p. 132.

Job: 1:8 p. 125, 4:17 p. 86, 19:23–24 p. 126, 23:12 p. 64.

Psalm: 14:1–3 p. 62, 18:28 p. Preface, 18:30 p. 61, 19:1 p. 90, 19:4 p. 29, 19:7 p. 61, 24:1 p. 78, 28:2 p. 74, 33:11 p. 29, 33:13–14 p. 135, 33:4 p. 4, 33:4–9 p. 85, 37:30–31 p. 140, 40:8 p. 140, 51:10 p. 75, 51:3–5 p. 62, 68:11 p. 81, 68:17 p. 74, 69:28 p. 146, 69:9 p. 165, 72:19 p. 90, 84:10 p. 81, 85:4 p. 184, 89:6 p. 86, 96:1 p. 6, 100:5 p. 30, 102:25–27 p. 66, 102:25–27 p. 88, 103:12 p. 30, 104:31–32 p. 135, 105:8 p. 134, 105:8 p. 24, 105:8 p. 96, 119:10–11 p. 141, 119:11 p. 190, 119:128

REFERENCE INDEX

p. 115, 119:133 pp. 12, 116, 119:160 p. 96, 12:6–7 p. 19, 12:7 p. 186, 121:7–8 p. 25, 125:2 p. 27, 138:2 p. Foreword, 139:15–16 p. 38, 143:8 p. 183, 146:5–10 p. 61, 147:5 p. 24.

Proverbs: 3:1–5 p. 79, 4:23 p. 75, 7:2–3 p. 140, 8:27 p. 27, 16:24 p. 101, 22:20–21 p. 96.

Ecclesiastes 3:1,11 p. 103, 7:20 p. 62, 12:13–14 p. 100.

Isaiah: 2:3 p. 67, Isaiah 4:3 p. 146, Isaiah 29:14, 17–19 p. 94–95, Isaiah 30:8 pp. 25, 151, Isaiah 40:2 p. 27, Isaiah 40:28 p. 66, Isaiah 40:6–8 p. 36, Isaiah 40:8 p. 88, Isaiah 45:18–19 p. 67, Isaiah 51:6 p. 30, Isaiah 55:11 p. 143, Isaiah 55:11 p. 188, Isaiah 57:15 p. 135, Isaiah 64:6 p. 63, Isaiah 65:17 p. 6, Isaiah 66:2 p. 6, Isaiah 66:23 p. 67.

Jeremiah: 16:21 p. 184, 29:32 p. 161, 31:33 p. 140, 36:17–18 p. 174, 36:3 p. 173, 51:58 p. 172, 51:64 p. 172.

Ezekiel: 1:24–25 p. 155, 3:10 p. 79, 36:24–27 pp. 6, 63.

Daniel: 4:37 p. 145, 5:22–24 p. 150, 5:5, 25–28 pp. 149–150, 8:26 p. 144 9:2 p. 160.

Malachi 3:6 pp. Foreword, 65, 88.

Matthew: 4:4, 7, 10 p. 154, 4:23 p. 185, 8:27 p. 185, 9:19–22 p. 45, 10:1 p. 184, 10:29–31 p. 15, 11:28–30 p. 160, 11:4–6 p. 94, 13:13–15 p. 95, 22:29–32 p. 59, 24:35 p. Foreword, 28:18–20 pp. 109, 143.

Mark: 7:20–23 p. 63, 16:2, 5-6, 9 p. 5.

Luke: 10:20 p. 146, 18:31–33 p. 115, 18:40–43 p. 45, 19:10 p. 7, 21:33 p. 92.

John: 1:1 p. 169, 1:1–3 p. 3, 1:3 p. 85, 1:32 p. 86, 2:22 p. 165, 4:21–24 p. 189, 5:24 p. 80, 5:4 p. 4, 6:63 p. 81, 6:68 p. 81, 6:68–69 p. 66, 7:37–38 p. 46, 11:22–27 p. 46, 17:17 p. 180, 17:7–8 p. 112, 18:37 p. 184, 19:30 p. 118.

Acts: 1:11 p. 185, 7:38 - 7:40 p. 76, 8:37 p. 109, 10:34–38 p. 186, 11:4 p. 13, 13:2 p. 113, 13:46–49 pp. 47, 113, 17:11 p. 60, 17:24 p. 136, 17:26–28 p. 10, 17:29 p. 53, 18:28 p. 165, 26:23 p. 5.

Romans: 3:1–2 p. 76, 3:28–31 p. 77, 5:12 p. 43, 5:15 p. 43, 5:18–19 p. 43, 5:20–21 p. 44, 5:8 p. 149, 10:8–11 pp. 8, 37, 74, 80, 10:14–15 p. 48, 10:17 pp. Foreword, 8, 11:36 p. 86.

1 Corinthians: 1:25–27 p. 28, 14:40 pp. 14, 116, 15:3–4 pp. 5, 111.

2 Corinthians: 3:1–3 p. 142, 5:17 p. 6, 6:2 p. 102.

Galatians: 3::8 p. 186, 3:11 p. 39.

Ephesians: 1:7, 13–14 p. 141, 2:8 p. Foreword, 6:17 p. 88.

Colossians: 1:15–18 pp. 4, 7, 12, 1:25–29 p. 91, 3:16 p. 141.

1 Thessalonians: 2:13 p. 50.

1 Timothy: 1:17 p. 31, 2:1 p. 5, 3:16 pp. 52, 87.

2 Timothy: 2:3–4 p. 88, 3:14–17 pp. 55, 190, 4:13 p. 111.

Hebrews: 1:1–4 pp. 89, 114, 1:10–12 p. 114, 2:3 p. 5, 4:12 p. 75, 5:9 p. 66, 9:16–17 p. 104, 9:27–28 pp. 102–103, 10:16–17 pp. 30, 140, 11:1 p. 39, 11:3 p. 85, 11:4 p. 43, 11:6 p. 33, 13:8 pp. Foreword, 29, 66, 88.

James: 1:17 p. 15, 1:25 p. 180.

1 Peter: 1:22–25 p. 37, 4:11 p. 77, 5:8 p. 88.

2 Peter: 1:2–3 p. 14, 1:20 p. 60, 3:5–7 p. 78, 3:9 p. 92.

1 John: 1:1–3 pp. 7, 14, 81, 5:11 pp. 13, 148, 5:6 pp. 86, 148, 5:8 p. 148, 5:9 p. 147.

Jude: v. 1 p. 25.

Revelation: 1:3 p. 16, 1:8 p. 29, 4:8–11 p. 29, 11:19 p. 32, 15:5, 8 p. 32, 20:15 p. 147, 21:1 p. 6, 21:6 p. 7, 21:22–23 p. 90, 21:27 p. 146, 22:13 p. 7, 22:18–19 p. 58.

Scripture Reference by Chapter

In order of appearance.

Preface: Psalm 18:28.

Foreward: 1 Peter 1:23; Ephesians 2:8; Hebrews 13:8; John 17:17; Malachi 3:6; Matthew 24:35; Psalm 138:2; Romans 10:17.

Chapter 1: 1 Corinthians 15:3–4; 1 John 1:1; 1 Timothy 2:1; 2 Corinthians 5:17; Acts 26:23; Colossians 1:16–17; Colossians 1:18; Exodus 20:11; Ezekiel 26:1; Ezekiel 29:17; Ezekiel 31:1; Ezekiel 32:1; Ezekiel 36:26–27; Hebrews 2:3; Isaiah 65:17; Isaiah 66:2; John 1:1–3; John 5:4; John 6:35, 48; Luke 19:10; Mark 16:2, 5-6, 9; Matthew 3:15; Psalm 1:2–3; Psalm 104; Psalm 119:160; Psalm 33:4; Psalm 33:4; Psalm 96:1; Revelation 21:1; Revelation 21:6; Revelation 22:13; Romans 10:17–18; Romans 10:8.

Chapter 2: 1 Corinthians 14:40; 1 John 1:1; 1 John 5:11; 1 Samuel 17:49; 1 Timothy 3:15; 2 peter 1:2–3; Acts 11:4; Acts 17:26–28; Colossians 1:15–18; Ephesians 4; Exodus 40:4; Hebrews 4:12; James 1:17; Job 32:8; John 19; John 21; Judges 20:16; Matthew 10:29–31; Philippians 1; Psalm 119:133; Psalm 121; Psalm 19; Revelation 1:3; Revelation 2–3.

Chapter 3: 1 Corinthians 1:25–27; 1 Kings 7:23; 1 Kings 9:3; 1 Timothy 1:17; 2 Chronicles 7:16; Hebrews 10:17; Hebrews 13:8; Isaiah 30:8; Isaiah 40:2; Isaiah 51:6; Joshua 6:15; Jude v. 1; Proverbs 8:27; Psalm 100:5; Psalm 103:12; Psalm 105:8; Psalm 12:6–7; Psalm 121:7–8; Psalm 125:2; Psalm 147:5; Psalm 19:4; Psalm 33:11; Revelation 1:8; Revelation 11:19; Revelation 15:5; Revelation 15:8; Revelation 4:8–11.

Chapter 4: 1 Peter 1:22–25; 2 Corinthians 4:18; Acts 13; Acts 13:46–49; Galatians 3:11; Genesis 12:5; Genesis 7:4; Hebrews 11:1; Hebrews 11:3; Hebrews 11:4; Hebrews 11:6; Hebrews 11:7; Isaiah 40:6–8; jeremiah 32; John 1; John 11:22–27; John 7:37–38; Luke 18:40–43; Luke 8; Matthew 9:19–22; Psalm 139:15–16; Romans 10:14–15; Romans 10:8–9; Romans 5:12; Romans 5:15; Romans 5:18–19; Romans 5:20–21.

Chapter 5: 1 Corinthians 2:13; 1 Samuel 17:45; 1 Thessalonians 2:13; 1 Timothy 3:16; 2 Chronicles 30:5–9; 2 Chronicles 7:14; 2 Peter 1:20; 2 Peter 3:2; 2 Samuel 23:1–4; 2 Timothy 3:14–17; Acts 17:11; Acts 17:29; Acts 3:21; Deuteronomy 4:2; Deuteronomy 4:39–40; Ecclesiastes 7:20; Ephesians 4:11–12; Exodus 2:11–15; Exodus 3; Ezekiel 36:24–27; Hebrews 1:1–2; Isaiah 64:6; Job 23:12; John 18:10; Luke 1:70; Mark 7:20–23; Matthew 22:29–32; Matthew 5:48; Psalm 119:89; Psalm 138; Psalm 14:1; Psalm 14:2–3; Psalm 146:5–10;

Psalm 18:30; Psalm 19; Psalm 19:7; Psalm 51:3–5; Revelation 22:18–19; Romans 10:13–15; Romans 15; Romans 3:12; Romans 5.

Chapter 6: 1 John 1:1–3; 1 Kings 6:22; 1 Kings 6:27; 1 Kings 6:5; 1 Kings 7–8; 1 Kings 7:10; 1 Kings 7:48–50; 1 Kings 8:3–4, 6–7; 1 Kings 8:6; 1 Kings 8:8; 1 Peter 4:11; 2 Chronicles 34:30–31; 2 Chronicles 5:8; 2 Kings 8:8; 2 Peter 3:5–7; 2 Samuel 16:23; Acts 6–7; Acts 6:8; Acts 7; Acts 7:38 - 7:40; Deuteronomy 16; Deuteronomy 27; Deuteronomy 27; Ezekiel 3:10; Genesis 29:2; Hebrews 13:8; Hebrews 4:12; Hebrews 5:9; Isaiah 2:3; Isaiah 40:28; Isaiah 45:18–19; Isaiah 66:23; Jeremiah 15:16; John 5:24; John 6:63; John 6:68; John 6:68–69; Joshua 8:30–32; Joshua 8:34–35; Malachi 3:6; Matthew 27:59–60; Proverbs 3:1–5; Proverbs 4:23; Psalm 102:25–27; Psalm 24:1; Psalm 28:2; Psalm 51:10; Psalm 68:11; Psalm 68:17; Psalm 84:10; Romans 10:8–11; Romans 10:8–9; Romans 3:1–2; Romans 3:28–31.

Chapter 7: 1 John 1; 1 John 5:6–8; 1 Peter 1; 1 Peter 5:8; 1 Timothy 3:16; 2 Peter 1; 2 Peter 1; 2 Peter 3; 2 Peter 3:5–7; 2 Peter 3:9; 2 Timothy 2:3–4; Acts 28:25–27; Colossians 1:25–29; Deuteronomy 31; Deuteronomy 31:8; Ephesians 6:17; Exodus 32; Hebrews 1:3; Hebrews 11:3; Hebrews 13:8; Isaiah 29; Isaiah 29:14; Isaiah 29:17–19; Isaiah 40:8; Isaiah 46:9–11; Isaiah 66:1; Job 4:17; John 1:14; John 1:3; John 1:32; Luke 21:33; Malachi 3:6; Mark 7; Matthew 11:4–6; Matthew 13:13–15; Matthew 6; Philippians 2; Proverbs 22:20–21; Psalm 102:25–27; Psalm 104; Psalm 105:8; Psalm 119:160; Psalm 19:1; Psalm 33:4–9; Psalm 72:19; Psalm 89:6; Revelation 21:22–23; Romans 11:36.

Chapter 8: 1 Corinthians 14:40; 1 Corinthians 15:3–4; 1 Corinthians 15:9; 1 Timothy 1:15; 2 Chronicles 31:2; 2 Chronicles 8:14; 2 Corinthians 2:17; 2 Corinthians 6:2; 2 Timothy 4:13; Acts 13:15; Acts 13:2; Acts 13:48–49; Acts 8:37; Ecclesiastes 12:13–14; Ecclesiastes 3; Ecclesiastes 3:1; Ecclesiastes 3:11; Exodus 24:3–4; Exodus 40:4; Galatians 1:11–18; Genesis 1:26; Genesis 6; Genesis 7:21–23; Habakkuk 1:5; Hebrews 1:1–4; Hebrews 1:10–12; Hebrews 9:16–17; Hebrews 9:27; Hebrews 9:28; Isaiah 49:6; Isaiah 55:3; Jeremiah 31; John 17:7–8; Leviticus 24; Luke 11; Luke 18:31–33; Matthew 15:2–9; Matthew 23; Matthew 28:18–20; Matthew 6; Proverbs 16:24; Psalm 119:128; Psalm 119:133; Psalm 139:13–16; Psalm 16:10; Psalm 2:7.

Chapter 9: 1 Chronicles 22:5; 1 Chronicles 27; 1 Chronicles 28; 1 Chronicles 28:19; 1 Chronicles 9:1; 1 Kings 11; 1 Kings 12:15–17; 1 Samuel 1:11; 1 Samuel 1:15; 1 Samuel 3:10; 1 Samuel 3:21; 2 Chronicles 1:12; 2 Chronicles 7:1–4; 2 Chronicles 7:16; 2 Samuel 7:19; 2 Samuel 7:21; 2 Samuel 7:7; Acts 2; Esther 10:2; Esther 2; Exodus 20; Exodus 24; Exodus 24:12; Exodus 24:4; Exodus 3; Exodus 3:13–14; Exodus 3:20; Exodus 31:18; Exodus 32; Exodus 32:15–16; Genesis 1:3; Genesis 11; Genesis 8:13; Genesis 8:21 - 8:22; Job 1:8; Job 19:23–24; John 19:30; Mark 13:31; Matthew 22:36–40; Matthew 24; Psalm 105:8.

Chapter 10: 1 Chronicles 28:12; 1 Chronicles 28:19; 1 Corinthians 3:13–15; 1 John 1:2, 5; 1 John 3:11; 1 John 4:14; 1 John 5:11; 1 John 5:6; 1 John 5:6–7, 9–11; 1 John 5:8; 1 John 5:9; 2 Chronicles 7:1–2; 2 Corinthians 3:1–3; Acts 17:24; Acts 9; Colossians 3:16; Daniel 12:1; Daniel 4:37; Daniel 5:22–24; Daniel 5:24; Daniel 5:25–28; Daniel 5:5; Daniel 8:17; Daniel 8:19; Daniel 8:26; Deuteronomy 9; Daniel 8:27; Ephesians 1:13–14; Ephesians 1:7; Exodus 31; Exodus 32:31–32; Exodus 32:33; Exodus 8; Hebrews 10:16–17; Isaiah 30:8; Isaiah 4:3; Isaiah 55:11; Isaiah 57:15; James 1:17; Jeremiah 31:33; Luke 10:20; Matthew 28:19–20; Philippians 4:3; Proverbs 7:2–3; Psalm 104:31–32; Psalm 119:10–11; Psalm 33:13–14; Psalm 37:30–31; Psalm 40:8; Psalm 69:28; Revelation 20:12; Revelation 20:15; Revelation 21:27; Romans 5:8.

Chapter 11: 1 Corinthians 15; 2 Chronicles 17; 2 Chronicles 30; Acts 17;2; Acts 18:28; Acts 8; Daniel 9; Daniel 9;2; Daniel 9:26; Deuteronomy 11; Deuteronomy 17:18–20; Deuteronomy 27:3, 8; Deuteronomy 28:14; Deuteronomy 28:8; Ezekiel 1:24–25; Ezra 4:12; Ezra 4:24; Ezra 4:4–5; Ezra 5:11; Ezra 6:1–2; Ezra 7:10; Ezra 7:13; Ezra 7:27–28; Ezra 9:4; Isaiah 53:5; Jeremiah 29; Jeremiah 29:32; John 2:22; Joshua 8:30–31; Joshua 8:32; Joshua 8:34; Luke 4; Matthew 11:28–30; Matthew 4:4, 7, 10; Psalm 69:9.

Chapter 12: 1 Samuel 10:25; 1 Samuel 8:21–22; 1 Samuel 9:15–16; 1 Samuel 9:17; 2 Kings 22–23; 2 Kings 23:2; Deuteronomy 28–29; Exodus 32:14–16; Exodus 34:27; Genesis 1:1; Jeremiah 36; Jeremiah 36:17–18; Jeremiah 36:3; Jeremiah 51:58; Jeremiah 51:64; John 1:1; Proverbs 25:11.

Chapter 13: 1 Chronicles 28:21; 2 Kings 18:4; 2 Kings 7:14; 2 Peter 1; 2 Timothy 3:16–17; Acts 1:11; Acts 10:34–38; Colossians 1:17; Colossians 4:5–6; Deuteronomy 11:18–21; Deuteronomy 31:28; Galatians 3:8; Galatians 5; Isaiah 55:11; James 1:25; Jeremiah 16:21; John 17:17; John 18:37; John 4:21–24; Joshua 18:4–6; Matthew 10:1; Matthew 4:23; Matthew 8:27; Philippians 1:27; Psalm 119:11; Psalm 12:7; Psalm 143:8; Psalm 85:4; Titus 3:5.

Afterword: 1 Corinthians 15:3–7; John 3:16–18; Romans 3:10–18; Romans 6:23; Acts 2:21; Acts 4:12; Romans 5:8; Romans 10:8-11; Luke 13:5; Romans 10:13.

www.ingramcontent.com/pod-product-compliance
Lightning Source LLC
Chambersburg PA
CBHW051342040426
42453CB00007B/373